MW00737353

Benjamins Transl

The BTL aims to stir
studies. The Libra
sometimes be
pedagogic
gradu

The Critical Link 5

Quality in interpreting – a shared responsibility

Edited by

Sandra Hale
University of Western Sydney

Uldis Ozolins
Royal Melbourne Institute of Technology University

Ludmila Stern
The University of New South Wales

John Benjamins Publishing Company

Amsterdam / Philadelphia

Library of Congress Cataloging-in-Publication Data

International Conference on Interpreting in Legal, Health, and Social Service Settings (5th
: 2007 : Parramatta, N.S.W.)
The critical link 5 : quality in interpreting : a shared responsibility / edited by Sandra Hale,
Uldis Ozolins and Ludmila Stern.
p. cm. (Benjamins Translation Library, ISSN 0929-7316 ; v. 87)
Includes bibliographical references and index.
1. Translating and interpreting--Congresses. I. Hale, Sandra Beatriz. II. Ozolins, Uldis,
1948- III. Stern, Ludmila. IV. Title.
P306.I448   2007b
481'.02--dc22   2009033364
ISBN 978 90 272 2431 6   (Hb ; alk. paper)
ISBN 978 90 272 8884 4   (Eb)

John Benjamins Publishing Co. · P.O. Box 36224 · 1020 me Amsterdam · The Netherlands
John Benjamins North America · P.O. Box 27519 · Philadelphia pa 19118-0519 · usa

Table of contents

Acknowledgements

We would like to thank all the authors for their valuable contribution to this volume. We would also like to thank the many reviewers who acted as blind referees for all the submissions. We would especially like to thank Elizabeth Friedman, Aviva Friedman and Rosali Harland from the UWS Interpreting and Translation Research Group, and Patricia Leplae from John Benjamins Publishing Company for their invaluable help in completing the volume.

The editors

CHAPTER 1

Quality in interpreting

A shared responsibility

Uldis Ozolins and Sandra Hale
Royal Melbourne Institute of Technology University /
University of Western Sydney, Australia

The Critical Link

It is generally agreed that the first Critical Link (CL) conference in 1995 marked the beginning of an era in Community Interpreting (Pöchhacker, 1999; Martin & Valero-Garcés, 2008). Brian Harris called it "an historic event in the evolution of professional interpreting" (1997, p. 1). The first Critical Link conference, which took place in Orillia, Canada, brought together practitioners, educators and researchers from around the world who up until that time had been working in almost complete isolation from each other. The first Critical Link conference with the theme "Interpreting in Legal, Health and Social Service Settings", served as an introduction to the international state of affairs. It became immediately apparent that while many of the same challenges were shared by all countries, some were at a much more advanced phase of development than others. The most common challenges identified at this first gathering were: the lack of recognition for the need for professional interpreters in the community, the scarcity of government funded services, the need for universal accreditation or certification systems and the need for a well defined role for community interpreters. Australia and Sweden in particular, stood out among the other countries in terms of widespread service provision, availability of formal education, national accreditation systems and a generally accepted interpreter role. However, twenty years after the inception of such initiatives, these countries were still struggling with issues of status, quality of services and professionalism. It was also around this time that research into Community Interpreting began to emerge, especially in the specialized sub fields of court and medical interpreting (Berk-Seligson, 1990; Wadensjö, 1992, 1998; Hale, 1996, 1997, 1999).

The success of CL1 led to CL2, held in Vancouver, Canada, with the theme "Standards and ethics in Community Interpreting. Recent Developments". The focus of this conference was on attempts to raise the standards in interpreting service provision by identifying the need for adequate interpreter training. CL3, with the theme "Interpreting in the Community: The Complexity of the Profession", recognized the many complex issues that surround Community Interpreting, much of which was now learned from the results of the ever growing body of research into the field. Data-based research was able to empirically demonstrate the complex nature of the interpreting process, and of the difficulties in achieving accuracy and impartiality amidst the many conflicting demands placed on community interpreters (Morris, 1999; Roy, 2000; Davidson, 2000; Hale, 2001).

Nine years after the initial Critical Link conference, the theme of CL4 was "Professionalisation of interpreting in the community". Although improvements were evident in many parts of the world, the sad reality was that attempts to professionalise Community Interpreting had reached a plateau in the more developed countries, such as Australia, Canada and the USA. Compulsory pre-service formal university education for community interpreters was still far from being a reality anywhere in the world; confusion over the interpreter's role continued to dominate the discussions; and working conditions, job security and rates of pay were still not adequate anywhere in the world (Rudvin, 2007).

It is generally recognized that being able to communicate in the country in which one lives and to access basic services, is a fundamental human right. The denial of this right can lead to total social and political disempowerment for those who do not speak the mainstream language. Community interpreters are the critical link between the mainstream community and the minority language speakers. However, there is still no recognition that community interpreters need specialized training in order to acquire the knowledge and skills necessary to provide quality interpreting. Such lack of awareness can lead to the provision of inadequate interpreting services, which can have more damaging consequences than if the service had not been provided at all.

CL5 was held from 11 to 15 April 2007, in Parramatta, Sydney, which not only is the heart of multicultural Australia but also the place where the first Reconciliation conference between the new settlers and the Australian Aborigines took place in 1805. The theme for CL5 was "Quality in Interpreting: A shared responsibility". The organizing committee believed that in order to achieve improvements, it was time that all participants involved in interpreted events, took some of the responsibility for quality. As one of the pioneers in Community Interpreting, Australia can demonstrate important achievements: thirty years of a national accreditation system, twenty years of a national professional association, twenty years of formal university degrees in community Interpreting and

Translation, and widespread government funded services. However, as in most other parts of the world, pre-service training is a choice rather than a requirement; there is little incentive for formal education; those who use interpreting services very rarely understand the complexities of the process or the role of the interpreter; and working conditions and remuneration levels are generally not commensurate with the high level skills and vast knowledge necessary for quality interpreting.

All of these issues impinge on quality in interpreting. Research (Berk-Seligson, 1990; Davidson, 2000; Hale, 2004; Angelelli, 2004) has demonstrated that the quality of community interpreting practice needs to improve in order to offer equitable services to those who require interpreting services. The reasons for this are many. Although there is a core of qualified, competent practising interpreters, there are also those who lack the necessary knowledge and skills to provide quality services. It has been argued (see Hale, 2005) that for the practice to improve, and for the status of the profession to be raised to the level of other professions, formal research based pre-service university training and in-service professional development should be mandatory and adequately rewarded. It is also critical for all participants in interpreted encounters to have a mutual understanding of each other's roles and needs. The best interpreters will not be able to provide quality services if unrealistic demands are placed on them; similarly the best lawyers or doctors, will not be able to render their services adequately if the interpreter is unaware of their needs and the interpretation is of poor quality. Similarly, the provision of suitable working conditions and adequate remuneration are also essential in ensuring high quality services. For all this to happen, a concerted unified approach needs to be taken. There is little point in researching Community Interpreting if researchers do not make their research practical, applicable and accessible and if the results will not be read and implemented by practitioners and educators. There is little point in offering training if it will not be accessed by those who will practice. There is little point in producing highly competent, skilled interpreters if they will not find satisfying, well-remunerated employment.

Quality in interpreting cannot be regarded as the sole responsibility of interpreters. All parties need to assume responsibility: each speaker needs to assume responsibility for what they say and how they say it; employers need to assume responsibility for providing suitable conditions and remuneration; the different systems need to assume responsibility for ensuring that minimum standards are demanded; educational institutions need to assume responsibility for providing adequate resources and support; researchers need to assume responsibility for making their research relevant, applicable and accessible to practitioners; and interpreters need to assume responsibility for their own professional development and professionalism.

Critical Link 5 provided the opportunity to take stock of the current situation; to seriously evaluate what has been done, where we are at, and where we need to go from here.

The papers

The focus on shared responsibility is well sustained by the papers in this collection. In the first section, *Quality in interpreting: a shared responsibility – the policy dimension*, papers address the macro environment of specific social policy contexts – law, health and international political organisations – in each case teasing out professional, institutional and sometimes political factors that need to be addressed so that interpreting can assist in realising the aims of these institutions, rather than be seen as an unfortunate necessity or even hindrance.

Justice Len Roberts-Smith of Western Australia made a remarkable contribution to Critical Link 5 by being there - for its duration. Readers may well reflect on how often they have seen a senior legal official stay for the whole of an interpreting conference, rather than just their own presentation. Having a long-standing interest in legal interpreting issues, first as a lawyer and then as a sitting judge, he outlines the often tortuous legal reasoning used to define the role of interpreters in court settings, and the particular difficulties of court systems in addressing issues of provision and competence of interpreters. While the rights of defendants to have interpreters is no longer seriously questioned, further issues of process and competence reveal inconsistent practices on the part of judges and lawyers, and much discretion in how communication issues will or will not be addressed. Roberts-Smith concludes with some strong recommendations for educating both lawyers and interpreters to enable more effective working by interpreters and more understanding of their role by the legal fraternity.

Eva Ng takes up similar themes in her Hong-Kong based study, paying attention to problematic translation as well as interpreting, in a legal system attempting to meld its traditional British legal heritage with Chinese approaches to codification. The attempted blending of these systems has meant interpreters often face insuperable problems where terms have been defined not on the basis of their acceptability to and understandability by those involved in legal process, but on forced constructions and neologisms that hope to semantically map the equivalent English term. Ng asks "Is it always possible for a Chinese term to be considered both adequate in the representation of its English equivalent and acceptable/comprehensible at the same time?" She outlines how it is often the translators and interpreters that are left to make individual and sometimes invidious decisions.

A surprising variation of the Hong Kong experience is that faced by interpreters in large international organisations, in this case the European Parliament as reported in *Stephanie Jo Kent*'s intriguing paper. Here, interpreters are faced by the contradiction of a language policy of statutory multilingualism, where all languages of member states can be used, and the growing move by many delegates to insist on speaking not in their first language but in English (and very occasionally French) of highly variable quality. The interpreters here need to make sense of speech that can be either deliberately or accidentally vague, evasive, cryptic or incoherent, occasioning at times complete mystification on the part of interpreters needing to convey the speakers' meaning, as well as a growing feeling of marginalisation of the whole interpreting enterprise as its supposed prime users abandon it in favour of an often inadequate *lingua franca*. Lest it be thought this strays far from issues of interpreting in the community, increased anecdotal evidence can also be gathered of this phenomenon of difficult to grasp English (in the case of English-speaking countries) of significant numbers of professionals, themselves migrants, who increasingly provide the workforce in public health systems and elsewhere, leading to problems for interpreters no less than for many English-speaking patients.

The many sessions on health interpreting at CL5 continued the solid contributions of earlier congresses, health being the single largest area of participation from delegates. But if the field is large, and undoubtedly developing in terms of professionalism and research and sophistication of analysis, there is also a feeling in many countries that an uneasy stage has been reached where the need for health interpreting is recognised but crucial issues of policy development in the broader context of healthcare can have unintended consequences for interpreting, and ultimately act as a disincentive to often the most competent interpreters. *Pam Garrett* from Australia asks bluntly in her paper "Is healthcare interpreter policy left in the seventies?" and analyses why intended policies of enabling universal access to language services for all non-English speakers in health settings are continually confounded – in Australia's case, Garret argues, "mainstream healthcare policy has shifted focus from 'access and equity' to 'efficiency', 'effectiveness', 'health outcomes', and 'patient safety'", and increased service demand has been "coupled, somewhat uncomfortably, with financial constraint". Yet empirically, those policies of universal access to language services remain unfulfilled: a study of a new pilot hospital shows continual use of family and friends to interpret, patchy reports of professional interprets being called, and even in the most highly complex treatment cases significant numbers of non-English speakers did not get professional interpreters, despite a sophisticated triage system that ostensibly included language needs.

If the first section of the book presents a perhaps sombre picture of real constrains in various policy environments that affect interpreting, the second section on *Investigations and innovations in quality interpreting* reveals a number of admirable cases of interpreters working together with their client institutions.

Michael Cooke from Australia shows the considerable steps that have been taken by judicial authorities to recognize communication issues in Australian indigenous communities and the extraordinarily complex situations with which interpreters have to deal. An earlier period of often absolute neglect of communication issues has now given way to a greater understanding by the legal system of the complex intersection of Australian and Aboriginal customary law and the way this also affects the interpreter role. Close kinship patterns of Aboriginal language groups mean that often interpreters will know or be related to the person requiring interpreting, at odds with standard interpreter or legal ethics demanding formal impartiality. And these same networks prescribe what language needs to be used in terms of respect and power, making it very difficult to interpret, for example, incisive questions in cross-examination, or questions about dead persons, or questions that seek explicit accounts of assault or sexual behaviour. The choice of interpreter, and the ability of lawyers, the court and interpreters to work together to achieve effective communication are paramount.

Three further papers in this section also break new ground. *Jemina Napier, David Spencer* and *Joe Sabolcec* look at the issue of how the Deaf can participate in the judicial process - as jurors. Normally, lack of competence in the language of the court would be a simple ground for disqualification of a juror, but the desire of the Deaf to participate in all areas of life of a normal citizen, and attendant disability discrimination laws, have now confronted courts with this new demand, and the authors analyse the accommodations both legalistic and logistical that were needed to allow Deaf jurors to function.

Franz Pöchhacker and *Waltraud Kolb*, in the course of a study of interpreter performance in asylum hearings in Austria, began to notice an unusual feature of interpreters' behaviour: many interpreters took particular note of how their renderings were taken down by the hearings' reporters – and then, how awareness of this written record began to influence their interpreting. The written record of testimony is the tangible evidence that remains of a hearing, so getting the record "right" in every way becomes crucial not only for the hearing reporter but for the interpreter, from simple things such as spelling out names or places to – perhaps – making testimony more coherent. The authors raise a nice question of whether interpreting for the record is the same as interpreting what one hears.

Erika Gonzalez and *Lurdes Auzmendi* give an account of the particular difficulties encountered in court cases of Basque separatists, where the deliberately metaphorical and evasive, sometimes circumlocutions and sometimes cryptic renderings of some speakers made it extremely difficult for interpreters to cope. The authors describe how, with the approval of the court, the interpreters introduced a simple but imaginative technological innovation which enabled them to literally hear the speaker twice, increasing the interpreters' understanding and rendering, but delivered in the normal time and mode, consecutively after the speaker.

Finally in this section, following on from the focus of Critical Link 4 in Stockholm, *Juan Miguel Ortega Herraez, Maria Isabel Abril Martí* and *Anne Martin* report on several surveys in Spain to show different degrees of professionalisation and understanding of role among interpreters in a variety of social settings – including health, welfare, immigration, administration, court and police work. In a number of cases interpreters clearly see themselves in a "helper" role, identifying strongly with the non-Spanish speakers and having little cognisance of professional imperatives of impartiality and role boundaries. Yet this was less so among the police and court interpreters: the authors' quiet conclusion is that in the police and court context interpreters have a far clearer recognition of their role and its limits because "the situation seems to be more controlled by the service provider". This allows us to draw parallels precisely with other areas of service provision where other professionals and workers seem happy, or even relieved (or, perhaps, contemptuous but uncaring) if the interpreter takes on any role in order to help the non-Spanish speaker. Paradoxically, the interpreter's role is enhanced by other professionals exercising such control, where control precisely ensures effective and clearly defined collaboration between interpreters and all other parties.

The final section of this book brings together several papers to address the themes of *Pedagogy, ethics and responsibility in interpreting*. The spread of training as a prerequisite for professional interpreting has been evidenced in successive Critical Link proceedings, but *Jieun Lee* from Australia identifies still a gross lack of literature and absence of settled views on the assessment of interpreting in educational programs. She presents a highly illuminating pilot study of how to rate interpreter performance, in this case for consecutive interpreting, bringing together the scant literature for interpreting and the more substantial literature on rating in language assessment *per se,* and shows a procedure which is able to clearly differentiate *accuracy, target language quality* and *delivery,* and achieve high inter-rater reliability. The lack of rigorous literature on interpreting assessment identified by Lee must give pause: have we mostly been doing it by intuition?

Giving another insight into pedagogy, *Raffaela Merlini* and *Roberta Favaron* present a multi-layered paper, taking a particular instance of interpreter behaviour – use of first or third person in a specific medical setting – and link it to broader issues of research, training, and most importantly self-awareness of interpreters and how interpreters can understand interpreting norms and negotiate variations based on sound professional judgment. Unlike almost all studies that focus on patient to medical professional interaction, they focus on interpreters working between English-speaking and Italian-speaking nurses in an international health facility in southern Italy. Transcripts of the interactions are used then in training sessions for these interpreters – a rare instance of such use of transcripts in interpreter training in Italy, enabling a grounded discussion of interpret norms and their contextual basis.

Pedagogy is also the concern of *Helen Tebble*'s paper, on what interpreters can learn from discourse studies, but the concerns here are perhaps a little unusual. While most studies of pedagogy in community interpreting attempt to identify some basic standards of educational outcomes to assure a minimum quality in the field, Tebble looks at what theoretical knowledge and awareness of discourse processes the very best interpreters need to perfect their interpreting. Concentration on the dynamics of the speech situations encountered can alert the interpreter to the intentions of both (or many) parties in an interpreting encounter, and alert them to the subtle moves in discourse – checking, quick verbal feedback, genre-specific moves, shifting topic, indicating turn taking – much of which may not be interpreted. She sees discourse studies as "fundamental to the knowledge and performance of the dialogue interpreter" for "the language use of the speakers arises out of the speech situation, so too must the interpreter's."

Ilse Blignault, Maria Stephanou and *Cassandra Barrett* turn the focus from pedagogy to ethics, performance and responsibility. As representatives of the New South Wales Health Care Interpreter Service – a service celebrating thirty years of operation, and whose members were prominent throughout Critical Link 5 – they studied the satisfactions that health interpreters derive from work in situations that, as mentioned in several previous papers, are less than ideal in terms of resourcing and recognition. While interpreters' technical and people skills were important in their self-esteem, so too were the occasions when they were regarded as a valued part of a health care team, establishing fruitful long-term relationships with both other health professionals and patients speaking their respective language.

And finally *Joseph Kaufert* and *Patricia Kaufert,* and *Lisa LaBine*, leaders in the field of ethics in health interpreting in Northern America, take their work in a further direction by looking at the use of interpreters in biomedical research, surveying researchers, relevant interpreters and ethics board members. An increasing number of medical researchers use interpreters when conducting research on multilingual populations, but the close attention and strict guidelines for issues such as informed consent among the mainstream medical profession, sometimes evaporates when researchers work with interpreters, often expecting the interpreters to undertake a large range of functions in relation to minority language patient populations. Equally, the authors found little understanding of the role of interpreters among ethics board members, and issues such as informed consent and responsibility for ensuring such consent remain loosely defined at best when interpreters are involved.

Conclusion

The papers thus serve to reinforce from many different perspectives the argument that achieving quality in interpreting must be a shared responsibility with the many actors and institutions interpreters work amongst. Taking these papers together, a slowly emerging perspective is that quality thus depends not only on the technical skills and ethics of interpreters, but equally upon the ethics and communication skills of all other professionals that serve multilingual populations. This collection of Critical Link papers, like its predecessors, provides a useful map to see the extent to which this awareness is – even if unevenly – nevertheless growing in an increasing number of countries around the world.

References

Angelelli, C. (2004). *Medical interpreting and cross-cultural communication*. Cambridge: Cambridge University Press.

Berk-Seligson, S. (1990/2002). *The Bilingual Courtroom. Court Interpreters in the Judicial Process*. Chicago: The University of Chicago Press.

Davidson, B. (2000). The interpreter as institutional gatekeeper: The social-linguistic role of interpreters in Spanish-English medical discourse. *Journal of Sociolinguistics, 4*(3), 379–405.

Hale, S. (1996). Pragmatic considerations in court interpreting. *Australian Review of Applied Linguistics, 19*(1), 61–72.

Hale, S. (1997). The treatment of register in court interpreting. *The Translator, 3*(1), 39–54.

Hale, S. (1999). The interpreter's treatment of discourse markers in courtroom questions. *Forensic Linguistics. The international journal of speech, language and the law, 6*(1), 57–82.

Hale, S. (2001). How are Courtroom Questions Interpreted? An Analysis of Spanish Interpreters' Practices. In I. Mason (Ed.), *Triadic Exchanges. Studies in Dialogue Interpreting* (pp. 21–50). Manchester: St. Jerome.

Hale, S. (2004). *The discourse of court interpreting. Discourse practices of the law, the witness and the interpreter*. Amsterdam and Philadelphia: John Benjamins.

Hale, S. (2005). The interpreter's identity crisis. In J. House, M. R. Martín Ruano & N. Baumgarten (Eds.), *Translation and the construction of identity* (pp. 14–29). Seoul: International Association for Translation and Intercultural Studies.

Harris, B. (1997). Forward. A landmark in the evolution of interpreting. In S. Carr, R. Roberts, A. Dufour & D. Steyn, (Eds.), *The Critical Link: Interpreters in the community* (pp. 1–3). Amsterdam/Philadelphia: John Benjamins.

Martin, A. & Valero-Garcés, C. (2008). Introduction. In C. Valero-Garcés & A. Martin (Eds.), *Crossing borders in community interpreting* (pp. 1–7). Amsterdam/Philadelphia: John Benjamins.

Morris, R. (1999). The gum syndrome: predicaments in court interpreting. *Forensic Linguistics, 6*(1), 6–29.

Pöchhacker, F. (1999). The evolution of community interpreting. *Interpreting 4*(1), 125–140.

Roy, C. (2000). *Interpreting as a discourse process*. New York and Oxford: Oxford University Press.

Rudvin, M. (2007). Professionalism and ethics in community interpreting. *Interpreting 9*(1), 47–69.

Wadensjö, C. (1992). *Interpreting as interaction. On dialogue interpreting in immigration hearings and medical encounters*. Linkoping: Linkoping University.

Wadensjö, C. (1998). *Interpreting as interaction*. London & New York: Longman.

PART I

A shared responsibility

The policy dimension

CHAPTER 2

Forensic interpreting

Trial and error

Len Roberts-Smith
Court of Appeal, Supreme Court of Western Australia

This chapter reviews a number of key cases from different English speaking countries where poor interpretation created legal problems. The author attributes these problems to three major reasons: (1) The complete absence of an interpreter; (2) the provision of unqualified bilinguals or interpreters in the wrong language; and (3) the services of "professional accredited" but untrained interpreters who do not possess the required high level skills to perform as legal interpreters. The author argues that monocultural or Anglophone lawyers and judges often lack an understanding of the interpreting process and the work of interpreters, which may lead to forensic error. The chapter ends with recommendations for the way forward.

1.   Introduction

Competent interpreting in court is fundamental to justice. The lack of competent interpreting in a criminal trial where an accused person does not speak any, or sufficient, English, may amount to denial of a fair trial and result in the quashing of a conviction. Where the inadequacy of the interpretation is not recognised, the result may be wrongful conviction or acquittal. Courts have the primary responsibility for ensuring the fairness of trials. But what can they do if there are no suitably qualified interpreters in the language(s) needed? How are courts or lawyers to know if an interpreter is competent? Is accreditation sufficient? What standards of competency are there? Arrangements for obtaining interpreters to work in courts and tribunals in Australia are largely ad hoc. Judges, lawyers, witnesses and parties are often not experienced in working with interpreters. Their expectations are often unrealistic. There is a serious risk trial outcomes will be affected as a consequence. This paper will provide an overview of key cases with interpreting issues, discuss the critical practical consequences of these problems and suggest ways in which they might be addressed.

2.   The jurisprudential basis of the role of the interpreter

The jurisprudential basis of the role of the court interpreter is that of a cipher or medium of communication. The leading Australian case is *Gaio v The Queen*. A patrol officer in Papua New Guinea had interviewed a suspect through a native interpreter. The legal point taken was that the evidence of the patrol officer was inadmissible because it was hearsay. The High Court held that the patrol officer's account of what the interpreter had told him the accused had said was not hearsay and so was admissible evidence. That was because the process was analogous to talking through a machine which interpreted from one language to another. So regarded, the patrol officer was in reality recounting what the accused had said directly to him.

What the High Court said in *Gaio* is often misunderstood. The comments of the members of the Court likening an interpreter to a "language machine" were not directed to the linguistic, cultural or social aspects of the interpretation process, but to the jurisprudential theory of the interpreter's role as a matter of legal admissibility. The reasoning in *Gaio* was consistent with a very much earlier decision of Lord Kenyon, albeit on a different point, in *Du Barré v Livette*. Lord Kenyon held the relationship between the defendant and his lawyer was privileged and because it was necessary to have an interpreter, everything said before that interpreter was equally in confidence as if said to the lawyer when no interpreter was present. The interpreter was the organ through which the defendant conveyed information to the lawyer.

3.   The right to an interpreter

3.1   The right to an interpreter in civil cases

In Australia, the view has generally been that in the absence of a written law (statute) providing otherwise, no-one has a right to an interpreter in a civil case.

In 1963 the High Court of Australia in *Dairy Farmers Co-operative Milk Company Ltd v Acquilina* held that a witness is not entitled to give evidence in their native tongue through an interpreter. In a joint judgment, the five Judges of the High Court said: "The general proposition that a witness is entitled to give evidence in his native tongue is one that cannot be justified..."

Interestingly, in the earlier case of *Filios v Morland* the court said that the primary consideration was that what the witness had to say should be put before the Court as fully and accurately, and as fairly and effectively, as the circumstances permitted. Brereton J accepted that it may be that a witness with an imperfect understanding of English could not achieve this by using that language, but his Honour then added:

> It is not always the case that it will be better achieved by the use of an interpreter. For evidence given through an interpreter loses much of its impact, and this is so in spite of the expert interpretation now readily available. The jury do not really hear the witness, nor are they fully able to appreciate, for instance, the degree of conviction or uncertainty with which his evidence is given; they cannot wholly follow the nuances, inflections, quickness or hesitancy of the witness; all they have is the dispassionate and inexpressive tone of the interpreter. Moreover, even today it is all too common an experience to hear the interpreter giving the effect instead of giving a literal translation of questions and answers, and of his own accord interpolating questions and eliciting explanations. These matters may operate unfairly either to the advantage or to the disadvantage of the witness involved. Moreover, and especially where the witness has some knowledge of English, the cross-examiner is placed at a grave disadvantage.

The notion that a court or tribunal is better able to assess the credibility of a witness if there is no interpreter interposed between them was articulated again in *Johnson*. On an appeal against the trial judge's decision refusing to allow a co-conspirator (Chan) to be recalled to give the entirety of his evidence again through an interpreter, Shepherdson J said that if the position had been that the appellant could not understand the evidence given by Chan and consequently was unable to properly instruct his lawyer, the outcome might have been different, but that was not suggested. His Honour said the "guiding star" is to ensure a fair trial for an accused. In that respect there are two needs to be considered: that for the jury to hear and understand a witness's evidence, and that of an accused person to hear and understand a witness's evidence.

Williams J commented that a reading of the cross-examination did indicate that from time to time counsel and the witness were at cross-purposes, but observed "that is not an unusual feature of a lengthy cross-examination in a criminal trial". Later, his Honour said:

> … In practice it will generally be obvious whether or not the assistance of an interpreter is required… *Experience has generally shown that the tribunal of fact can make a better assessment of a witness if there is no interpreter transposed between it and the witness.* In this case I am not convinced that the language difficulties experienced by Chan were such as necessitated the use of an interpreter. (My emphasis)

The third Judge, Derrington J, said:

> In deciding whether to have an interpreter for any witness, the only consideration is the interests of justice in the case, it being remembered that the accused is on trial and his interests must be properly protected. But that does not mean that an interpreter should be used if it is unnecessary *for the intervention of an interpreter tends to render it more difficult to ascertain the truth.* (My emphasis)

Also in 1987, in *Singh (Heer) v Minister for Immigration and Ethnic Affairs*, the Federal Court quashed a decision to deport an Indian Sikh woman because of procedural unfairness involving the taking of a record of interview with her while she was in custody. Mrs Heer succeeded on a ground which concerned the conduct of a record of interview with her by a departmental officer. That interview took place two days after her arrest. The officer saw her in the prison where she was being held. His purpose was to complete a pro forma report. When he arrived, Mrs Heer had visitors. One of them was a 15-year-old girl by the name of Amarjit who was there with her parents. She was fluent in Punjabi (the applicant's native language) and spoke much better English than her parents and the applicant. A prison officer suggested she could act as interpreter and the departmental officer agreed. In the course of the interview, Mrs Heer did need interpreter assistance from Amarjit about 25 per cent of the time. About two and a half pages into the six-page interview questionnaire, Amarjit had to leave. That was noted on the form, as "interpreter quit here". The questions and answers continued for another one and a half pages. Then, with one page left to complete, the departmental officer was required to leave the prison. He had Mrs Heer sign at the foot of each of the completed pages without having them further read or interpreted to her. During the interview, Mrs Heer was frequently upset and in tears. The officer left the sixth page with the prison authorities who arranged the following day for a prison officer to complete the interview with her without an interpreter. When Mrs Heer gave evidence about this in the Federal Court through an interpreter, she said she repeatedly told the prison officer that she did not understand his questions and asked him to get an interpreter. However, the prison officer said the form had to be filled in that day, and he continued. Foster J found the action of the prison officer was most unfair to Mrs Heer. Furthermore, no answers were recorded to some critical questions. The Judge concluded:

> It seems to me that the manner of conducting the interview, the last two and a half pages being without the assistance of an interpreter and the important questions on page six not being answered and no explanation given for this other than Mrs Heer's, suggests that the manner of conducting the interview was seriously unfair to Mrs Heer.

Gradidge v Grace Bros Pty Ltd was a case in the Compensation Court of New South Wales. This was a case stated to the New South Wales Court of Appeal.

The appellant was deaf. In the Compensation Court, an interpreter was sworn to interpret in sign language. While the appellant was giving his evidence, objection was taken to a question. Legal argument followed. Counsel for the respondent noticed the interpreter was interpreting the argument to the appellant and objected to that. The appellant's own counsel indicated he did not require that to be interpreted to the appellant. The Judge directed the interpreter to desist. The interpreter refused, telling the Judge that she saw it as her function to interpret to the appellant everything which took place in the court. The Judge was not prepared to continue on that basis. He adjourned the hearing and stated questions of law for the opinion of the Court of Appeal concerning his ruling.

The Court of Appeal held the Judge had erred in directing the interpreter to desist. The appellant was a party and entitled to know what was happening. Unless excluded from the court, she was entitled to have the proceedings interpreted to her.

Kirby P saw it as an important issue of due process. His Honour said that in early times when Australia was comprised of a generally homogeneous English speaking population, there was less sensitivity than now to the difficulties of people appearing in courts without the advantage of proficiency in the English language, but times have changed. He added:

> The criticisms of the decisions in *Acquilina* and *Filios* have appeared in a large number of legal commentary. They have generally been directed at the assumption, which appears to lie behind the reasoning of those decisions, that the task of an interpreter is purely mechanical, that is, it involves the word for word translation into the English language from another language and vice versa. Greater knowledge of language and communication teaches that this is not so…

Samuels J A agreed. He thought the principle was clear enough, it being that any party who was unable for want of some physical capacity or for lack of knowledge of the language of the court, to understand what is happening must, by the use of an interpreter, be placed in the position in which he or she would be if those defects did not exist. His Honour emphasised:

> The task of the interpreter in short is to remove any barriers which prevent understanding or communication. This must, of course, be subject to the overriding right of the judge, first to determine whether those barriers exist and, second, to decide in what way the corrective mechanisms may be applied without disrupting or adversely affecting the forensic procedures which he is charged to undertake.

His Honour further emphasised that the task of the interpreter is not restricted merely to passing on the questions when the party is giving evidence, but must be extended also to apprising a party of what is happening in the court and what procedures are being conducted at a particular time. He said it is quite wrong to imagine that all an interpreter is supposed to do is to interpret questions for a person in the witness box.

In *Adamopoulos v Olympic Airways SA* the New South Wales Court of Appeal held that a party to legal proceedings does not have a legal "right" to an interpreter; whether a party should be allowed an interpreter is a matter within the discretion of the court. Relevant considerations may include whether an interpreter is required for a fair hearing; whether a party may be disadvantaged by the absence of an interpreter; the interest of the other party; the time at which the application for an interpreter is made; whether an interpreter is needed and whether there is any extraneous or ulterior motive for the request. This remains the law. An attempt to circumvent it was made unsuccessfully in *Re East & Ors; Ex parte Nguyen*. That concerned an application made directly to the High Court which it was claimed arose under a treaty.[1] The appellant failed, because the High Court held the application was not a justiceable matter arising under a treaty (that is, the Court had no jurisdiction to deal with it).

3.2   The right to an interpreter in criminal cases

The position is different in relation to criminal cases, although substantial difficulties remain.

In *R v Lee Kun*, a Chinese man who spoke no English was tried for murder and convicted. There was no interpreter at his trial. The lawyer who represented him at trial had also done so in the preliminary hearing of the charge before a Magistrate. There the evidence had been interpreted for him by an interpreter. The evidence given at trial was the same. The appeal was on the basis that the omission to interpret the evidence at trial was such a serious irregularity that the conviction should be quashed. The English Court of Criminal Appeal refused leave to appeal, because they were satisfied no substantial miscarriage of justice had actually occurred. That was because if the evidence had been interpreted, the same verdict would inevitably have resulted. Nonetheless, as to the principle generally, Lord Reading CJ said:

> When a foreigner who is ignorant of the English language is on trial on an indictment for a criminal offence and is undefended, the evidence given at the trial must be translated to him. If he states that he understands part of the evidence and does not wish that part translated, unless the judge in his discretion thinks

---

1.   The High Court of Australia has original jurisdiction in matters arising under a treaty: s 75(i) *Constitution*.

otherwise, it need not be translated, because the object of the translation is already achieved … If he does not understand the English language, he cannot waive compliance with the rule that the evidence must be translated; he cannot dispense with it by express or implied consent, and it matters not that no application is made by him for the assistance of an interpreter. It is for the Court to see that the necessary means are adopted to convey the evidence to his intelligence, notwithstanding that, either through ignorance or timidity or disregard of his own interest, he makes no application to the Court. (pp. 340–341)

His Lordship based these remarks squarely on the requirement for an accused person to be present at their trial so as to hear the case made against them and have the opportunity of answering it. This encompassed not only physical presence, but the capacity to hear, to understand and to respond.

There was a different outcome in *Begum*. That was a case in which the English Court of Appeal made some trenchant comments about who had responsibility for ensuring a non-English speaker had access to a competent interpreter. In that case the appellant had pleaded guilty to the murder of her husband and was sentenced to life imprisonment, but three years later she appealed on the ground everyone had spoken to her in English, which was a language she did not understand. At the conclusion of argument, the court immediately announced its finding that the trial had been a nullity and that it would give its reasons later. The reasons subsequently given included:

> *It is beyond the understanding of this court that it did not occur to someone from the time she was taken into custody until she stood arraigned that the reason for her silence, in the face of many questions over a number of interviews upon the day of the hearing and upon many days previously at various times, was simply because she was not being spoken to in a language which she understood. We have been driven to the conclusion that that must have been the situation... The effect of what has happened in such a situation as that, is that no proper trial has taken place. The trial is a nullity... The failure here both by solicitor and counsel was to realise that the reason for the apparent lack of communication lay in the inadequacy of interpretation. Yet not once does it appear to have occurred to either of them to question the interpreter so as to ascertain whether or not he was understanding what the appellant was saying to him and whether he, the interpreter, had the impression that she was not comprehending the language he was talking to her.* (My emphasis)

The theme which runs through the cases on the entitlement of an accused to an interpreter in a criminal trial, is that such entitlement is an aspect of the right of an accused to a fair trial.[2] Denial of a fair trial constitutes a miscarriage of justice and a conviction which occurs in those circumstances will be quashed. The right to a fair trial was discussed by the High Court in *Dietrich v The Queen*. Although that was not about interpreters, Deane and Gaudron JJ each mentioned the denial of an interpreter to an accused in a criminal trial who needed one, as an example of a circumstance which would constitute an unfair trial. So it was that in *Saraya* the New South Wales Court of Criminal Appeal held the interpretation of the appellant's evidence at trial was so deficient as to amount to a denial of a fair trial.

The Court said:

> Where an accused person is unable adequately to give evidence in the English language, the right to the use of an interpreter for the purpose of his giving evidence must ... be regarded as an essential incident of a fair trial; and the trial will be unfair if an interpreter is not provided: *Dietrich v The Queen* (1992) 177 CLR 292. Equally, it would be unfair if the interpreter lacks the skill and ability to translate [*sic*] accurately the questions asked by counsel and the answers given by the accused person.

Also in 1993 the Privy Council decided *Kunnath v The State*. The appellant was an uneducated Indian peasant, working as a cleaner in a Bombay guest-house. His employer persuaded him to travel to Mauritius and deliver a bag to a person whose identity would be revealed to him on arrival. When he arrived in Mauritius, Customs officers found heroin in a false bottom of his bag and he was arrested. He claimed he was unaware that the bag contained heroin. His native language was Malayalam. His trial was conducted in English. He was represented by legal counsel. The interpreter was under the impression he could interpret only on the instruction of the Judge. He interpreted the charge to the appellant at the beginning of the trial and the appellant's statement to the court from the dock, but none of the evidence. In his statement from the dock, the appellant stated that he had not understood what the witnesses had said. He was convicted and sentenced to death. The Privy Council said:

> It is an essential principle of the criminal law that a trial for an indictable offence should be conducted in the presence of the accused ... As their Lordships have already recorded, the basis of this principle is not simply that there should be corporeal presence but that the accused, by reason of his presence, should be able to understand the proceedings and decide what witnesses he wishes to call, whether or not to give evidence and, if so, upon what matters relevant to the case against

---

2.   Or as Deane J observed in *Jago v The District Court of New South Wales* (1989) 168 CLR 23 at 56, the right not to be tried unfairly.

him … An accused who has not understood the conduct of proceedings against him cannot, in the absence of express consent, be said to have had a fair trial.

A seminal case examining an accused's right to an interpreter in a criminal trial and the standards of interpretation by which the fulfilment of that right may be gauged is *R v Tran*, a Canadian case. In that case Lamer CJ traced the evolution of the fundamental right of an accused at common law to the assistance of an interpreter in a criminal trial, not as a separate right, but as an incident of the right to a fair trial. On the notion of fairness he said:

> It is clear that the right to the assistance of an interpreter of an accused who cannot communicate or be understood for language reasons is based on the fundamental notion that no person should be subject to a Kafkaesque trial which may result in loss of liberty. An accused has the right to know in full detail, and contemporaneously, what is taking place in the proceedings which will decide his or her fate. This is basic fairness. Even if a trial is objectively a model of fairness, if an accused operating under a language handicap is not given full and contemporaneous interpretation of the proceedings, he or she will not be able to assess this for him or herself. The very legitimacy of the justice system in the eyes of those who are subject to it is dependent on their being able to comprehend and communicate in the language in which the proceedings are taking place.

3.3   Denial of access to interpreting services

In 1994 things were not going quite so well in Australia so far as judicial recognition of the need for interpreters was concerned. In *Cucu v District Court of New South Wales* the claimant made an application to give his evidence through an interpreter. The Judge seemed to think this was a pretence and refused it. In his judgment on the application to quash the order made in the District Court, Kirby P said the Judge:

> … seems to have been unfavourably affected by the application of the claimant to give his evidence through an interpreter. Sadly, in our multilingual society, there remains a great deal of resistance on the part of judges and other legal practitioners, to this facility. It must be said again that the majority (including the majority of lawyers) who are exclusively Anglophone show an enduring resistance to the needs of non-Anglophone parties and witnesses in court. The linguistic skills adequate for work and social intercourse frequently evaporate in stressful, formal and important situations …

Later, his Honour said:

> No doubt there are some parties and witnesses who seek to take improper advantage of the facility of a court interpreter. But the risk that this is the case must be weighed against the serious injustice, and breach of fundamental human rights, which is involved by denying that facility to a person who reasonably requests it and who may need it in the peculiar setting of a court proceeding.

Sheller JA said that he agreed with the reasons given by Kirby P, subject to one reservation. That concerned what Kirby P had to say about interpreters. On that topic, Sheller JA said:

> Inevitably evidence must be presented to the Court in the English language. In a civil case where English is not the first language of a witness it will be for the judge to decide whether the evidence should be given by the witness in English or through an interpreter. Normally where a witness has difficulty speaking English and requests the assistance of an interpreter this will be permitted. However this course adds another dimension to the Court's task in eliciting the truth. *A judge may feel that a direct account in English even badly spoken is fairer to the witness and to the parties*: see *Filios v Morland* [1963] SR (NSW) 331 at 332–334 approved by the High Court in *Dairy Farmers Co-operative Milk Co Ltd v Acquilina* (1963) 109 CLR 458 at 464. *Moreover it should be borne in mind that for many people brought up in other countries with different systems of education it is natural to understand and speak several languages including English. Judges will in weighing the evidence take account of the witness's language difficulties.* (My emphasis)

Given the judicial views sometimes expressed that interpreters may actually detract from or interfere with the capacity of a court to assess a witness' evidence and credibility, it is interesting to note the observations of Gray in *Kathiresan v Minister for Immigration & Multicultural Affairs* at [48] and [49].

> [48] In an area in which cross-cultural communications occur, there is danger in giving too much rein to the "subtle influence of demeanour" ... Judging the demeanour of the witness from the tone of the interpreter's answers is obviously impossible. Judging the demeanour of the witness from the witness's own answers in a foreign language would require a high degree of familiarity with that language and the cultural background of its speakers ...
> [49] A witness whose answers appear to be unresponsive, incoherent, or inconsistent may well appear to lack candour, even through the unresponsiveness, incoherence or inconsistencies are due to incompetent interpretation.

The notion that an accused's inability to understand the proceedings means in effect the trial is not being conducted in their presence, was developed in a particular statutory context in *Ebatarinja v Deland*, where the accused was a deaf Aborigine who was charged with murder. The relevant statute required the magistrate to conduct the preliminary hearing "in the presence or hearing of the defendant".

The High Court held this was not a mere formality. Further, if the defendant, even though physically present, was unable to understand what had been put against him or her, the hearing would be a nullity. That was the situation in this case. There being no interpreter capable of communicating with the defendant, the prosecution was abandoned.

The lack of an interpreter where one is necessary can obviously result in injustice. But courts have historically tended to the view that they have had little choice but to continue trials where they consider the accused has a "sufficient" understanding.

3.5   Standards of forensic interpreting

Of particular significance is the standard by which forensic interpretation should be assessed to determine whether it falls so far short of such as to constitute an effective denial of a fair trial. The Chief Justice of Canada has said the relevant standard is that of continuity, precision, impartiality, competency and contemporaneousness.[3] On the need for precision (which he thought was "self-evident"), Chief Justice Lamer quoted with approval a comment from Steele "Court Interpreters in Canadian Criminal Law":

> The interpretation must be, as close as can be, word for word and idea for idea; the interpreter must not "clean up" the evidence by giving it a form, a grammar or syntax that it does not have; the interpreter should make no commentary on the evidence; and the interpretation should be given only in the first person, e.g., "I went to school" instead of "He says he went to school".

The necessity for precision is an additional reason why summaries of oral testimony are insufficient. Chief Justice Lamer recognised that there are no universally acceptable standards for assessing interpreter competency, but observed that an interpreter must at least be sworn by taking the interpreter's oath before beginning to interpret the proceedings. He said that where there is a legitimate reason to doubt the competency of a particular interpreter, a court would be well advised to conduct an inquiry into the interpreter's qualification. I have elsewhere expressed the view that it would ordinarily be prudent for an interpreter to be required to state their qualifications for the record before being sworn or affirmed. That also recognises the principle at common law that it is the responsibility of the trial Judge to ensure that adequate interpretation is afforded the accused or witness.

---

3.   RvTran [1994] 2 SCR 951.

One "trap" in attempting to assess quality of interpretation from a subsequent account given or reading of a transcript in the target language, is that answers which are apparently compatible with and responsive to the questions, may actually not have been. That was the situation in *Lars*. After all the accused were arrested, a "competent, qualified and ticketed interpreter" ("Mr B") employed on call by the Department of Immigration and Ethnic Affairs in Queensland was sent specifically to assist in communicating between the police and the appellant (Da Silva). Mr B then interpreted in a brief conversation between them and Da Silva. He was called to give evidence at the trial. Mr B said that in that conversation Da Silva denied knowledge of a co-accused's (Larsen) drug manufacturing activity, of the nature of the drug, amphetamine, and of the fact it was an illegal drug. Her explanation of how she came to be there was consistent with her innocence.

Mr B left after that and Da Silva was not formally interviewed by the police officer for another three days. They had difficulty in obtaining the services of another Portuguese interpreter. The police found a local resident, an engineer ("Mr C") "who had a good working acquaintance with the Portuguese language". He had spent some 3½ years in Brazil in the late 1970s into the 1980s; however he had not kept up his Portuguese studies for some ten years before the interview.

As the Court of Appeal observed, Mr C was not able to say his interpretation of what was said between Da Silva and the police was "absolutely accurate" – the most he was able to say was that he did so to the best of his ability and he believed his interpretation was accurate. It was clear from his evidence that he had no occasion to suspect there was any misunderstanding between himself and Da Silva, but:

> What is, however striking is that, if [Mr B's] evidence is accepted, the accused had in his presence denied any guilty knowledge of the criminal activities of Larsen and his associates whereas what is conveyed by the interview as translated [*sic*] by [Mr C] is a series of significant admissions of such guilty knowledge.

How that might possibly have come about was explained by the court as follows:

> Another possible explanation, however, is that there was a real problem of interpretation in the course of the significant inculpatory interview; and that is what is claimed by the accused and by her counsel on her behalf.

The court proceeded to examine and analyse the series of questions and answers as written in English in the record of interview. They noted many of the questions were so complex as to "present to a person not perfectly skilled in the Portuguese language considerable difficulty in translation [*sic*] from English into Portuguese."

The court added that this aspect in particular, made it unfair to Da Silva to use the record of interview against her at her trial: "…in circumstances where it came into existence through the efforts of an interpreter less than perfectly skilled in that difficult art."

Da Silva claimed that the questions asked of her were much simpler and shorter than those set out in English in the record of interview. The court thought, given Mr C was:

> … not absolutely competent in the Portuguese language, and able to render into that language every fine detail of an English sentence, it would be natural that he would distil from the English what appeared to him to be the nub of the question and put it to the accused in the form of a brief and simple question in Portuguese. We find it entirely believable that, as the accused said, many questions were put to her in Portuguese in a very short and simple form which is not reflected in the English text recorded in the record of interview.

Their Honours went on to conclude:

> It appears to us with respect that his Honour failed to appreciate, as we have said, the significance of the fact that questions expressed by the police officers in a long and complex form may have been conveyed to the accused in a simple and briefer form which may have elicited from her an answer different from that which she would have given had she the full question properly before her.

The competence of an interpreter was directly called into question again in *Perera v Minister for Immigration and Multicultural Affairs*. The applicant had been re-fused refugee status. He made an application to the Refugee Review Tribunal for judicial review of the refusal. Kenny J first summarised the effect of the legal principles established by the case law. Her Honour said that in criminal trials there is a rule that an accused must be physically present in court. The rule is intended to ensure the accused is able to hear the case against him or her and to have an opportunity to answer it. The same rationale is said to inform the approach taken in the criminal courts with respect to the use of interpreters. In the case of an accused who is not sufficiently proficient in English to understand the proceedings or to make themselves understood, the trial Judge must, as part of his or her duty to ensure a fair trial, see to it that the accused receives the assistance of a competent interpreter. For similar reasons, there may be the need for the services of an interpreter in a civil proceeding.

Her Honour began with a consideration of the role of the interpreter in a tribunal hearing and the standard of interpretation appropriate to that role. She said the function of an interpreter is to convey in English what has been said in another language, and *vice versa*, so as to place the non-English speaker as nearly as possible in the same position as an English speaker. She then pointed out that interpretation is not a mere mechanical exercise, but one which involves both

technical skill and expert judgment. Her Honour noted that perfect interpretation may be impossible – no matter how accurate the interpretation is, the words,
style, syntax or emotion are not those of the witness and some words are culturally
specific and incapable of being interpreted. Finally, recognising that a particular
interpretation may be less than perfect but nonetheless sufficient, her Honour
asked how bad must an interpretation be to render reliance on it a reviewable
error; and by what criteria is the quality of the interpretation to be assessed? To
answer those questions, Kenny J noted the criteria identified in *Tran*.

The question whether the applicant needed an interpreter at all did not directly arise in that case as it was accepted the applicant did. Her Honour noted it
is apposite to recognise that some understanding, or even some degree of fluency,
in the English language does not necessarily mean a person does not require an
interpreter to adequately understand the case and to adequately convey their own
evidence to the court.[4] Kenny J concluded that there had been a relevant depar-
ture from the standard of interpretation in *Perera*.

3.6   Quality of interpreting: A recent case

The quality of interpreting at the appellant's trial was a major focus of an appeal
by a convicted drug importer in *De La Espriella-Velasco v The Queen*. The arrangement made for interpretation at trial was not entirely satisfactory from the
start. The court provided an English/Spanish interpreter, ("Mr C"). Although no
reference to his qualifications or experience appears on the trial transcript, he
was accredited at NAATI Level 3. He was appropriately sworn at the commencement of the trial. However, a Ms Baroud, at the appellant's request, was allowed
by the trial Judge to sit in the dock with the appellant. The appellant thus had two
interpreters, one on each side. Indeed, it was apparently Ms Baroud who performed the bulk of the interpreting duties. This was explained by the Judge to the
interpreter and Ms Baroud. That was entirely inappropriate. Ms Baroud was not
sworn to act as an interpreter for the court. Furthermore, not only by then was
she the appellant's wife, but she had been personally involved in the activities out
of which the charge arose. Finally, the explanation given by the Judge was given
not to the appellant, to whom it should have been directed, but to the interpreter,
who was then asked to summarise what his Honour had said.

---

4.   The difficulties confronted by persons with sufficient English for most daily purposes, but
who are confronting unusual or stressful situations are discussed generally in Hale. S. (2004).
The Discourse of Court Interpreting. John Benjamins Publishing Co.

There were numerous grounds of appeal, including one that the defence of duress ought to have been left to the jury, but the one which is presently pertinent was that the trial miscarried as a result of the poor quality of the "translation" [*sic*] service provided to the appellant by the court-appointed interpreter.

After the appellant's conviction and sentence, his lawyers engaged a Spanish/English interpreter in Florida, a Mrs Esther Crespo, to review the transcript and the taped recording of the appellant's evidence at trial. That exercise took her some three months, following which she produced a very extensive report. She included as an appendix a revised version of the transcript in which she set out the original transcript as it appeared in English, and then inserted what had been said by the interpreter and the appellant in Spanish and her own interpretation (in Spanish or English) where that differed from the trial interpreter. This appendix occupied some five volumes of appeal books. Mrs Crespo gave evidence on the appeal by video-link from Florida.

All members of the court accepted that forensic interpretation, especially in court proceedings, is a complex and sophisticated process. For example, after a discussion of the authorities already mentioned above:

> I respectfully endorse the approach taken by Kenny J in *Perera* (at [29]) that the interpreter must express, in the target language, as accurately as that language and the circumstances permit, the idea or concept as it has been expressed in the source language. The individual aspects of this expression of what is required, are important. The reference to the "idea or concept" being expressed acknowledges that the process of interpretation is not merely the substitution of a word in one language for an equivalent word in the other and that there is often a lack of semantic equivalence. That, and social or cultural differences may mean that even the "idea or concept" itself has no equivalent in both societies. The point sought to be made about the expression *"patrón de Puerto"* in this case seems to be an example of this. It also acknowledges that, as Ms Crespo explained, language interpretation deals with units or "bundles" of meanings, not words, or what is described as "literal" interpretation. "The circumstances" obviously include the pressures of time and lack of opportunity for the interpreter to consider, determine and convey precise meaning. The requirement that the idea or concept be interpreted as it has been expressed in the source language includes the notion of appropriate register, or conservation of meaning. That is to say, the form and level of expression of what the interpreter says in the target language should reflect the form and expression used by the witness in the source language.

In his judgment, Miller AJA illustrated the complexity and sophistication of forensic interpretation by setting out a number of passages from the evidence of Mrs Crespo given on the appeal.

Mrs Crespo's opinion, broadly, was that the testimony of the appellant was negatively impacted by the failure to provide adequate interpretation. She said her review had revealed 588 errors and 539 omissions. She expressed the opinion that Mr C was not a trained experienced interpreter. She considered that his performance was severely impeded by fatigue or inexperience and his ability to understand process and convey linguistically precise statements when interpreting to and from the pertinent languages, was less than satisfactory. She continued:

> [Mr C] failed to conserve register. Questions and answers included additions or omissions, verb tense errors, gender transposition, incorrect interpretation of numbers, overuse of third person instead of first person, literal translation, false cognates, or failure to translate terms, statements instead of questions, hemming, hawing and hedging; and last but not least, the interpreter [Mr C] became defensive and chatted with the accused.
>
> Mr De la Espriella stated his answers in correct Spanish, did not hedge, make grammatical or linguistic errors, expressed himself clearly and only misspoke a couple of times. Peculiar to his patterns of speech is the use of present verb tenses in narrating things that have already happened, which was not reflected by the interpreter. Additionally, very much in keeping with custom, Mr De la Espriella is formal in addressing the court, the attorneys, and also precedes names with Mr or Mrs, as the case may be.
>
> The accuracy, register and level of language were not conveyed by the interpreter; rather, the court record of his testimony reflects grammatical errors, distortions, omissions and a significantly lower level of language – a far cry from the original testimony. Furthermore, the jury was exposed to the witness challenging the interpreter in his frustration, and the interpreter's defensiveness, which could lead the jury to develop a negative or erroneous impression of the accused.

Many specific examples from Mrs Crespo's report are given in the judgment; they make interesting reading. Ultimately, however, the appeal did not succeed. The court held that although there were deficiencies in the interpretation, they were not so serious as to have the effect of denying the appellant a fair trial.[5]

---

5. *De la Espriella-Velasco*, [107]–[113] per Roberts-Smith J. A. The case incidentally demonstrates one of the deficiencies of the Australian adversarial system where it is left to the parties to choose what evidence they wish to put before the court. Mrs Crespo's claims about the inadequacies of interpretation at trial were not challenged. The trial interpreter was, of course, not represented on the appeal, and counsel for the respondent chose to deal with this ground of appeal by arguing that even if Mrs Crespo's criticisms were well-founded, they did not show the interpreting had been so bad as to cause the trial to miscarry.

4.   Consequences of communication failure

It is apposite at this point to review the sample of cases given above (and they are just a sample) to see if we can identify first the consequences of communication failure and then perhaps some of the causes.

The consequences of failure in that sample alone have included committal proceedings for murder being permanently stayed; orders for forfeiture of bail, or for deportation being set aside; and convictions for murder, or serious drug offences being quashed. Serious as those consequences are, what must be of even greater concern is the likelihood (if not inevitability) of wrongful convictions of innocent people, or wrongful acquittals of guilty people, or wrongful decisions across the whole gamut of decisions made by courts and tribunals, by reason of an unappreciated lack of communication with those involved.

Some of the apparent causes of forensic error in the sense I use that term here, again as gleaned from the foregoing sample, include lack of understanding of the problem by monocultural or Anglophone lawyers and Judges.

The first and most obvious cause is not having anyone able to interpret at all. Next would be utilising the services of persons who are either not qualified interpreters at all or interpreters in the wrong language or interpreters who simply are not up to meeting the necessary standard of forensic interpretation. The continuing perception amongst many, if not most, Judges and lawyers is that interpreters are actually an obstacle to communication.[6] Some of these perceptions are due to a lack of appreciation of linguistic or cultural differences or what the process of interpretation entails. Unfortunately, many are also the product of practical experience. Sometimes that is because the interpretation has been done by unqualified persons because the process of interpretation has not been understood, or because no qualified person has been available,[7] or because a "qualified" or "accredited"

---

6.   Described by Ruth Morris as the "typical judicial suspicion of interpreters" in her 1999 paper The Face of Justice: Historical Aspects of Court Interpreting. *Interpreting, 4*(1), 97–123, John Benjamin's Publishing Co. in which she discusses many of the cases mentioned above. See also Morris, R (1999). The gum syndrome: predicaments in court interpreting. *Forensic Linguistics, 6*(1), University of Birmingham Press, and analyses of appellate cases involving interpreting issues in an essentially comparable judicial system, namely, that of the USA (e.g., Berk-Seligson, S. (2000). Interpreting for the Police: Issues in Pre-trial Phases of the Judicial Process. *Forensic Linguistics: The International Journal of Speech, Language and the Law, 7*(2), 213–38.

7.   An example is that given in Laster, K. and Taylor, V. (1994). *Interpreters and the Legal System.* Federation Press, pages 43 and 91. A cleaner was called upon to interpret in Italian in a Brisbane court. Her services were dispensed with as unsuitable (as were those of a second "interpreter") when the Judge realised she had insufficient English to perform the task.

interpreter is not able to perform to the necessary standard.[8] There is an obvious danger, which has on occasion been realised in the past. That is raising the expectations of the judiciary and the legal profession, and then not being able to meet them. The damage done by that tends to be very long-lasting. The problem here is two-fold. Some of it is failure on the part of those whose responsibility it is to provide an adequate interpreter; the other part lies with the interpreter profession and those who set the professional standards. I shall return to this below.

One of the most critical needs for forensic interpretation in Australia is in the field of Aboriginal languages. The diversity of Aboriginal languages and the cultural complications evident in the forensic setting have been discussed elsewhere. In its final report on Aboriginal customary laws The Law Reform Commission of Western Australia (LRCWA) has made some excellent recommendations on what government, police, the courts and the legal profession can do in this area. Most of the recommendations concerning Aboriginal interpreting are just as applicable to forensic interpreting generally.

There is a patchwork of legislation relating to forensic interpretation across Australian jurisdictions. The provisions are not comprehensive, they are not consistent and they have other deficiencies. Some statutory provisions in Australia allow for an interpreter to be provided at the broad discretion of the court or decision-making body "if the court is satisfied the interests of justice so require". Some statutes simply provide that a person "may", or has a "right" to have an interpreter during proceedings.[9] Some statutes qualify the right by reference to language proficiency.[10] The statutes which use the terms "may use" or "right to" an interpreter are typically silent on who assesses the language proficiency of the witness or party and on the question of who is responsible for the provision of the

---

8.   See the discussion in *De la Espriella-Velasco, supra*.

9.   *Victorian Civil and Administrative Tribunal Act 1998* (Vic), s 49; *State Administrative Tribunal Act 2004* (WA), s 41 – unless the tribunal directs otherwise, a party may be assisted in a proceeding by an interpreter or other person necessary or desirable to make the proceedings intelligible to that party. *Anti-discrimination Act 1991* (Qld), ss 162 and 284: a person has a right to use a professional or voluntary interpreter at a conciliation conference and tribunal proceeding.

10.   A witness may give evidence about a fact through an interpreter unless the witness can understand and speak the English language sufficiently to enable the witness to understand, and to make an adequate reply to, questions that may be put about the fact: *Evidence Act 2001* (Tas), s 30; *Evidence Act 1995* (NSW), s 30; *Evidence Act 1995* (Cth), s 30; *Administrative Decisions Tribunal Act 1997* (NSW), s 71(6). The *Magistrates' Court Act 1989* (Vic), s 103(5) provides that if the court is satisfied that a party to an arbitration does not have a knowledge of the English language, that is sufficient to enable the party to understand, or participate in, the arbitration, the court may allow a competent interpreter to interpret the arbitration.

interpreter. It is implicit that it is for the court or tribunal to make the assessment of language proficiency. Where the assessment is that an interpreter is required, then if the court or tribunal does not have the power or authority to provide one, it will presumably not allow the proceedings to continue unless and until someone else does.

Some statutes express the obligation negatively as a prohibition.[11] Some statutes make no reference to interpreter standards, for example defining "interpreter" merely as a person who attends court to interpret the testimony of a witness. Others (more often in criminal proceedings) require a "competent" interpreter, but in the absence of some recognised standard of competence, the problem in leaving that to the court to determine is obvious. Some recognised standard or qualification is necessary. The only measure presently available is accreditation by NAATI.[12] Thus, some statutes define a qualified interpreter for the purposes of forensic interpreting, as one who is accredited by NAATI.[13]

---

11. (1) In a proceeding for a child, the Children's Court must, as far as practicable, ensure the child's parents and other parties to the proceeding (including the child if present) understand the nature, purpose and legal implications of the proceeding and of any order or ruling made by the court.

(2) If the child, parent of a child or other party to a proceeding has a difficulty communicating in English or a disability that prevents him or her from understanding or taking part in the proceedings, the Children's Court must not hear the proceeding without an interpreter to translate [*sic*] things said in the proceeding or a person to facilitate his or her taking part in the proceeding: *Child Protection Act 1999* (Qld), s 106.

12. NAATI: National Accreditation Authority for Translators and Interpreters. There are currently four levels of accreditation (Laster & Taylor, supra, page 33-34). The first is the "paraprofessional interpreter". This represents a level of competence in interpreting for the purpose of general conversations. Paraprofessional interpreters generally undertake the interpretation of non-specialist dialogues. The next level is "translator and/or interpreter". This is the first professional level. It represents the minimum level of competence for professional interpreting or translating. Interpreters at this level are capable of interpreting across a wide range of subject involving dialogues at specialist consultations. They use the consecutive mode of interpretation. The third level is that of "advanced translator and/or conference interpreter". This is the advanced professional level, representing competence to handle complex/technical/sophisticated interpreting and translating. Interpreters at this level practice both consecutive and simultaneous interpreting and convey the full meaning of conflicts information from the source language into the target language in the appropriate style and register. The fourth level is that of "advanced translator (senior) and/or conference interpreter (senior)". This level reflects both competence and experience at the highest level.

13. An example of this, which recognises the practical situation where a NAATI accredited interpreter is not available, is reg 8 of the *Law Enforcement (Powers and Responsibilities) Regulations 2005* (NSW) which deals with interviews by police officers:

5.   Quality through qualified interpreters

NAATI has made an enormous contribution to the development of an interpreter and translating profession in Australia and the establishing of a system of national accreditation. However, there are serious limitations to NAATI accreditation. None of the NAATI levels of accreditation involve specialist examination or legal interpreting accreditation. All are generalist levels, although individuals may choose to specialise in particular areas such as law, medicine, social work or the like. The majority of interpreters currently working in the courts in Australia are in fact accredited at "interpreter" level (the old level 3). Further, there is a strong academic view that the NAATI examination, at any level, is not adequate to test court interpreters. Practical experience bears this out. A single test (or short series of tests) is simply not capable of ensuring that an individual's knowledge, language and other skills are adequate to enable them to perform competently to the standard required for forensic interpreting. I have worked with many interpreters with NAATI accreditation at the "interpreter" level, yet only rarely have they demonstrated the standard of competency which should be expected. This is not a criticism of the interpreters, who have almost without exception been highly motivated and have performed to the best of their ability and experience. The problem is systemic. The system must provide better training to interpreters, at a specialist level, and must recognise that merely linguistic ability is not enough. Being an excellent linguist is no guarantee an individual either understands translating or interpreting or is capable of performing either role.

The difficulty is not necessarily with the current NAATI levels of accreditation as such. They appropriately describe the competencies translators and interpreters at those levels should have. The difficulty is that the present system of accreditation simply does not guarantee those competencies, and they are often not demonstrated in practice. I wholeheartedly support the move to establish national competency standards. These should apply to both training and performing. Training courses, institutions and individual translators and interpreters should be accredited in accordance with a recognised and accepted academic and professional regime. The legislatures could then embody in statute law, the necessary

---

"a.   a police officer should bear in mind that a person with some ability in conversational English may still require an interpreter in order to ensure that the person understands his or her legal rights.

b.   a qualified interpreter should be preferred over a person who speaks the detained person's language but is not a qualified interpreter. A qualified interpreter is one who is accredited to professional levels by the National Accreditation Authority of Translators and Interpreters in the language concerned.

c.   An interpreter should not be used as a support person."

professional standard required for interpreters in law, health, social work or any other area, by reference to a national standard which actually guaranteed competency. The courts, the legal profession, the police and other law enforcement agencies would have a national frame of reference for determining competence objectively, without being forced into the unacceptable position of having to make assessments of competence they are not equipped to make.

My own vision is that such national competency standards would be sourced through all elements of the translating and interpreting profession, academic, practising and regulatory. It would be nationally approved and implemented. Recognition of competence or qualification accreditation must be at a national level and must be consistent across Australia.

I suggest the move now to such a national competency standard model is critical to the future of the translating and interpreting profession in Australia. All else really depends upon it. Pay levels will never be commensurate with the real demands and skills of the work without standards which are nationally recognised by appropriate professional qualifications. Courts, governments, businesses and others will never uniformly insist on the employment of professionally qualified interpreters unless and until they can do so by reference to a national standard which they have confidence will give them interpreters with the levels of competency they require. Translating and interpreting will never be recognised as a profession until its members can show they have a professional structure of recognised and guaranteed competencies, underpinned by a construct of professional ethics and a national organisation representing them as a profession.

Once national competency standards are in place, it then becomes easy to see what others can do. Courts, legislatures and governments can establish minimum standards needed for forensic interpreting. A court could simply require, as a minimum, a certificate of interpreting in the appropriate language. For a particularly complex criminal trial, or complex civil litigation, they would know to require an interpreter with a graduate degree, or better. They would have a frame of reference which would require them to make no assessment of the competence of the individual interpreter. They would have the confidence that the interpreter with the qualification actually had the competencies including a professional ethical framework. In conjunction with a national regime which guarantees interpreting and translating competence, governments would implement policies of the kind recommended by the Law Reform Commission of Western Australia.

6.   Conclusion

Unlike most European and some Asian countries familiar with a multiplicity of languages, Australians are generally completely unfamiliar with working with interpreters and have little understanding of what is involved. Accordingly, educational and training packages targeted to particular institutions and professional groups are fundamentally important. It is not enough for only some of the participants in the forensic profession to have an understanding of the need for, and role of, the interpreter. All must obtain such understanding. Police require training in the context of interviewing suspects and witnesses. The judiciary need to understand that communication is facilitated by sound interpreting, not hindered by it; they need an understanding of when a party or witness is being disadvantaged by lack of language fluency and they need to understand how to work with interpreters in court. Lawyers need to understand the importance of communicating with their clients or witnesses or other parties through interpreters, and how to work with them effectively. These educational and training packages would include not only the matters I have mentioned generally above, but also such points as the need to brief the interpreter (because interpretation is about context) and to provide appropriate working conditions (including appropriate breaks or having more than one interpreter where long periods are involved). So it is that the theme of this volume "Quality in Interpretation: A Shared Responsibility", is indeed an accurate statement of the only way we can achieve this goal.

References

Berk-Seligson, S. (2000).Interpreting for the Police: Issues in Pre-trial Phases of the Judicial Process. *Forensic Linguistics: The International Journal of Speech, Language and the Law,* 7(2), 213–38.

Cook, M. (2005). Caught in the middle: Indigenous Interpreters and Customary law. In Law Reform Commission of Western Australia. (January 2006). *Aboriginal Customary Laws; Discussion Paper* pp. 397–407. Project No 94.

Hale, S. (2004). *The Discourse of Court Interpreting.* John Benjamin's Publishing Co.

Laster, K. and Taylor, V. (1994). *Interpreters and the Legal System.* Federation Press.

Law Reform Commission of Western Australia. (September 2006). *Final Report; Aboriginal Customary Laws – The Interaction of Australian Law with Aboriginal Law and Culture.*

Morris, R. (1999). The Face of Justice: Historical Aspects of Court Interpreting. *Interpreting,* 4(1), 97–123. John Benjamin's Publishing Co.

Morris, R (1999). The gum syndrome: predicaments in court interpreting. *Forensic Linguistics,* 6(1). University of Birmingham Press.

Cases cited

Adamopoulos v Olympic Airways SA (1991) 25 NSWLR 75.

Administrative Decisions Tribunal Act 1997 (NSW), s 71(6).

Anti-Discrimination Act 1991 (Qld), ss 162 and 284.

Begum (1991) 93 Cr App Rep 96.

Child Protection Act 1999 (Qld), s 106.

Criminal Code 2002 (ACT), s 700.

Cucu v District Court of New South Wales (1994) 73 A Crim R 240.

Dairy Farmers Co-operative Milk Company Ltd v Acquilina (1963) 109 CLR 458.

De La Espriella-Velasco v The Queen (2006) 31 WAR 291; [2006] WASCA 31 at [74].

Dietrich v The Queen (1992) 177 CLR 292.

Du Barré v Livette 170 ER 96.

Ebatarinja v Deland (1998) 194 CLR 444; [1998] HCA 62.

Evidence Act 1977 (Qld), s 131A(1); r 34(3)(g) Criminal Procedure Rules 2005 (WA).

Evidence Act 1995 (Cth), s 30.

Evidence Act 1995 (NSW), s 30.

Evidence Act 2001 (Tas), s 30.

Filios v Morland (1963) 63 SR (NSW) 331.

Gaio v The Queen (1960) 104 CLR 419.

Gradidge v Grace Bros Pty Ltd.

Johnson (1987) 25 A Crim R 433.

Kathiresan v Minister for Immigration & Multicultural Affairs, unreported; FCA(Gray J); VG 305/1997; 4 March 1998 at 6.

Kunnath v The State [1993] 1 WLR 1315.

Lars (1994) 73 A Crim R 91.

Law Enforcement (Powers and Responsibilities) Regulations 2005 (NSW).

Magistrates' Court Act (Vic), s 40.

Perera v Minister for Immigration and Multicultural Affairs (1999) 92 FCR 6; [1999] FCA 507, [18]–[19].

Re East & Ors; Ex parte Nguyen (1998) 196 CLR 354; [1998] HCA 73.

R v Lee Kun [1916] 1 KB 337.

R v Tran [1994] 2 SCR 95.

Saraya (1993) 70 A Crim R 515.

Singh (Heer) v Minister for Immigration and Ethnic Affairs (1987) 15 FCR 4, Forster J.

State Administrative Tribunal Act 2004 (WA), s 41.

Steele, "Court Interpreters in Canadian Criminal Law", (1992), 34 Crim LQ 218 at 240–241.

Uniform Civil Procedure (Fees) Regulations 1999 (Qld), reg 8.

Victorian Civil and Administrative Tribunal Act 1998 (Vic), s 49.

CHAPTER 3

The tension between adequacy and acceptability in legal interpreting and translation

Eva N. S. Ng
The University of Hong Kong

For over a century, English was the only language in which law was practiced in Hong Kong, yet the handover of Hong Kong to China in 1997 has made legal bilingualism inevitable. In translating existing laws into Chinese, the Law Drafting Division emphasises the need to establish a semantic mapping between the Chinese statutes and their English counterparts, and to strive for both adequacy and acceptability when selecting a Chinese term or expression to represent a common-law concept. This paper examines how legal translators and interpreters resolve the tension between adequacy and acceptability, and concludes that the effort to achieve adequacy at the expense of acceptability may not always pay off.

1. Introduction

Hong Kong has inherited the English common-law system, which remains in force despite the changeover of her sovereignty from Britain to China in 1997. The continuation of the common-law system is guaranteed by constitutional provisions, i.e. the Basic Law, which came into effect on the establishment of the Hong Kong Special Administrative Region (HKSAR) on 1 July 1997 and provides that:

> The laws previously in force in Hong Kong, that is, the common law, rules of equity, ordinances, subordinate legislation and customary law shall be maintained, except for any that contravene this Law, and subject to any amendment by the legislature of the Hong Kong Special Administrative Region (Article 8).

English remained the only official language in Hong Kong until 1974, when the Official Languages Ordinance (Cap 5) was passed, establishing both English and Chinese as the official languages for the purposes of communication between the Government and the general public, as well as for court proceedings (Official Languages Ordinance, Section 3, Cap 5, Laws of Hong Kong).

Recommendations for the laws of Hong Kong to be translated into Chinese were made as early as 1972 by the Legal Sub-committee under the Chinese Language Committee, chaired by Sir T. L. Yang, then a High Court Judge (Thomas, 1988, p. 16). Following the recommendations, some of the statutes were translated into Chinese for information purposes, although these translated Chinese versions did not enjoy any legal status. Subsequent to the signing of the Sino-British Joint Declaration on the Question of Hong Kong in 1984 – which provides in its Annex I that "in addition to Chinese, English may also be used in organs of government and in the courts in the Hong Kong Special Administrative Region" – in 1986 the Hong Kong Royal Instructions, a set of former constitutional instruments, were amended to allow laws to be enacted in English or Chinese. Cap 5 was amended accordingly and a new section (10B) was added to the Interpretation and General Clauses Ordinance (Cap 1) in 1987 providing that the bilingual versions of an ordinance "shall be equally authentic" and that "the provisions of an Ordinance are presumed to have the same meaning in each authentic text." These amendments in effect paved the way for the later development of bilingual legislation.

April 1989 saw the enactment of the first bilingual Ordinance – the Securities and Futures Commission Ordinance (Cap 24), which also marked the commencement of the bilingual legislation program, undertaken by the Law Drafting Division of the Legal Department (now Department of Justice), whose responsibility is to prepare the two language texts of all ordinances and subsidiary legislation introduced by the Government. Apart from drafting new legislation in bilingual versions, the Law Drafting Division also completed, by May 1997, the Chinese translation of all the statutes originally enacted in English only. These Chinese versions of the statutes were declared authentic under Section 4B of Cap 5 by the former Governor in Council after consultation with the Bilingual Laws Advisory Committee. The orders declaring the authenticity of the Chinese texts were laid on the table of the former Legislative Council for negative approval under Section 34 of Cap 1 (Law Drafting Division, 1998). Today Hong Kong's statute book is entirely bilingual.

As the common-law system relies primarily on legal precedents in the form of judgments handed down by the courts over the years in common-law jurisdictions around the world, it is considered "unnecessary, unrealistic and not cost-effective" to have all these legal reports, originally written in English, translated into Chinese (Judiciary, 2003, p. 2). The language of the case law thus remains largely English, though a small number of selected judgments delivered in English and considered to be of great public and media interest have been translated into Chinese since 1996, and since 1999 judgments of "jurisprudential value" delivered in Chinese have had their English translations made available for the benefit of non-Chinese speaking legal practitioners both inside and outside Hong Kong (Judiciary, 2003, p. 2). The translated version of a judgment, however, does not have the legal status as a judgment. The only authentic version of a judgment is the one in its original language, be it English or Chinese. In other words, the principle of equal authenticity does not apply to case law.

2.   The bilingual Hong Kong courtroom

For over a century, English remained the only language in which trials were conducted at all levels of courts until 1974, when the Official Languages Ordinance was passed to establish Chinese as one of the official languages. It was the year when the requirement to use only English in courts was lifted at Magistrates' courts. This language restriction was later removed at the other levels of courts in stages from 1996 to 1997 (Appendix 1).

When a case is heard in English, court interpreting services are almost indispensable because, given the fact that over 90% of the population in Hong Kong is Cantonese-speaking Chinese (Appendix 2), a court case inevitably involves people testifying in Cantonese or other Chinese dialects, and all common-law courts recognise the right of the witnesses to testify in their native languages and to be provided with interpretation services. Thus court interpreters have long played an essential role in facilitating the communication between the legal personnel and the people who are involved in the court proceedings but do not speak the language of the court, resulting in what Thomas (1988) refers to as a "limited bilingual legal system." Note that in Hong Kong, court interpreting services, save the services by part-time interpreters, have long been provided for the linguistic majority, instead of the linguistic minority, as is the usual case in other courtroom settings.

Although the liberty to use Chinese as one of the court languages as the court sees fit has resulted in an increasing use of Chinese for trial hearings over the past decade, especially in lower courts, English remains a dominant court language in the High Court. Statistics from the Judiciary show that in 2006, some ten years after the restriction on the use of Chinese was lifted at all levels of courts, over two thirds of the cases in the High Court and about 60% of the District Court cases were still conducted in English, whereas one third of the cases in the Magistrates' courts were conducted in English (Appendix 3).

It thus appears that English still plays and will continue to play an important role in the courtroom, as is provided by Article 9 of the Basic Law that "in addition to the Chinese language, English may also be used as an official language by the executive authorities, legislature and judiciary of the Hong Kong Special

Administrative Region." As English continues to be used as one of the official court languages, court interpreting services cannot be dispensed with. As of to-day, the Court Language Section of the Judiciary still gathers the largest pool of interpreters in Hong Kong.[1]

3.   Adequacy and acceptability in legal interpreting and translation

The bilingual courtroom has a much longer history than the bilingual statute book in Hong Kong. That is, long before the bilingual legislation program started in 1989, court interpreters had been doing what legal translators were later doing. Like the legal translator, the court interpreter has to work with the language of the law, for example, to sight-translate legal documents such as particulars of offences, or provisions of ordinances cited by counsel, although through a different medium. In other words, a repertoire of Chinese translations of legal terminology was built up over the years before the subsequent implementation of bilingual legislation. While a number of these translations (such as *mousha* 謀殺 for "murder," *wusha* 誤殺 for "manslaughter," and *daoqie* 盜竊 for "theft") have been adopted as the of-ficial Chinese translations, there are some which have, however, failed to gain entry into the bilingual statute book, for one reason or another. For example, *feili* 非禮 (a translation for "indecent assault"), *cangyou dupin* 藏有毒品 or *cangdu* 藏毒 for short (for "possession of dangerous drug"), *ouda* 毆打 (for "common assault") and *baoqie* 爆竊 (for "burglary") have been translated otherwise in the bilingual Hong Kong statute book, either because of the need to maintain terminological consis-tency, or in an effort to strive for higher accuracy: "Indecent assault" as *weixie qin-fan* 猥褻侵犯, "possession of dangerous drug" as *guanyou weixian yaowu* 管有危險藥物, "common assault" as *putong xiji* 普通襲擊 and "burglary" as *ru wu fanfa* 入屋犯法. The customary translations, which have gained wide currency over the years, nonetheless continue to thrive in the courtroom. The official translations, however adequate the legal translator believes they represent the meanings of their English counterparts, sound alien, especially to laypeople. Thus, when putting a charge to a defendant – one without legal representation in particular – the court interpreter often has to resort to the customary translation, or to supplement the official translation with the customary one for fear that the defendant might think

---

1.   In 2007, the Court Language Section of the Judiciary had 167 full-time interpreters, provid-ing interpreting services among English, Cantonese and Mandarin at all levels of courts (Judi-ciary, 2007); and the 2006 Judiciary Annual Report shows that the establishment was supple-mented by a total of 411 part-time interpreters, who speak a variety of Chinese dialects or other foreign languages.

s/he is being charged with a different offence. For example, a drug addict, repeatedly found in possession of dangerous drug, who is used to being charged with the offence *cangdu* would definitely be taken by surprise to hear the charge *guanyou weixian yaowu*. In other words, when interpreting legal terms or expressions, the court interpreter is concerned not only about the accuracy or adequacy of the interpretation, but also the comprehensibility and acceptability of the interpretation. The nature of face-to-face interaction makes it possible for court interpreters to sense any breakdown in communication and to adjust their strategies accordingly. In other words, in the process of interpreting, court interpreters benefit from a known or well-defined audience, which allows them to adopt a more flexible interpreting approach depending on whom they are interpreting for.

In legal translation, however, due to the requirement to maintain terminological consistency in the statutes, such flexibility is to a large extent restricted. The equally authentic status which the Chinese translation is accorded further renders legal translators no other choices but to prioritise accuracy over acceptability. In other words, the ultimate goal of the legal translator is to establish a semantic mapping between the English and the Chinese texts.

There are two ways of semantic mapping used by legal translators in Hong Kong when translating a legal term. One is to employ an existing Chinese term to represent a common-law concept while the other involves the coining of a new Chinese legal term by combining existing morphemes if no readily available term can be found in the Chinese language (Law Drafting Division, 1999, p. 39). The translation of "possession" as *guanyou* is an example of coinage of this kind. The Law Drafting Division (ibid.) also maintains that legal translators have to consider both the adequacy and acceptability of the term/expression when selecting a Chinese term/expression to represent a common-law concept, that is, whether the term/expression denotes the full meaning of its English counterpart, and whether it is acceptable and comprehensible under the grammatical and usage rules of the Chinese language. Is this idealism always realised in legal translation? That is, is it always possible for a Chinese term to be considered both adequate in the representation of the English original and acceptable and comprehensible at the same time?

Of the two methods of semantic mapping, the former usually results in high acceptability, whereas the latter often leads to poor acceptability. For example, *daoqie* 盜竊, which means "stealing" or "theft," is a readily available term in the Chinese language selected to represent the common-law concept of "theft," which is defined in the Theft Ordinance, Section 2, Cap 210, Laws of Hong Kong as follows:

(1) A person commits theft if he dishonestly appropriates property belonging to another with the intention of permanently depriving the other of it; and "thief (*qiezei* 竊賊)" and "steal (*touqie* 偷竊)" shall be construed accordingly.

(2) It is immaterial whether the appropriation is made with a view to gain, or is made for the thief's own benefit.

Section 4 of the same ordinance defines "appropriate" as:

(1) Any assumption by a person of the rights of an owner amounts to an appropriation, *and this includes, where he has come by the property (innocently or not) without stealing it, any later assumption of a right to it by keeping or dealing with it as owner* (emphasis mine).

(2) Where property or a right or interest in property is or purports to be transferred for value to a person acting in good faith, no later assumption by him of rights which he believed himself to be acquiring shall, by reason of any defect in the transferor's title, amount to theft of the property.

Obviously the term "theft" as construed in the statutes connotes a broader sense than the Chinese term *daoqie*, as "theft" encompasses the meaning of appropriating property one has come by "(innocently or not) without stealing it," and "any later assumption of a right to it by keeping or dealing with it as owner," whereas *daoqie* has a narrower meaning, which according to the *Xiandai hanyu da cidian* 現代漢語大辭典 (Great Contemporary Chinese Dictionary) is "to rob or snatch; to steal, now used to mean stealing only" (my translation). In this case, the legal translator has opted for a term with low adequacy but high acceptability.

Other cases exemplify the other way round. The term "burglary," which used to be translated and commonly accepted in Hong Kong as *baoqie* 爆竊 (meaning "breaking in to steal"), has now been rendered in the Chinese version of the Theft Ordinance as *ru wu fanfa* 入屋犯法 (literally "entering a house to commit an offence therein") because the Chinese term *baoqie* carries only a partial meaning of the common law concept of "burglary," which is defined in the Theft Ordinance, Section 11, Cap 210, Laws of Hong Kong as:

(1) A person commits burglary if
   (a) he enters any building or part of a building as a trespasser and with intent to commit any such offence as is mentioned in subsection (2); or
   (b) having entered any building or part of a building as a trespasser he steals or attempts to steal anything in the building or that part of it or inflicts or attempts to inflict on any person therein any grievous bodily harm.

(2) The offences referred to in subsection (1)(a) are:
   (a) stealing anything in the building or part of a building in question;

(b) inflicting on any person therein any grievous bodily harm or raping any woman therein; and

(c) doing unlawful damage to the building or anything therein.

(3)   References in subsections (1) and (2) to a building shall apply also to an inhabited vehicle or vessel, and shall apply to any such vehicle or vessel at times when the person having a habitation in it is not there as well as at times when he is.

(3A) The reference in subsection (2)(c) to doing unlawful damage to anything in a building includes

(a) unlawfully causing a computer in the building to function other than as it has been established by or on behalf of its owner to function, notwithstanding that the unlawful action may not imair the operation of the computer or a program held in the computer or the reliability of data held in the computer;

(b) unlawfully altering or erasing any program, or data, held in a computer in the building or in a computer storage medium in the building; and

(c) unlawfully adding any program or data to the contents of a computer in the building or a computer storage medium in the building (added 23 of 1993 s. 6).

As the offences stated in subsection (2) comprises not only stealing, but also the infliction of grievous bodily harm on any person in the building or the raping of any woman therein, as well as unlawfully damaging the building in question, *baoqie* was considered an inadequate rendition of the common-law concept "burglary." A more inclusive term *ru wu fanfa* was thus adopted and considered a more adequate term to represent the meaning of "burglary" as it is defined in the statutes. However, the acceptability of *ru wu fanfa* remains low. As of today *baoqie* remains an oft-cited term both inside and outside the courtroom. In courts, it is not uncommon for court interpreters to supplement *ru wu fanfa* with the old customary term *baoqie*. Similarly, the news media use the term *baoqie* – instead of *ru wu fanfa* – most of the time in reporting burglary cases.[2] It is interesting to note that *baoqie* is used even in the press release issued by the Hong Kong SAR government in reporting burglary cases ("Police Charge," 2001, 2004). Only when the specific section of the Theft Ordinance is cited can one expect to see the official translation *ru wu fanfa* in use.

Obviously the rendition of "burglary" as *ru wu fanfa* illustrates an approach different from that used for the translation of "theft." The question is, if *daoqie*

---

2. "Man Arrested," 2007; "Four Farmers," 2006; "Two Men," 2006; "Burglary," 2007.

is considered an adequate translation of "theft," there is no apparent reason why "burglary" could not have been translated as *baoqie*. As a matter of fact, the historical common-law meaning of "burglary" has changed over time. In *A New Law Dictionary* (Holthouse, 1850, p. 58), "burglary" is defined to be "the breaking and entering into a house or dwelling in the night, with the *intention* of committing a felony," a definition based on the following explanation of "burglary" by Blackstone (1770, p. 223):

> Burglary, or nocturnal housebreaking, *burgi latrocinium*, which by our ancient law was called *hamescken*, as it is in Scotland to this day, has been always looked upon as a very heinous offence: not only because of the abundant terror that it naturally carries with it, but also as it is a forcible invasion and disturbance of that right of habitation, which every individual might acquire even in a state of nature; …

The definition of "burglar" given by Coke (1648, p. 63) is:

> A burglar (or the person that committeth burglary) is by the Common law a felon, that in the night breaketh and entreth into a mansion house of another, of intent to kill some reasonable creature, or to commit some other felony within the same, whether his felonious intent be executed or not. We call it in Latin Burglaria…

While the term "burglary" remains in use to this day, the historical elements of the offence like "breaking," "mansion house," "forcible invasion," and "in the night" have ceased to be the necessary components in the makeup of the modern-day "burglary." As is provided in Cap 210, the "unlawful damage to the building or anything therein" now even includes changing the configuration of a computer, erasing, altering or adding any program to the computer therein. The building in question also refers to an inhabited vehicle or vessel. That being the case, *ru wu fanfa* is not that accurate or adequate a translation as a "mansion house" (*wu*) is no longer a required element. It thus appears that there is no such a thing as a forever accurate translation of "burglary," whose meaning has changed and can be expected to change as time goes by, with more judicial precedents created over time.

As a matter of fact, *ru wu fanfa* is not a product of the bilingual legislation campaign launched in late 1980s. In *A Police Officer's Guide to the Theft Ordinance*, *ru wu fanfa* instead of *baoqie* was already used in the unofficial Chinese translation of the guide (Fletcher et al., 1970). That means that as far back as 1970, some conscious efforts were made to replace *baoqie* with *ru wu fanfa*, which has however failed to gain any currency or acceptability so far, despite its status as an official translation of "burglary." Even in the *Glossary of Terms Commonly Used*

in the Hong Kong Police Force (*Jingwuchu changyong cihui* 警務處常用辭彙),
co-edited by the Hong Kong Police Force and the Civil Service Training and
Development Institute in 2001, *baoqie* is still used as the Chinese translation of
"burglary." Other conventional translations like *feili* and *ouda* are also found in
this glossary book. One possible explanation is that this book is intended for general readers like police officers and other civil servants rather than legal professionals, and thus commonly accepted rather than esoteric terms are adopted for
the sake of better accessibility. Whatever the reason, low acceptability of the new
official translations of the terms cited above is evident.

4.   Conviction lost in translation

The establishment of the equal authenticity of the bilingual statutes suggests that
both the Chinese and the English versions of the statute book are semantically
equivalent and that one may refer to either the Chinese or the English version of
the same piece of legislation during a legal debate, and arrive at a judicial decision based on that. In other words, any discrepancy in the bilingual statutes can
have grave implications for legal practitioners and litigants, or any other person at
stake, especially where a legal term is not expressly defined in the statutes, but, as
in most cases, has to be elucidated through a judicial interpretation, for example,
by referring to legal precedents.

On 31 October 1996, the *South China Morning Post,* an English newspaper in
Hong Kong, reported a court case with the headline "Conviction Lost in Translation," when the High Court Judge, Justice Wally Yeung Chun-kuen, overturned
the convictions of a defiant fish shop owner, Madame Tam Yuk-ha, who had been
found guilty of twice breaching the Urban Council by-laws, citing crucial differences in the English and the Chinese versions as the reason for quashing the
convictions ("Conviction," 1996).

"Tam Yuk-ha could have been guilty under the law in English but innocent
according to the Chinese translation," Justice Yeung was quoted as saying in the
newspaper.

Tam was summonsed before a special magistrate and found guilty for placing
metal trays, a chopping block and a table on the pavement outside her shop on
two visits made to her shop by health inspectors. An appeal against the special
magistrate's decision was filed and presided by Yeung.

The prosecution was brought against Madame Tam under By-law 35 of the
Food Business (Urban Council) By-laws, Cap 132. By-law 35(a)[3] reads as follows:

---

3.   Currently the Food Business Regulation, Section 34, Cap 132X, Laws of Hong Kong.

> After the grant or renewal of any licence, no licensee shall, save with the permission in writing of the Council, cause or permit to be made in respect of the premises to which the licence relates:
> (a) Any alteration or addition which would result in a material deviation from the plan thereof approved under by-law 33.

The crucial point in this case is the interpretation of the word "addition," and its Chinese translation *zengjian gongcheng* 增建工程 in the Chinese version of the by-law in question. In deciding whether the placing of items outside the shop would constitute "an addition to the approved plan," Yeung made references to the judgment by Justice Bewley on the *R v Cheng Chun-Yee* case, in which the placing of three tables and fourteen chairs on the pavement outside the restaurant by the restaurant owner was considered an addition to the approved plan. Yeung decided that if Bewley's judgment was to be followed, the placing of metal trays and other items outside the shop would clearly constitute an addition to the plan. However, when he reviewed the Chinese version of the by-law in question, he had the following comments:

> *Zengjian gongcheng* plainly means "building additional construction or building works." No one who understands the Chinese language would, by any stretch of the imagination, come to the conclusion that the placing of metal trays and other items in front of the shop would be a *zengjian gongcheng*.
> (Hong Kong Judiciary, 1996, pp. 9–10)

Yeung then decided that the English term "addition" was ambiguous and the Chinese language term *zengjian gongcheng* was clear and plain. He added that where there was a difference in the meaning of the two authentic texts, the court had to reconcile the difference "in such a way as to give effect to the authentic text which carries a clear and plain meaning over the one which is ambiguous" (Hong Kong Judiciary, 1996, p. 12), and further noted that "if the two authentic texts cannot be reconciled with one another, the only reasonable step to take is to give effect to the authentic text which favours the appellant" (Hong Kong Judiciary, 1996, p. 13).

Yeung then decided not to follow the decision of Bewley in the *R v Cheng Chun-Yee* case, pointing out further that as the defendant in that case had no legal representation, it was presumed that Bewley did not have the benefit of the Chinese language version of the by-law in question to assist him in reaching his decision.

Having regard to the Chinese term *zengjian gongcheng*, Yeung concluded that the placing of metal trays and other items outside the appellant's shop could not be *zengjian gongcheng*, but might constitute some other offence such as obstruction. A ruling was thus made in favour of the appellant with the convictions quashed and the sentences set aside.

5.   Semantic discrepancies in legal translation

If Yeung is not mistaken in his interpretations of the English and the Chinese texts, regardless of whether he is wrong in his ruling, there then exists a semantic gap between the English and the Chinese texts. Apparently few would dispute that the English term "addition" as construed in the English text has a broader semantic spectrum and thus permits a more liberal interpretation, whereas *zengjian gongcheng* involves the building or constructing of additional works to the approved plan and thus has a narrower meaning. This seems to run counter to the principle proposed by the Law Drafting Division (1999, p. 40), which suggests that "[i]f an English term can be interpreted to consist of a number of semantic meanings, then its Chinese translation should also be capable of being so interpreted."

The alleged difference in the meaning of the two texts was, however, dismissed by Justice Liu, who revisited the case and overturned Yeung's earlier ruling, supported by the other two co-judges, Justice Chan and Justice Wong. Liu disagreed to Yeung's view that the English text was ambiguous and suggested that "variation or expansion of spaces allocated under By-law 33(1) might be achieved without doing construction works or works of a structural nature" (Hong Kong Judiciary, 1997b, p. 3). He further pointed out that the use of the prepositional phrase "in respect of" instead of "to" was noteworthy, which was less restrictive in meaning and thus permitted a more liberal interpretation. His interpretation of the English text is however not necessarily in contradiction to that of Yeung as it is generally believed that an ambiguous term usually bears a wider connotation while a plain and clear one carries a narrower meaning (Fung, 1997, p. 222). Thus Liu's view that the English term "addition" is not restricted to "works of a structural nature" may actually coincide with Yeung's argument that the English term is ambiguous (and is thus broader).

To reconcile the two texts, Liu proceeded to interpret the Chinese term *zengjian gongcheng* by consulting a Chinese dictionary by the Commercial Press and came to the conclusion that this Chinese term did not necessarily refer to "the building or constructing additional works" but could actually be taken to mean "additionally erected work" (Hong Kong Judiciary, 1997b, p. 7). In doing so, he attached a broader meaning to the Chinese term *zengjian gongcheng*, thus dismissing the discrepancy between the two texts. His interpretation of the Chinese expression is nonetheless far-fetched and shared by few, if any.

Linguists and law draftsmen, on the other hand, strove to do the opposite to achieve the same objective, i.e. to prove the semantic equivalence between the two texts. Rather than broadening the meaning of the Chinese term to make it more congruent with the English term, they attempted to narrow down the meaning of the English term. Leung (2004, p. 99), while agreeing that "addition" has both an ordinary and a technical meaning, suggests that in a context where surrounding words like "alteration" and "plan" appear, it should be taken as technical (presumably what is rendered in the Chinese text). He further cites Sin's definition of the term (cited in Leung, 2004, p. 99) from the *Encyclopedia of Building and Construction Terms*, which defines "addition" as "a term used in Building Codes to mean new construction which adds to the physical size or floor area of an existing building or structure as opposed to 'alteration.'" So by interpreting "addition" to mean "new construction," semantic equivalence between the two texts is again established. The problem is, unlike its English "equivalent," the Chinese expression *zengjian gongcheng* has only a technical meaning and does not permit a liberal interpretation as to include "the placing of metal trays and other items outside the shop." Again this is not in line with the above-mentioned principle advocated by the Law Drafting Division. Could an expression that denotes a broader semantic spectrum have been used in the Chinese version?

Three members of the Bilingual Laws Advisory Committee, made up of legal practitioners and linguists, having independently studied the English and Chinese texts, decided that the two were semantically equivalent, and maintained that because the section was talking about "in respect of premises," the English phrase "alteration or addition" should not be taken to include the placing of items outside the premises ("Wrong Law," 1996). Similarly, a narrower meaning was attached to the English term "addition" to make it congruent with the Chinese translation *zengjian gongcheng*.

In the same report by the *South China Morning Post*, the Government Law Draftsman Yen resorted instead to the legislative intent in an attempt to dismiss the discrepancy between the two texts, asserting that the purpose of the Section of the by-law in question was to prevent people from making big changes such as construction works, not from obstructing a public place. The implication of his words is that a wrong law has been used to bring the prosecution against the defendant. Yen's remarks about the purpose of the Section, however, run counter to the view held by Chan, who opines that the purpose of the Section of the by-law is to "restrict the operation of the food business to the location, area and dimensions to the allocated space which is set out in the plan which formed the basis of the granting of the licence" (Hong Kong Judiciary, 1997b, p. 11).

In case of the semantic incongruence between the two texts of an Ordinance, the emphasis on legislative intent is clearly spelt out in Section 10B(3) of the Interpretation and General Clauses Ordinance (Cap 1), which provides:

> Where a comparison of the authentic texts of an Ordinance discloses a difference of meaning which the rules of statutory interpretation ordinarily applicable

> do not resolve, the meaning which best reconciles the texts, *having regard to the object and purposes of the Ordinance,* shall be adopted (emphasis mine).

The notion of legislative intent is, nonetheless, highly problematic, bearing in mind the controversy sparked off as a result of the repeated interpretations of the Basic Law by the Standing Committee of National People's Congress since the handover of Hong Kong's sovereignty in 1997. In literary criticism, there is a well established notion known as "intentional fallacy," a term first used by Wimsatt and Beardsley (1954) to describe the error of interpreting a work in terms of its author's professed intention in creating it. It is thus believed that unless intentions are realized and implied by the autonomous verbal structure itself, they are irrelevant and immaterial. Hence any statement about the author's intent must be subjected to the same scrutiny and to the same interpretive process as the text itself. In other words, it is the "autonomous verbal structure" or the "text" itself that matters in the interpretation of the author's intent.

In legislation, as Leung (2004, p. 101) aptly notes, the notion of intent is even more complicated as the process of legislation involves more than one author. It involves the process of drafting as well as passing before a piece of legislation can be made into law. So when we talk of the legislative intent, are we talking about the intention of the law draftsmen, that of the lawmakers, or the legislature which passes it and makes it into law?

6.   Common law as the semantic reference scheme and its implications

To rebut the view held by some that the common law is not translatable as there always exist certain common-law concepts for which no Chinese vocabulary can be found to fully express their meaning, the Law Drafting Division (1999, p. 39) maintains that one should not take a Chinese term literally to grasp its full meaning, but should always refer to its meaning in the common law:

> Even if a common law concept cannot be represented fully by any readily available Chinese term, it does not necessarily mean that the concept cannot be expressed in Chinese. What should be noted is the fact that when a Chinese term is used to express a common law concept, the full meaning behind the term cannot be grasped by merely taking the literal meaning of the term or deciphering its morphemic elements in the Chinese language. Reference must be made to the meaning as it is found in the common law. The common law must be taken as the semantic reference scheme.

An irresistible inference one is tempted to draw from the above remarks is: it is not the meaning of the Chinese term itself that matters at the end of the day;

what matters is the meaning as it is understood in the common law. To take the above remarks to one extreme, the Chinese translations of common-law expressions are reduced to be, as Wong (1999, p. 31) puts it, "mere symbols in the most unsophisticated sense of those words," and "have no meaning of their own, however beautifully rendered they might seem and however much their creator thinks they resemble the original."

As the case of Tam Yuk-ha demonstrates, it is the common-law meaning of "addition" as inferred from the case law (the language of which remains largely English, as has been pointed out above), not the Chinese translation, that eventually prevails.

It thus appears that there exists, as Wong (1999, p. 32) points out, an irresolvable "tension between the use of Chinese as a full equal of English as Hong Kong's legal language and the continuation of the common law." On the one hand, stress is laid on the equal authenticity of the bilingual versions of an ordinance (Section 10B, Cap 1, Laws of Hong Kong); whereas on the other hand, it is provided in Section 10C(1) of the same ordinance that:

> Where an expression of the common law is used in the English language text of an Ordinance and an analogous expression is used in the Chinese language text thereof, the Ordinance shall be construed in accordance with the common law meaning of that expression.

7.   Conclusion

Legal translators and interpreters perform a vital function in the administration of justice in a bilingual legal setting, and quality in legal translation and interpreting is essential to ensure effective communication between parties who do not speak the same language. For court interpreters, the ultimate goal is to get the message across in their effort to facilitate the communication between the court and those involved in the court proceedings yet not speaking the language of the court, in such a way that acceptability or comprehensibility of the interpretation weighs no less than its adequacy in representing the Source Language meaning. In legal translation, the stress on semantic equivalence of the bilingual statutes and the establishment of their equal authenticity push legal translators to strive for accuracy, often at the expense of acceptability and readability. However, given the emphasis on the common law as the semantic reference scheme, and the fact that the meaning of a common-law term may change with the times as new legal precedents are created, the meticulous efforts on the part of the legal translator to attain semantic mapping do not always seem to pay off. A seemingly adequate translation such as *ru wu fanfa* for "burglary" has failed to gain any currency, whereas the translation of "addition" as *zengjian gongcheng* – however precisely the legal translator thinks this term represents the meaning of the English original – fails its authenticity test, reducing the Chinese version of the legal text back to its former "for reference only" status. This reduced status of the Chinese legal text is underlined by the remarks of Liu: "[w]hat effect, if any, would the subsequently authenticated Chinese language text have on the English language text" (Hong Kong Judiciary, 1997b, p. 5). That being the case, it might not be worthwhile for legal translators to hold adequacy to the highest esteem, striving to reproduce a Chinese term with "identical" meaning as the English original, *at all costs*. Instead of providing a Chinese translation perceived to be accurate and adequate as its English original – in spite of its awkwardness and low acceptability to readers of the Chinese text – perhaps legal translators should re-evaluate their translation approach, and instead produce a Chinese text that is readable and comprehensible. In other words, the weighting of adequacy and acceptability should be adjusted so that fluency and readability of a text is by no means secondary.

References

Blackstone, W. (1770). *Commentaries on the Laws of England*, Volume 4. Oxford: Clarendon Press.

Burglary for Her Easy Rider – Teenage Girl Pleads Guilty (爲軟飯王爆竊少女認罪). (2007, January 25) *Apple Daily*. Retrieved from *http://appledaily.atnext.com/template/apple/art_main.cfm?iss_id=20070125&sec_id=4104&subsec_id=12740&art_id=6749761*

Coke, E. (1648). *The Third Part of the Institutes of the Laws of England: Concerning high treason, and other pleas of the crown, and criminal causes*. London: W. Lee, and D. Pakeman.

Conviction Lost in Translation. (1996, October 31) *South China Morning Post*, p. 1.

Fletcher et al. (1970). *A Police Officer's Guide to the Theft Ordinance*. Hong Kong: Government Printer.

Four Farmers from Jiangxi Province, Claiming to Have Come to Hong Kong to Escape Poverty, Sentenced to Three Years in Jail for Burgling Superb Hotels (江西農民專爆高級酒店　稱來港爲脫貧　四人各囚三年). (2006, February 11) *The Sun*. Retrieved from: *http://the-sun.on.cc/channels/news/20060211/20060211020908_0000.html*

Fung, S. (1997). Interpreting the Bilingual Legislation of Hong Kong. *Hong Kong Law Journal*, 27(2), 206–28.

Holthouse, H. J. (1850). *A New Law Dictionary*. London: Thomas Blenkarn.

Hong Kong Judiciary. (1996). *Judgment on the case between R and Tam Yuk Ha*. Magistracy Criminal Appeal No 933 of 1996. Hong Kong: Judiciary.

Hong Kong Judiciary. (1997a). *Use of Chinese in Court*. Paper presented at Panel on Administration of Justice and Legal Services Meeting on 13 October 1997. Hong Kong: Provisional Legislative Council.

Hong Kong Judiciary. (1997b). *Judgment on the case between the HKSAR and Tam Yuk Ha.* Magistracy Criminal Appeal No 1385 of 1996. Hong Kong: Judiciary.

Hong Kong Judiciary. (2003). *Translation of Judgments.* Panel on Administration of Justice and Legal Services. Legislative Council Paper No. CB(2)1856/02–03(01). Hong Kong: Legislative Council.

Hong Kong Judiciary. (2007). *Ratio of English and Chinese trials at different court levels.* The Judiciary Administrator replies to written questions raised by Finance Committee Members in examining the Estimates of Expenditure. Hong Kong: Judiciary.

Law Drafting Division of the Department of Justice. (1998). *A Paper Discussing Cases Where the Two Language Texts of an Enactment are Alleged to be Different.* http://www.legislation.gov.hk/eng/inprmain.htm

Law Drafting Division of the Department of Justice. (February 1999). The Common law and the Chinese Language. *Hong Kong Lawyer,* 39–43.

Leung, M. (2004). Assessing Parallel Texts in Legal Translation. *Journal of Specialised Translation, 1,* 89–105.

Man Arrested in Yau Ma Tei for Suspected Burglary (油麻地男子疑爆竊店舖被捕) (2007, April 3). *Mingpao News.* Retrieved from: *http://www.mpinews.com/htm/INews/20070403/gb20816w.htm*

Police Charge Two Men with Burglary (警方落案起訴兩名男子爆竊罪) (2004, May 8). Press release, The Government of the Hong Kong Special Administrative Region. Retrieved from: *http://www.info.gov.hk/gia/general/200405/08/0508011.htm*

Police Charge Three Men with Burglary (警方落案控告三名男子爆竊罪) (2001, July 7). Press release, The Government of the Hong Kong Special Administrative Region. Retrieved from: *http://www.info.gov.hk/gia/general/200107/07/0707294.htm*

Thomas, M. (1988). The Development of a Bilingual Legal System in Hong Kong. *Hong Kong Law Journal, 18,* 16.

Two Men Jailed for Burglary (兩名男子爆竊罪入獄) (2006, July 18). *RTHK News.* Retrieved from: *http://app2.rthk.org.hk/pda/news/content.php?id=326896*

Wimsatt, W. K. Jr. and Monroe C. B. (1954). *The Verbal Icon: Studies in the Meaning of Poetry.* Lexington: University of Kentucky Press.

Wong, D. H. M. (November 1999). The Myth of Legal Bilingualism in Hong Kong. *Hong Kong Lawyer,* 31–32.

'Wrong Law' Used to Get Tough on Food Outlets. (1996, November 8). *South China Morning Post,* p. 6.

Appendix 1: Use of Chinese in courts

Courts	Types of cases	Date on which Chinese could be used
Magistrates' Courts		1974
District Court & Lands Tribunal	Civil cases, matrimonial cases, employees' compensation cases, criminal cases and Lands Tribunal cases	16 February 1996
Court of First Instance of the High Court	Appeals from Magistrates' court, Labour Tribunal, Small Claims Tribunal and Obscene Articles Tribunal	1 December 1996
	Appeals from the Minor Employment Claims Adjudication Board	2 June 1997
	Any other cases including civil and criminal cases	27 June 1997
Court of Appeal of the High Court	Any appeal from the Court of First Instance of the High Court, the District Court and the Lands Tribunal	27 June 1997

Source: Information Paper, Provisional Legislative Council Panel on Administration of Justice and Legal Services Meeting on 13 October 1997.

Appendix 2: Population aged 5 and over by usual language in 2006

Usual Language	Number	Percentage of total
Cantonese	6,030,960	90.8
Putonghua	60,859	0.9
Other Chinese dialects	289,027	4.4
English	187,281	2.8
Others	72,217	1.1
Total	6,640,344	100.0

Source: 2006 Population By-census Office, Census and Statistics Department, HKSAR.

Appendix 3: Ratio of English and Chinese trials at different court levels in 2006

Court of Appeal
Criminal cases
English   65%
Chinese   35%
Civil cases
English   74%
Chinese   26%

Court of First Instance
Criminal cases
English   74%
Chinese   26%
Civil cases
English   85%
Chinese   15%
Appeal from lower courts
English   34%
Chinese   66%

District Court
Criminal cases
English   63%
Chinesw   37%
Civil cases
English   55%
Chinese   45%

Magistrates' Courts
Charge cases
English   32%
Chinese   68%
Summonses
English   5%
Chinese   95%

Source: Judiciary Administrator's Replies to Supplementary Questions by Finance Committee Members in Examining the Estimates of Expenditure 2007–2008, Judiciary.

CHAPTER 4

A discourse of danger and loss

Interpreters on interpreting for the European Parliament*

Stephanie Jo Kent
University of Massachusetts Amherst, USA

Community and conference interpreters are concerned by misunderstanding and for the preservation of linguistic diversity. Rather than emphasizing differences in context or mode, this chapter seeks to deepen parallels and similarities across the spectrum of professional simultaneous interpretation by describing a discourse of simultaneous interpreters within "the largest professional interpreting community in the world" (Interpreter #2). The multilingual and democratic institution of the European Parliament (EP) provides a unique venue to explore shared responsibility between interpreters and interlocutors. As policy makers who regularly use interpreters, the effectiveness of interpreted communication in the EP is of imminent interest to all participants in interpreted interaction. Because codes of ethics typically constrain interpreters' ability to provide coherent feedback to the interlocutors with whom we work, this paper summarizes one specific and situated interpreter concern. A contrast between the ritual and transmission views for conceptualizing the purpose of communication is used to illuminate the struggle in Interpreting Studies to clearly distinguish linguistic meaning from socially-emergent meaningfulness.

1.   Background

Community interpreting and conference interpreting are like identical twins separated at birth. Each type operates within its particular environment, shaped by situational constraints of rule and custom yet noticeably similar in activity and intention. Interpreters – regardless of language, mode, or use of technology – aim

* This research was funded in part by the Communication Department, the European Field Studies Program (Anthropology), and the Graduate School of the University of Massachusetts, Amherst.

to generate understanding among persons using multilingual communication. In this regard, simultaneous interpretation in any context is an intercultural communication practice that invokes identifications and relationships among participants while sharing information and ideas between them.

Professionally, interpreters are trained to draw a sharp line between our individual hope for certain outcomes and the material interlocutors give us to work with in order to achieve their desired results. Despite hierarchies of use, such as by elites in service of institutionalizing power or by common folk in order to get things done, each and every instance of interpretation encounters the core challenge of co-constructing meaningfulness from the spontaneous mixture of linguistic resources provided by interlocutors with the skill and experience provided by an interpreter. This concurrence of interaction is what most distinguishes interpretation from the written activity of translation. The texts of interpretation are utterances, spoken or signed, which anticipate immediate attention and response; simultaneous interpretation is not a frozen form to be consumed when convenient. As the American Deaf Community says if you become distracted and miss the punchline of a joke, "Train go, sorry!" (Hager, 1994).

Although not the subject of this chapter, I suggest that researchers of signed language interpretation have contributed significantly to our understanding of the sociocultural implications of simultaneous interpretation because Deaf users of signed languages insist upon their own rights as equal participants in bilingual and bicultural communication. As a linguistic minority group, Deaf people have refused to accept the domination of spoken English, leveling a consistent critique at the ways in which signed language interpreters either facilitate or interfere with establishing a linguistic field of equality. Decades of pressure from the Deaf community in the U.S. spawned a new model, known as the bilingual-bicultural or ally model, which appears in the literature in the early 1990s (e.g., McIntyre and Sanderson, 1993; Page, 1993). A dozen years later, Napier explains, "The current thinking is that [signed language] interpreters should present themselves as bilingual and bicultural mediators, who make linguistic decisions based on their cultural knowledge of the groups for whom they are interpreting, and their knowledge of interactional norms" (2005, p. 58).

The bilingual-bicultural model of simultaneous interpretation is a rebuke of the original conduit model, which presented interpreters as mere linguistic passageways. Seeds of the transition were evident in the 1980s, and perhaps earlier. Baker-Shenk, for instance, reports challenges to the concept of interpreter neutrality in 1986. The ethics that guide signed language interpreter's decision-making today had to undergo a deconstruction of what Metzger calls "the myth of neutrality" (2002) in order to improve the description of professional role enactment. The first conduit model stemmed from the definition of role provided by spoken language conference interpreters. Criticism directed by members of a linguistic minority group at the role enactment of community interpreters (Kent, 2002) can be considered to include an implicit critique of the interpreter's role as envisioned by spoken language conference interpreters.

Significantly, conference interpreters continue to set industry standards for ethical noninvolvement and representative accuracy even as they fight against being removed further and further from the scene of live human interaction by the constantly-increasing capabilities of technology. Already, for instance, a phenomenon that could be described as "documentary interpretation" (an idea arising from the work of the Centre for Translation & Interpreting Studies in Scotland, under the direction of Professor Graham H. Turner) is the norm during the European Parliament's full plenary sessions. "Documentary interpreting" refers to the realm of media not law: specifically, interpreters perform *for the show*. Documentary interpreting in this sense should not be confused with interpreting for the record. Although described as "debate," the speeches given by Members during plenaries are mainly directed to consumption by home country audiences via the internet, television, and radio rather than as engagement with colleagues who are in the same room.

The relative tensions encountered by the different subfields of Simultaneous Interpreting complement and contradict each other. The interpersonal becomes increasingly political, and politicians must engage greater interpersonal diversity. The need for qualified interpreters and quality interpreting for individuals and families displaced by global employment trends, environmental catastrophes, and war grows at alarming rates. Meanwhile, to the extent that simultaneous interpretation is recognized as a crucial communicative strategy, policies and resources are often skewed to provide for abstracted institutional processes more than for the living imperatives of individuals interacting with agents of governmental and social institutions. The goal of this chapter, therefore, is to contribute to bringing the professional subfields closer together so that each can teach the other and both can grow.

Europe has a proud tradition of spoken language interpreting. The field known as conference interpreting mythologizes its origin in Nuremberg at the landmark international tribunal of Nazi war criminals. Democratic justice, respect for speakers of different languages, and high standards of representative accuracy characterized those historic trials in the 1940s. These ethical precepts became institutionalized during the 1950s and 1960s in the first interpreter training programs and earliest infrastructure of what would become the European Union. One contemporary legacy of this high-stakes birthright is Rule 146 in the European Parliament's Rules of Procedure, which states:

> All Members shall have the right to speak in Parliament in the official language of their choice. Speeches delivered in one of the official languages shall be simultaneously interpreted into the other official languages and into any other language the Bureau may consider necessary. (2009)

This is a legal principle of linguistic equality on a scale that exists nowhere else in the world. Multilingualism is promoted throughout the European Union through various institutional policies, extensive funding for language learning, and official rhetoric linking the rights of language choice with democratic transparency and efficiency.

The European Parliament provides a perfect site for studying simultaneous interpretation as a practice of intercultural communication because of its heterogeneous composition and explicit mission. Although the United Nations deserves credit for its own multilingual interpreting tradition, the UN recognizes only six official working languages: Arabic, Chinese, English, French, Russian, and Spanish. The European Commission, the Council of Ministers, and the Court of Justice (core EU institutions alongside the European Parliament) also have reduced language regimes. Only in the European Parliament are all Member States' official languages authorized as actual working languages – totaling twenty-one during the specific time period of this data collection (two more countries – Bulgaria and Romania – and their languages became official in 2007).

In 2004, an enlargement of member countries nearly doubled the previous amount of working languages in the European Parliament (EP) from eleven to twenty (Maltese interpretation was not immediately available), exponentially increasing the number of source-target interpreting combinations, and requiring a vast increase of the interpreter corps. The enlarged language regime, as described by EP interpreters interviewed in the spring of 2005, does function. These interpreters do, however, acknowledge problems, challenges, and changes of institutional culture. The discourse analysis presented here highlights one perception of professional simultaneous interpreters concerning the quality of communication among the elected politicians (the MEPs, or "Members") as they craft legislation and advocate the interests of their respective nations and political parties.

2.   Theory: Critical links in professional interpreting

Much popular talk about interpreting involves a common sense notion of the relationship between language and meaning (e.g. Diriker, 2004). Napier (2005), relying on a definition from translation studies adopted by an American Sign Language (ASL) researcher, provides an example of how this common sense also pervades interpreting studies:

> Translation is often used as a generic term to refer to *the transfer of* thoughts and ideas *from* one language (source) *to* another language (target) regardless of the form of either language (written, spoken or signed). When the form of the source language is either spoken or signed, the *transfer process* is referred to as interpretation (Brislin, 1976 cited in Cokely, 1992a, p. 1).   (Emphasis added, 2005: viii)

This reduction of language to a tool or vehicle for the movement of "thoughts and ideas" from one place/person to another is encouraged by the modern fascination with technology.

James Carey describes one of the two well-known ways to conceive of communication: "Our basic orientation to communication remains grounded, at the deepest roots of our thinking, in the idea of transmission: communication is a process whereby messages are transmitted and distributed in space for the control of distance and people" (1975, p. 3). This basic assumption depicts meaning as an object (a message) to be physically moved, leading to a conceptualization of the interpreter's task as mere management – "translation" is a simple matter of distribution. The transmission view has become increasingly embedded in the popular common sense over the last three centuries because of metaphorical and literal linkages between physical infrastructures for transporting physical goods, from railways to jet airplanes, and ever-faster ways of receiving/sending information, from the telegraph to instant messaging (Mattelart, 1994, 2000).

The transmission view is similar to the debunked conduit model from Community Interpreting Studies, however the conduit model refers narrowly to the interpreter's *place* in the communication process. The transmission view of communication also defines the scope of interaction in *time*. Conceived of as a conduit, the interpreter is instrumentalized as a passageway; it is from the viewpoint of communication as transmission that the path is removed from consideration in terms of meaning. The conceptual mechanization of simultaneous interpretation as a basic transferal is disingenuous because the logic suffices whenever mutual understanding occurs without noticeable problem. However, the transmission metaphor only holds up if one neglects the numerous instances in which transparent transfers of meaning fail. In other words, if one ignores the evidence of misunderstanding (with or without simultaneous interpretation), one operates within a reduced framework that considers only the immediate utilitarian effects of language.

While thoughts, ideas, and feelings are indeed "transmitted" during communication, the habitual practices of language use are also establishing norms and identifications (component parts of culture) among individuals as they communicate with each other. In complement to the transmission view, Carey describes the ritual view of communication, which:

> ...exploits the ancient identity and common roots of the terms commonness, communion, and communication. A ritual view of communication is not directed toward the extension of messages in space but the maintenance of society in time: not the act of imparting information but the representation of shared beliefs. (1975, p. 6)

Coming to terms with a ritual view of communication means realizing interpreting as an on-going cultural invention. Carey illustrates the distinction between the two models with the example of a newspaper. He describes how a person reads for information (transmission of content) while simultaneously participating as a spectator of society: this is a ritual activity that, among other things, creates identifications with other newspaper readers. Simultaneous interpretation is not that different than newspapers, which Carey describes as:

> A form of culture invented by a particular class at a particular point of history ... an invention in historical time that like most other human inventions will dissolve when the class that sponsors it and its possibility of having significance for us evaporates. (1975, pp. 8–9)

The long-term cultural effects of members of a certain class selecting to use a *lingua franca* instead of simultaneous interpretation – in essence, of *de*-selecting SI – is a serious matter raised by interpreter's experiences and observations of providing interpretation services in the European Parliament.

3.   Methodology: Cultural communication and the matter of voice

While sticking to description of the empirical data, this paper aims for a dialogic effect by combining cultural communication theory (Carbaugh, 2005; Philipsen 1987) and critical discourse analysis (Blommaert, 2005) under the premises of the ritual model of communication (Carey, 1975). In other words, repetitions of patterns in interaction are taken as more meaningful than the specific content of linguistic messages. Cultural communication privileges the ritual view of communication (while still recognizing the role of transmission), and critical discourse analysis "focuses its critique on the intersection of language/discourse/speech and social structure... [by] uncovering ways in which social structure relates to discourse patterns (in the form of power relations, ideological effects, and so forth)" (Blommaert, 2005, p. 25).

This study's methodology is grounded in critical discourse analysis because the multilingual policies of the European Union expressly tie the overarching (transnational) institutional structure with individual language choice. "Giving everyone at the table a voice in their own language is fundamental to the democratic legitimacy of the European Union" (European Commission 2008). As defined by sociolinguist Jan Blommaert (2005), *voice* is the use of language to accomplish desired ends. The requirements of voice involve a combination of linguistic fluency and sociocultural knowledge. Do the language choices of Members of the European Parliament reflect a specific kind of sociocultural knowledge? Before engaging the Members, I sought to gain perspective from professional colleagues: the staff and freelance interpreters for the European Parliament. A strategy for analyzing what interpreters say about interpreting at the EP is provided by cultural communication theory as developed by Gerry Philipsen (1987) and utilized and enhanced by Donal Carbaugh (e.g. 2005).

Cultural communication theory builds on Dell Hymes' (1962) theory known as the ethnography of communication. "Cultural communication," describes Carbaugh, "can be understood as an approach to investigating the premises and practices of shared identity as these are active in conversation and cultural life" (2005, p. 26). Cultural communication theory not only outlines a means for identifying practices and describing patterns in social interaction but also provides a set of rigorous tools for deducing the premises that make cultural and conversational practices sensible to those engaging in (and engaged by) them. From this viewpoint,

> Culture is not a physical space, a social group of people, nor a whole way of living, although it does create, when used, mutually intelligible senses of place, persons, and patterns of living. What culture is, from this view, is a system of expressive practices that is fraught with feeling, and … alerts interlocutors to their common life, its particularities of place, people, and patterns of life, whether these exist in conflict or harmony. (Carbaugh, 2005, p. 60)

Some elements of mutual intelligibility about the place, persons, and patterns of interaction within the work environment of the European Parliament can be gleaned from repeated themes in talk about interpretation. The discourse of interpreters, in particular, provides a situated viewpoint on the intersection of language use and social structure that can be measured against publicized institutional goals of democracy, efficiency, and transparency. What follows is a selection from interviews with interpreters about interpreting at the EP in the spring of 2005. This was near the end of the EP's first full year after the 2004 Enlargement added ten new member nations (Cyprus, the Czech Republic, Estonia, Hungary, Latvia, Lithuania, Malta, Poland, Slovakia, and Slovenia). The interview corpus includes three interpreters from each active language, for a total of sixty-five interviews. Representative quotations from fifteen interpreters are cited in this paper. These particular interpreters work with varying combinations of Dutch,

English, Finnish, French, German, Greek, Hungarian, Italian, Lithuanian, Polish, Portuguese, Spanish and Swedish.

The interviews were open-ended conversations, loosely structured around questions concerning how interpreting is working or not working, and the interpreters' explanations of why. The course of conversation was initially devoted to helping the author grasp the general workings of the overall interpretation system within the European Parliament. Over time, the conversations served to clarify nuances and details of how the system is intended to function – and toward which goals – in comparison with how the system functions in actual practice. The guiding research question was to discover what interpreters had to say about interpreting and language choice as deliberate features of democratic policy creation. The one thematic finding developed here concerns Members' choice of source language and the accompanying dilemmas presented to interpreters.

4.   A discourse of danger and loss

> *"I'm talking about the magic of language that's being killed."*
> (EP Interpreter #3)

Much of the EP interpreters' discourse mirrors the European Union's public rhetoric about democracy and equality. Many interpreters are aware of criticisms that interpretation is merely symbolic and/or too expensive. Although neither the promotional rhetoric nor the debate over cost and symbolic value will be detailed here, it is worth noting that conference interpreters, like community interpreters, have failed to generate proactive arguments as to the immediate or long-term value of simultaneous interpretation. Interpreter discourse about interlocutors seems to be as full of complaints (and occasional compliments) about them as their discourse is about us. The following re-constructed discourse summarizes a specific EP interpreter concern about language use that appeared in nearly every interview: whether MEPs choose to use their best expressive language or to speak less fluently via a *lingua franca*. Research into the MEPs' own reasons was underway at the time of publication; the findings reported here are thus limited to only one angle. Every quotation provided below is from a professional interpreter for the European Parliament. Their descriptions and explanations are eloquent, requiring minimal exposition and spare commentary. Each of the selected quotations is a complement to similar sentiments; together they compose a compelling discourse about the choice of monolingualism (the use of a presumably shared language) over multilingualism (the collaborative use of many languages).

Interpreters for the European Parliament consistently and regularly complain about speakers' reading of prepared texts. "The difficulty here is...speed and badly spoken languages" (EPI #4). Comments range from critique of the delivery (fast reading of prepared text) to doubt regarding intention (such as MEPs seeking to say something without actually communicating). Mentioned by the majority of EP interpreters, the problems with MEPs' speed-reading-as-talk was not accompanied by as much frustration as MEPs' lack of fluency in a *lingua franca*. "It's Globe-ish again. It's bad English. It's sometimes bad French" (EPI #2). The general view is represented by this interpreter's comment: "People are getting used to a lower level of quality and a kind of communication that relies on broken English" (EPI #8).

Table 1. Epithets for English

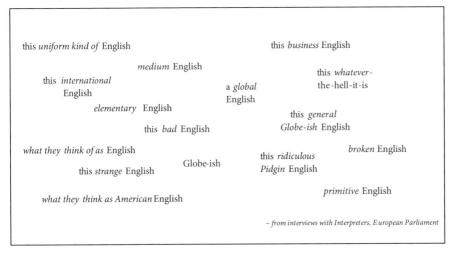

"[T]he English-speaking look-alikes" (EPI #9) are described by interpreters in detail:

> It's not as if it's English spoken by Englishmen. That's one kind of English, but... it's mainly another kind of...Pidgin English that's spoken by...non-natives. Many of the new member states have sometimes a very proximate knowledge of English and that makes for a completely different kind of English, a kind of jargon. Sometimes they don't know the value of certain words or expressions, and that's a danger.
> (EP Interpreter #6)

The sentiment of danger was common among EP interpreters, because "you're not really sure they know what they're saying" (EPI #6). Consequently, the output from interpreters into the target language "might be slightly different. It might not be exactly what the speaker is trying to say. Obviously you aren't doing this on purpose, but are desperately trying to understand something and then say something in the target language" (EPI #13). These three dangers arise repeatedly:

1. Interlocutors possibly *not knowing what* they are saying;
2. Interlocutors being *unaware of* the full range of *implications* of what they are saying;
3. Interpreters inadvertently saying something *other than* what the speaker *intended*.

Accompanying the danger of reduced understanding and actual misunderstanding, many interpreters also talk about a related loss.

"You lose the implications of what they say, the turns of phrase that indicate that something special is going on" (EPI #8). What that "something special" might be was described primarily along the dimension of national culture. "The fact that a Greek tells you something, or a Swede tells you something, gets lost" (EPI #15). Interpreters do not mean the symbolic label or name of the nation; rather, they are referring to something ineffable, a subtle yet distinct quality of mind:

> When you speak a language, you implicitly accept the categories of that language. What you can express is limited by the categories that exist in that language. That means you might find yourself in a position where your political discourse is dictated by what is accepted, what is fashionable or not fashionable in a given language. For example, the Anglo-Saxon way of expressing yourself carries with it a certain perception of the world. When a Lithuanian or a Greek or a Portuguese uses English, in some way I think they are giving up part of their world and replacing it with a sort of internationalized sort of worldview.
>
> (EP Interpreter #8)

Comments about the relationship between language and conceptualization appear frequently throughout the interview transcripts. Usually the naming of variation in worldview is accompanied by a tone of grief (sometimes articulated, sometimes implied) that the scope of meaningfulness possible from the interactions of these cultural differences is being reduced. At the same time, some interpreters try to argue in support of MEPs' use of a *lingua franca* instead of simultaneous interpretation:

> If everybody has a *lingua franca* where there are no advantages or privileged positions among the speakers, then why should they use interpreters? But that is also never the case. You always have someone who speaks native, mother tongue whereas others are required to have this foreign language, and you don't have this equality any more…If someone is struggling with the language you can lose very important points, or a debate.　　　(EP Interpreter #7)

Likewise,

> Native speakers are not bothered by people speaking their language wrong be-
> cause they know it's not their mother tongue and they will try and understand
> and grasp the meaning of what the person who is speaking is saying. I think that
> all the other people who share that language as a tool will not be bothered too
> much by the fact that that person speaks badly. I think the only people who are
> bothered by it are the interpreters because they actually hear where the commu-
> nication breaks down once in a while.   (EP Interpreter #3)

5.   Digression: Transmission model, reprise

Professional interpreters are trained to (try to) avoid or minimize confusion in
the co-production of meaning. A curious juxtaposition exists between the application of interpreter skill and interlocutors' perceptions of the simultaneous
interpretation process. The extremes range from blasé acceptance of unskilled
or under-trained interpreters (S. Hale, personal communication, 29 May 2008)
to highly critical condemnation of the slightest perceived deviation from "the"
intended message. What unites these opposed judgments is that both rely on assumptions that language is simple and meaning unproblematic. Those that accept
interpreted utterances without question seem to presume transparency (or can't
be bothered to work at mutual understanding), while those who expect telepathy
presume any variation from expectation is evidence of incompetence. As long as
the unique multilingual character of simultaneous interpretation is measured by
standards of monolingual interaction, a culture that devalues simultaneous interpretation is being created and reinforced.

6.   Resumption of the discourse of danger and loss

> *"communication breaks down once in a while"*
> (EP Interpreter #3)

What do European Parliament interpreters mean by communication breakdowns?
The same issues are repeated with more specificity: "We see that [MEPs] lexicon
is reduced by seventy or eighty percent when you venture into another language"
(EPI #2), and "[MEPs] can't tackle important things with their bad language"
(EPI #14). These factors can lead to palpable problems, such as "misunderstandings, embarrassment, or no reaction at all, when the speaker obviously would like
some reaction from the audience" (EPI #13). The frequency of such breakdowns is

unclear from the current corpus of data, because while some interpreters observe such instances of breakdown only "once in a while" (EPI #3), others say, "We witness the contradictions every day – the mistakes – every day" (EPI #2).

Why does a norm of using a weak *lingua franca* instead of the fully expressive rhetorical range of one's best official language exist in a political context of international decision-making? Clearly the perspective of the MEPs themselves is necessary to glean a full picture, but interpreters do speculate: "People tend to think better of themselves than they are. Then what happens is they decide to abandon their mother tongue and speak in one of the foreign languages because they think they know it, when they don't know it, or [don't] know it adequately" (EPI #10). Some interpreters are also unwilling to pass ultimate judgment: "They have the impression to communicate better, but do they communicate better? I don't know. It's getting across general ideas, but the finesse, the nuances get completely lost" (EPI #4).

The question of consequence returns, what is being lost when a less-fluent language is used? What is being gained by this language choice? How much will the loss cost? What benefits accrue from what is gained? "If it's a Polish speaking bad English, I have no clue [what they mean]. And this is becoming part of our work more and more. The English that we have to translate from is second or third language English – from people who do not *think* in that language" (EPI #8). If speakers are not fluent enough to think in the language they are using, "It's like Finnish and English: you need to be a Finn to understand that kind of English" (EPI #1), or, "…a kind of Swenglish that will not be easily understood by the interpreters unless they have Swedish or Danish…because they won't understand the structure behind or why they use certain words" (EPI #6). The combinations are myriad: "Unless you know Spanish grammar, [their English is] very difficult to follow" (EPI #5). Sometimes this happens in community interpreting contexts, where the minority language speaker adopts false cognates from the mainstream language, causing confusion for the interpreter. For example, when a Spanish speaker uses the term "*asalto*", it can be unclear to the interpreter working into English whether they intend "assault" as a general category or the specifically Spanish meaning of "armed robbery" (Hale, 2004).

It seems that interpreters are observing language users in the European Parliament in the process of convergence to a monotone form of English. What interpreters observe as MEPs move toward *lingua francas* (especially English) and away from their best language is that "the nuances are lost and everybody gets to something grey. The passion is lost. It becomes more generalized because that's all you can say in that kind of language" (EPI #3). Not only is the content and complexity of conversation reduced, but "people pretend that they understand and they don't. Because they're too embarrassed to admit they don't know English" (EPI #2).

Interpreters find "it's difficult to say [to an MEP], 'Look, don't speak English anymore'" (EPI #1). "Trying to do so? It's very, very delicate..." (EPI #6). Interpreters agree with the democratic principle that language choice is an actual and legitimate right: "You can't stop people from speaking other languages. They're quite proud about it" (EPI #4). "Senior officials from member states want to show off their language skills" (EPI #12). Such desires and pressures add up: "It's very hard to tell them, 'Look, with your English, you're better to not speak it if you can't say it'" (EPI #1). How does the right of language choice translate into practical, democratic equality? Economist Amartya Sen (1992) proposes that we need to determine the actual individual achievements that are promoted by the given field. On-going research pursues this question.

It is premature at the time of publication to make a statement regarding how well Members of Parliament and/or the Parliament's permanent administrative staff either understand or are aware of the perspective detailed here concerning danger and loss associated with practices of language choice within the European Parliament. Nonetheless, it does seem that the evidence is present and available to be recognized and acted upon by interlocutors.

> This is an environment where the illusion of being understood correctly easily gets created. For example, if you are in a meeting and have to say something, you'll probably be referring to a text that has been talked about in three, four, or five previous meetings, so everybody knows what you're talking about. That's a great advantage because even if you don't express yourself exactly, the listener knows what you're talking about and can fill in the gaps, so you get the illusion of being understood if you speak English. This is very dangerous because then you think that with your medium English, you get understood and you don't need all these interpreters...I even had my doubts, but the proof is they don't understand each other. You see it especially when there's a new topic. People who think their English is good have to speak in their mother tongue because they can't cope with speaking in English – the new terms, new reality they don't know.
>
> (EP Interpreter #12)

Learning the reasons and questioning the outcomes and effects of these language choices from the Members of Parliament themselves could provide an excellent opportunity for building shared responsibility for the quality of SI as a collaborative practice of intercultural communication. Research funded by a U. S. Fulbright Grant (2008–2009) enabled action research concerning the system of simultaneous interpretation in the European Parliament, centering on the views of Members. Summaries of some fieldnotes are posted in the category "Parliamentary Adventures" at the author's weblog, www.reflexivity.us.

7.   Turning to a new paradigm

Interlocutor language choice is a matter of great significance to interpreters because of the relationship between fluency and meaning. The more fluent a speaker is in the language they are using, the more sensible their meaning, hence, the more readily interpretable into another language. A concern raised by the interpreter discourse shared here regards the linguistic advantaging and disadvantaging of MEPs based upon varying levels of fluency, particularly in terms of the interpreter's ability to generate intention and effect through SI, and generally as a concern for the effectiveness of the institution as a whole. Interpreters for the European Parliament convey a sense of danger and loss because of an insufficient accomplishment of deep linguistic equality as measured by each MEP's accomplishment of voice. This theme in interpreter discourse draws attention to the individual decisions and cumulative effects of Members' language choices in relation to their effectiveness at policy-making and their modeling of a common culture utilizing the practice of simultaneous interpretation.

If interpreters and interlocutors share the refusal to reduce the location of meaning to content alone (a transmission model of communication), we can discover meaningfulness and responsibility in the habits and routines of simultaneously-interpreted interaction. The locus of this alternative paradigm is the social construction of cultural commonalities over time through identifying with each other in the process of shared communication practices. This perspective privileges a collective – rather than personal – origin of meaning without denying the individual's unique perspective, experiences and potential. Instead, the ritual model goes beyond temporary, immediate, and static meaning by examining the effects of repetition in the medium of use (monolingual *lingua franca* or simultaneously-interpreted multilingualism). Such a perspective on the aggregative effects of language choice is a necessary complement to the transmission-based assignment of limited meaning to a discrete utterance at a closed point in time.

As a ritual activity, the message in the medium of language choice for members of the European Parliament ultimately regards the co-production of democratic equality among speakers of different languages. Will the mode of monolingualism be preferred (no matter which language is the one being shared)? Or will multilingualism be implemented at the cultural level through the spread of simultaneous interpretation? The urgent discourse of EP interpreters flags concerns shared by professional interpreters of all stripes in every venue. I advocate a profession-wide move of "constitutive thinking" such as that advocated by Ryan Commerson in *Re-defining Deaf* (2009). Contemporary social theory is clear in its lessons that meaning is only fixed when ideology and power seek to make it so.

In addition to the transmission of information, the larger and deepest purpose of simultaneous interpretation is to generate common culture among people *who are* maintaining different cultures.

References

Baker-Shenk, C. (1986). Characteristics of Oppressed and Oppressor Peoples. In M. McIntyre (Ed.), *Interpreting: The Art of Cross-Cultural Mediation* (pp. 43–53). Silver Spring, MD: RID Publications.

Blommaert, J. (2005). *Discourse: A Critical Introduction.* Cambridge University Press: Cambridge.

Carbaugh, D. (2005). *Cultures in Conversation.* Mahwah, NJ: Lawrence Erlbaum Associates.

Carey, J. W. (1975). A cultural approach to communication. *Communication, 2,* 1–22.

Commerson, R. (2009). *Re-defining Deaf.* Retrieved 6 April 2009 from www.mosinternational.com.

Diriker, E. (2004). *De-/Re-Contextualizing Conference Interpreting: Interpreters in the Ivory Tower?* Amsterdam/Philadelphia: John Benjamins.

European Commission. (February 2008). Interpretation Policies. *Europa: Gateway to the European Union.* Retrieved 6 April 2009 from http://europa.eu/languages/en/chapter/39

European Parliament. (2009). *Rules of Procedure of the European Parliament* 16th edition. Retrieved 2 April 2009 from http://www.europarl.europa.eu/sides/getDoc.do?pubRef=-//EP//NONSGML+RULES-EP+20090309+0+DOC+PDF+V0//EN&language=EN

Hager, L. C. (1994). *Train Go Sorry.* Boston: Houghton-Mifflin.

Hale, S. (2004). *The Discourse of Court Interpreting: Discourse practices of the law, the witness and the interpreter.* Amsterdam: John Benjamins.

Hymes, D. (1962). The Ethnography of Speaking. In T. Gladwin & W. C. Sturtevant, (Eds.), *Anthropology and Human Behavior* (pp. 13–53). Washington: The Anthropology Society of Washington.

Kent, S. J. (2002). Sign Language Interpreters and the Practical Management of Communication: "In" and "Out" of Role. *Views: A monthly publication of the Registry of Interpreters for the Deaf, 19*(6), 8–9. Silver Spring, MD: RID Publications.

Mattelart, A. (1994). *Mapping World Communication: War, Progress, Culture.* Translated by S. Emanuel and J.A. Cohen. Minneapolis/London: University of Minnesota Press.

Mattelart, A. (2000). *Networking the World: 1794–2000.* Translated by L. Carey-Libbrecht and J. A. Cohen. Minneapolis/London: University of Minnesota Press.

McIntyre, M. and Sanderson, G. (1993). Bye-Bye! Bi-Bi! Questions of empowerment and role. *A confluence of diverse relationships: Proceedings of the 13th National Convention of the Registry of Interpreters for the Deaf,* 94–118. Silver Spring, MD: RID Publications.

Metzger, M. (2002). *Sign Language Interpreting: Deconstructing the Myth of Neutrality.* Washington, DC: Gallaudet University Press.

Napier, J. (2002/2005). *Sign language interpreting: Linguistic coping strategies.* Gloucestershire, England: Douglas McLean.

Page, J. (1993). In the sandwich or on the side? Cultural variability and the interpreter's role. *Journal of Interpretation, 6,* 107–126.

Philipsen, G. (1987). The Prospect for Cultural Communication. In D.L. Kincaid (Ed.), *Communication Theory: Eastern and Western Perspectives* (pp. 245–254). San Diego: Academic Press.

Sen, A. (1992). *Inequality Reexamined.* Cambridge, Massachusetts: Harvard University Press.

CHAPTER 5

Is healthcare interpreter policy left in the seventies?

Does current interpreter policy match the stringent realities of modern healthcare?

Pamela W. Garrett

Simpson Centre for Health Services Research, University of NSW, Australia

This chapter explores healthcare interpreter policy in the wider context of broader healthcare agendas and changing multicultural policies. It questions whether the interpreter policy objective of universal access for limited English speakers is viable in the context of the rapidly changing modern healthcare environment. This chapter reviews some interesting new material derived from my research on modes of language facilitation in a pilot hospital and the experiences of patients with limited English proficiency. The chapter makes a series of challenging suggestions for future healthcare interpreter service policy.

1.   Policy background

The 1970s and 1980s in Australia were characterized by an enthusiastic commitment to multiculturalism, with the attendant access and equity policy ideals, guiding the development of language services in healthcare (Garrett and Lin, 1990). Access and equity were comprehensively defined in the national government's *Galbally Report* (Galbally, 1978) as:

- Equality of opportunity
- Right to maintain and express one's culture
- Ethno-specific service development
- Self-help or voluntarism

This time was characterized by a celebration of cultural and linguistic diversity, strong health and welfare support for "ethnic minorities", and a governmental commitment to the rights of minorities.

It was within this optimist context that Australian states developed interpreter policy and specialized healthcare interpreting services in hospitals, first in the state of New South Wales and then later across Australia (Garrett and Lin, 1990; Reid and Boyce, 1995). Initially small groups of interpreters were employed in large metropolitan teaching hospitals. By the 1980s, with the help of *Galbally Report* funding supplemented by state health funds, interpreter services began to develop based on geographical regions, often providing services to networks comprising up to twelve major public hospitals and associated community services. Interpreters were booked by providers (doctors and nurses) through a central booking office. They travelled by car or taxi to the required healthcare service from one of a series of interpreter offices located in different hospitals. The quality of interpreter services was gradually improved through promoting an emphasis on professional qualifications, rigorous in-service training, peer review, a requirement for interpreters to attain accreditation from a national credentials body, and managerial accountability.

Healthcare interpreter policy was frequently nested within multicultural health policy, which sought to alter mainstream health service structures and culture. Policies outlined the required procedures for appropriately booking and using professional interpreters, with specification of healthcare situations in which it was imperative to call a professional interpreter. Examples of these situations included admission, discharge, consent for surgery/procedures, assessment/diagnosis, major medical events, emergency department attendance, and counseling. Universal access to interpreters for those with limited English was assumed in policy. Related multicultural policy strategies included: appointing a senior person in each hospital as the Ethnic Services Coordinator; provision of cultural awareness (cultural competency) education to health care staff; changes in data collection to ensure country of birth and language spoken were recorded in the patient's record; ongoing consultation with ethnic community groups and organizations; and the modification of hospital services (such as food services) to take into account cultural preferences (Health Department of NSW, 1983). The core content of these policies constructed in the 1970s and 1980s essentially remains policy to this day.

2.   The changing healthcare and diversity context

The 2006 Australian Census indicated that over half a million people (561, 413) or 2.8% of the total population spoke English not well or not at all (ABS, 2006). Of these, 29% were aged sixty-five years or older (ABS, 2006), the age at which hospital and health services are highly used. It has been frequently noted that the ethnic population is ageing at a more rapid rate than the general population (MacCallum, 1990). At the 2006 census, more women (57%) than men spoke English poorly or not at all and the majority of people with limited English were of low socio-economic status. The major languages spoken at home by the population with poor English proficiency in 2006 were Chinese languages, Vietnamese, Arabic, Italian and Greek. Low English proficiency has been associated with poorer health and greater use of medical services (Kliewer and Jones, 1997). Needless to say, the population of people with limited English is extremely heterogeneous, with different nationalities, religions, languages, education levels, lengths of residency, and political and social affiliations.

The context for interpreter policy and service provision has become increasingly complicated. By this first decade of the 21st century, there has been a discernible shift in the way Australian governments view multiculturalism, with the term now abandoned in official national discourse. This ideological shift has been accompanied by a retraction in parts of the governments' multicultural welfare and service role (Klinken Whelan and Noble, 2000; Castles, 1999). At the same time, mainstream healthcare policy has shifted focus from "access and equity" to "efficiency", "effectiveness", "health outcomes", and "patient safety" (Lazarus, 1998; Lapsley, 2000; Eagar et al., 2001). This healthcare reform has been influenced, if not driven, by increased service demand coupled, somewhat uncomfortably, with financial constraint (Bloom, 2000). Mainstream healthcare has increasingly targeted services specifically to those in greatest need, and emphasized a requirement for "evidence" in relation to both policies and services.

Local research exploring the effectiveness of healthcare interpreter services is sparse. However, international evidence is increasingly emerging, particularly from the USA, where the racial and ethnic disparity debate has led change. Professional interpreters have been linked with increased patient satisfaction, greater patient involvement, improved understanding, greater compliance with treatment, improved access, and reduced medical errors (Brach and Fraser, 2000; Timmins, 2002; Jacobs et al., 2001; Flores et al., 2003; Baker et al., 1996; Flores et al., 2005). The literature warns against using "ad hoc" interpreters (friends and relatives) in healthcare (Vasquez and Jarvier, 1991; Phelan and Parkman, 1995; Timmins, 2002; Flores et al., 2003; Calderon and Beltram, 2004; Morales et al., 2006). However, the available evidence is frequently descriptive (Yeo, 2004). While accurate communication in healthcare should not require high-level evidence, higher level studies would undoubtedly promote legitimacy and greater understanding of the issues. There is arguably a need for more Australian and international evidence in respect of language services.

3.   Research on language facilitation

The following section provides an outline of policy-related outcomes from pilot research undertaken in a tertiary hospital in the western suburbs of Sydney involving 258 patients with limited English proficiency. The data was derived from a Multilingual Telephone Survey and a subsequent Medical Records Audit (Garrett et al., 2008a). The purpose of the study was to determine the modes of language facilitation used by patients with limited English proficiency. A further study developed a method for identifying the relationship between a patient's clinical complexity and their usage of interpreters (Garrett et al., 2008b). Subsequently focus groups were held with forty-nine patients with limited English and ten carers to qualitatively examine their experience of hospital care (Garrett et al., 2008c; Garrett et al., 2008d).

3.1   Usage of professional interpreters (Garrett et al., 2008a)

Only about a third of patients with limited English had actually used an interpreter in hospital. There is an underlying assumption in interpreter policy that universal access to healthcare interpreters is available when patients with limited English attend the hospital.

About half of those who spoke limited English reported that they were offered an interpreter in hospital, possibly suggesting that more may have used interpreters if their need had been identified.

Usage of interpreters was particularly limited in the Emergency Department (ED), the primary care point at which diagnosis is established and treatment/care paths determined. Only about 13% of ED patients had used a professional interpreter, suggesting that alternative approaches to language facilitation may be required in this high volume, busy, stressful environment.

About 60% of those patients who were admitted to the hospital had used an interpreter. Most patients, whether they were admitted or emergency department patients, saw an interpreter only once during their hospital stay. However, interpreter policy assumes that admitted patients would have an interpreter at least three times (admission, diagnosis/ assessment, and discharge).

3.2   Data collection and documentation

The study indicated that the documentation of language facilitation modes was deficient in the medical records. There is no requirement to document the usage of language facilitators such as bilingual staff and family/friends. Further, it is likely that some patients with limited English may not be identified as requiring an interpreter as no-one is required to ask, and document the important question: "How well do you speak English?" Current policy requires that a sticker be affixed to a medical record if an interpreter is required, however, the identification of the need for interpreters on presentation to hospital is quite poor.

3.3   Usage of family and friends to interpret ("ad hoc" interpreters)

The study showed that about half of the patients with limited English proficiency "preferred" to use their relatives as their interpreter. The usage of family and friends to interpret was a more frequent event than the usage of professional interpreters. Family and friends played a particularly active role in the hospital care of patients with limited English, although the policy warns against this practice.

3.4   Patient's healthcare complexity and usage of interpreters
         (Garrett et al., 2008b)

In seeking to discover whether those patients most in need had accessed a professional interpreter, we developed an empirical measure of clinical complexity which we called the "Communication Complexity Score". This scale was developed for each patient by summing a number of single item scores each of which was weighted for clinical severity. The scored items used for Admitted Patients were the following: Admitted Score (if admitted, the score was higher), Urgency-on-Admission Score (more urgent, then the score was higher), Medical Emergency (MET) Score (if a medical emergency was recorded, then the score was higher), Intensive Care/High Dependency Admission Score (if admitted to the ICU or HDU, then the score was higher), Medication Score (more new medications, then the score was higher), Procedure Score (if procedures were invasive, then the score was higher), and Diagnosis Score (if the diagnosis was more life-threatening, then the score was higher). The scored items used for Emergency Department Patients were, Triage Category Score (if greater urgency, then the score was higher), Medication Score, Procedure Score, and Diagnosis Score. These items were chosen as they reflected notions of complexity outlined in interpreter policy documents (e.g. NSW Health, 2006). Statistical tests showed the scale had good psychometric properties, was internally consistent and that the resulting model had good predictive powers.

This study found that patients with moderate and high complexity scores were significantly more likely to use professional interpreters. However, there were also a significant number of patients with high complexity scores who did not obtain an interpreter. This indicates that the current approach is failing to identify all of those limited English patients with greatest clinical and communication needs.

3.5   Patient experience (Garrett et al., 2008c)

The Focus Groups explored the experience of healthcare from the perspective of the patient with limited English proficiency. While the majority of patients seemed positive about their hospital experience, the theme of powerlessness appeared central to many patient experiences. Appropriate language facilitation was the most pressing and prevalent issue. Inattention to specific cultural mores and racism in some instances contributed to negative experiences. Patients primarily valued positive engagement, information and involvement, kind, compassionate and respectful treatment, and the negotiated involvement of their family. Respect for cultural, religious and personal beliefs was highly valued by some patients as was supportive systems for healthcare provision. Professional interpreters were very highly valued and at critical times in a healthcare episode, "sorted out" the problems for the patient.

3.6   "Happy Migrant Effect"– reluctance to assert healthcare rights (Garrett et al., 2008d)

In the Focus Groups, patients with limited English proficiency reported some negative events. Inability to communicate in English, poor patient and family involvement with staff, a lack of control or powerlessness, staff shortages, staff negligence or incompetence, and treatment delays were reported by some patients. Other patients discounted and minimized the significance of similar experiences, suggesting an emergent construct which we called, "The Happy Migrant Effect". This construct indicated that patients appeared to be "happy" and satisfied with their healthcare experience, despite reporting experience of very negative events. The "Happy Migrant Effect" was related to a range of factors including: extreme powerlessness related to being unable to communicate, the positive comparison of healthcare in Australia compared with their country of origin, patriotism for their new country, cultural norms that proscribed acceptance, politeness or social desirability, self-denigration for not having learned English, and, for a few, a fear of reprisals if they spoke out in complaint.

4.   Policy in the future

4.1   Interpretation in the Emergency Department

The most appropriate way to provide language services in the Emergency Department requires a well-considered review. This high-pressure environment needs ease of access to language services and it is clear that the current approach is totally inadequate. Consideration should be given to telephone interpretation at triage so as to ensure proper assessment in all cases where patients speak limited English. Beyond that, decisions should be made as to the need for face-to-face interpreting based on clinical complexity and need.

4.2   Telephone interpreting and new technology for inpatients

While some intensive face-to-face interpreting session should be provided for each inpatient, consideration could be given to providing greater access to telephone interpreting for patients.

4.3   Data

At the point of presentation at the health service, the patient's self-assessed English proficiency should be documented, along with their country of birth, their preferred language, and their need for an interpreter. This data should be routinely collected and collated. Documentation of all modes of language facilitation (including interpreters, bilingual staff and family/friends) needs to be mandated.

The data on which to base an assessment of complexity is not available. "Urgency at presentation" is likely to be the best (currently) available indicator(s) of the patient's clinical complexity and therefore, the best indicator of the need for professional interpretation. Patients with limited English whose urgency level is recorded as medium to high should automatically warrant the services of a professional interpreter. (This would require several procedural changes in both assessment services and interpreter services). Beyond this it is clear that there should be a better mainstream indicator of healthcare complexity than "urgency at presentation".

4.4   Family and friends

Interpreter policy warns against the use of family and friends as interpreters, without recognizing the many instances when family and friends are helpful and required for basic or urgent communication with the patient. Family and friends have a viable role in advocating, facilitating language, and in interpreting in situations where a professional interpreter is not available. The policy should proscribe situations in which it is never acceptable for family and friends to interpret (e.g. signing a consent for surgery form). Further, patients with limited English should have (at least) one opportunity to discuss their diagnosis, treatment and care without their family being present. Policy needs to recognize that while many families are loving and benevolent, there are instances where the interests of the family and the patient may diverge. The important role of the interpreter as a "checker" of information provided by families and friends needs to be clearly outlined in policy. The use of family and friends as interpreters needs to be incorporated into policy in a more considered way.

4.5   Advocacy

The recognition that patients with limited English are amongst those least likely to complain about poor language facilitation, even if it results in negative events, leads to a need for a stronger advocacy role for professional interpreters, bilingual staff, and mainstream providers (Garrett et al., 2008d).

5.   Where to in the future?

A major issue affecting current healthcare language services is this apparent gap between the ideals of policy and the reality of the day-to-day clinical environment. Healthcare interpreter policies were built on the assumption that people with limited English have the right to a professional interpreter. Our pilot study findings indicate that only a third of patients with limited English proficiency are receiving professional interpreter services.

Yet, the question remains as to whether universal access to interpreters for patients with limited English proficiency was ever attainable. More importantly, the question is whether the ideal of universal access can realistically be retained in the modern, highly demanding healthcare environment. If universal access is to remain the policy, and there are very compelling safety, equity and quality arguments to support this, then our pilot research indicates that very considerable changes are needed in procedures, processes, and (most importantly) resources. If, on the other hand, priorities are to be set based on resource availability, then there is a case for ensuring that those with the greatest clinical complexity and need receive due priority. The third alternative, of maintaining an ill-considered, ad hoc gap between ideology (policy) and practice is the worst of the three options.

Realistic, attainable goals need to be determined for interpreter services. Such goals need to be collaboratively set with the healthcare providers, so as to ensure they are relevant, feasible and achieve the best use of the available resources. In some cases, such as in the Emergency Department, interpreter services may need to be re-aligned to meet patient's need.

In order to achieve such a collaboration, interpreter service policy needs to become firmly situated within the healthcare discourse related to quality, safety and effectiveness (Garrett et al., 2008d; Johnstone and Kanitsaki, 2006). It cannot be maximally effective and remain vested in the ideology of access and equity which was most popular in the 1970s. Interpreter service research, resource allocation and policy need to move out of the seventies into the new millennium and establish strong linkages between language ability, patient safety and equity which will ensure a vibrant, adequately resourced and viable future.

References

Australian Bureau of Statistics. (2006). *Census of Population and Housing*. Retrieved from www.abs.gov.au.

Baker, D., Parker, M., Williams, M., Coates, W. and Pitkin, K. (1996). Use and Effectiveness of Interpreters in an Emergency Department, *JAMA, 275*(10), 783–788.

Brach, C. and Fraser, I. (2000). Can Cultural Competency Reduce Racial and Ethnic Health Disparities? A Review and Conceptual Model. *Medical Care Research and Review, 75*(1), 181–217.

Bloom, A. (2000). *Health Reform in Australia and New Zealand*. Melbourne, Oxford University Press.

Calderon, J. and Beltran, R. (2004). Pitfalls in Health Communication: Healthcare Policy, Institution, Structure, and Process. *MedGenMed*, Jan-March: 6(1), 9.

Castles, S. (1999). Globalisation, multicultural citizenship and transnational democracy. In G. Hage and R. Couch (Eds.) *The Future of Australian Multiculturalism: reflections of the twentieth anniversary of Jean martin's The Migrant Presence* (pp. 31–41). Sydney, University of Sydney.

Eagar, K., Garrett, P. and Lin, V. (2001). *Health Planning: an Australian perspective*. Sydney. Allen and Unwin.

Flores, G. et al. (2003). Errors in medical interpretation and their potential clinical consequences in pediatric encounters, *Pediatrics, 1*(1), 6–14.

Flores, G., Abreu, M. and Tomany-Korman, S. (2005). Limited English proficiency, primary language at home, and disparities in children's health care: how language barriers are measured matters. *Public Health Rep, 120*(4), 418–30.

Galbally, F. (chair) (1978). *Migrant Services and Programs: report of the review of post-arrival programs and services for migrants (Galbally Report)*. Volumes 1 and 2, Canberra, AGPS.

Garrett, P. and Lin, V. (1990). Ethnic health policy and service development. In J. Reid and P. Trompf (Eds.) *The Health of Immigrant Australia* (pp. 339–380). Sydney, Harcourt Brace Jovanovich.

Garrett, P., Forero, R., Dickson, H. G. and Klinken Whelan, A. (2008a). How are Language Barriers Bridged in Acute Hospital Care? The Tale of Two Methods of Data Collection. *Australian Health Review.*

Garrett, P., Forero, R., Dickson, H. G. and Klinken Whelan, A. (2008b). Communication and Healthcare Complexity in People with Little or No English: The Communication Complexity Score. *Ethnicity and Health, 13*(3), 203–217.

Garrett, P., Dickson, H. G., Young, L., Klinken Whelan A. and Forero, R. (2008c). What do Non-English-Speaking Patients Value in Acute Care? Cultural Competency from the patient's perspective: a qualitative study. *Ethnicity and Health, 13*(5), 479–496.

Garrett, P., Dickson, H. G., Young, L. and Klinken Whelan, A. (2008d). 'The Happy Migrant Effect': perceptions of negative experiences of healthcare by patients with little or no English: a qualitative study across seven language groups. *Journal of Quality and Safety in Healthcare, 17*(2), 101–103.

Health Department of New South Wales. (1983*). Guidelines to Improve Migrant Access to Hospitals.* (Circular 83/60), Sydney, NSW Health Department.

Jacobs, E., Lauderdale, D., Meltzer, D., Shorey, J., Levinson, W. and Thisted, R. (2001). Impact of Interpreter Services on Delivery of Health Care to Limited-English-proficient Patients. *J Gen Intern Med, 16*, 468–474.

Johnstone, M. and Kanitsaki, O. (2006). Culture, language, and patient safety: making the link, *International Journal for Quality in Health Care, 18*(5), 383–388.

Kliewer, E. and Jones, R. (1997). *Immigrant Health and the Use of Medical Services,* Canberra, DIMA.

Klinken Whelan, A. and Noble, C. (2000). Difference in Health: Is Multicultural Health Still an Issue? In J. Collins and S. Poynting (Eds.) *The Other Sydney* (pp. 297–231). Melbourne, Common Ground Publishing.

Lapsley, H. (2000). Quality Measures in Australian Health Care. In A. Bloom (Ed.) *Health Reform in Australia and New Zealand* (pp. 282–292). Melbourne, Oxford University Press.

Lazarus, R. (1998). Health-related Outcomes. In C. Kerr, R. Taylor and G. Heard (Eds.) *Handbook of Public Health Methods* (pp. 6–9). First Edition. Sydney, McGraw-Hill.

McCallum, J. (1990). The mosaic of ethnicity and health in later life. In J. Reid and P. Trompf (Eds.) *The Health of Immigrant Australia* (pp. 312–338). Harcourt Brace Jovanovich, Sydney.

Morales, L., Elliott, M., Weech-Maldonado, R. and Hays, R. (2006). The Impact of Interpreters on Parents' Experiences with Ambulatory Care for Their Children. *Medical Care Research and Review, 63*(1), 11o–128.

NSWHealth. (2006). *Interpreters - Standard Procedures for Working with Health Care Interpreters,* (Circular PD2006_053). Sydney: NSWHealth.

Phelan, M. and Parkman, S. (1995). How to Do it: Work with an Interpreter. *BMJ, 311*, 555–557.

Reid, J. and Boyce, R. (1995). Reconciling Policy and Practice: Australian multicultural health policy in perspective. *Policy and Politics, l23*(1), 3–16.

Timmins, C. (2002). The impact of language barriers on the health care of Latinos in the United States: A review of the literature and guidelines for practice, *Journal of Midwifery and Women's Health, 47*(2), 80–96.

Vasquez, C. and Javier, R. (1991). The Problem With Interpreters: Communicating With Spanish-Speaking Patients. *Hospital & Community Psychiatry, 42*, 163–165.

Yeo, S. (2004). Language barriers and access to care. *Annual Review of Nursing Research, 22*, 59–73.

PART II

Investigations and innovations in quality interpreting

CHAPTER 6

Interpreter ethics versus customary law

Quality and compromise in Aboriginal languages interpreting

Michael S. Cooke
Intercultural Communications, Australia

This is is an exploration of the tensions between interpreting ethics and customary law distilled from interviews with interpreters in Aboriginal languages as part of research commissioned by the Law Reform Commission of Western Australia (2006). While accuracy, impartiality and confidentiality are key principles in interpreting ethics, it was found that for Australian Indigenous interpreters each of these principles may be seriously compromised in practice by rules of customary law. Suggested strategies for resolving potential conflict between interpreting ethics and customary law include: Indigenous communities requiring public education about the interpreter's role; health and legal professionals undertaking cultural awareness training; requiring use of trained and accredited interpreters; and an expanded role for interpreters to occasionally act as cultural broker.

1. Introduction

Australian Aboriginal interpreters sometimes face overwhelming tension between their professional role and their responsibilities and restrictions under customary law. Here, I focus on the impacts of Aboriginal customary law on the integrity and practice of the interpreting code of ethics and on implications for quality in interpreting. Issues facing Aboriginal interpreters may arise simply from having relatives as clients or from false community perceptions about an interpreter's role (that can, for example, lead to their being blamed for the outcome of criminal justice proceedings). These and other pressures are great enough so that competent and experienced interpreters often refuse to work in serious criminal matters where they may be most needed.

Before proceeding further, a few contextual explanations are required.

Firstly, my knowledge and experience limit me to dealing with interpreting issues in respect to Aboriginal languages and communities rather than those of the Torres Strait Islanders of far north Queensland.

Secondly, my own experience as an interpreter has mainly been in criminal justice contexts using the Djambarrpuyngu language, one out of many Aboriginal languages still in use today. It is spoken by about 5,000 people across half-a-dozen communities along the eastern coast of the Northern Territory (NT). This makes it a large language in Aboriginal contexts, since many other languages have speaker populations of only several hundred (and in some cases, much fewer).

Thirdly, most of my professional interaction with Aboriginal interpreters has been in the NT – with a population of about 60,000 Aboriginal people, most of whom speak one of thirty or so Aboriginal languages as their first language. My role has mainly been that of a trainer for most of the 130 or so interpreters regularly engaged by the government-run Aboriginal Interpreter Service. However, while the NT is home to the largest number of remaining actively-spoken Aboriginal languages, there are also significant pockets of Aboriginal language speakers in remote communities in some other Australian states.

Fourthly, the formal research base for this presentation is founded in a project I undertook for the Law Reform Commission of Western Australia in contributing a background paper on Indigenous interpreters and customary law to its investigation of the interaction of Western Australian law with Aboriginal law and culture (Cooke, 2006). The body of this research, funded by the Commission, was a series of twenty interviews/discussions I conducted in the NT and Western Australia (WA) – mainly with Aboriginal languages interpreters, but also including trainers, administrators, police, lawyers and a magistrate. Numerous excerpts from my background paper are included here.

2.   Background to Aboriginal languages interpreting

The need for effective communication between Europeans and Australian Aboriginal people was evident from the earliest days of European settlement at Sydney in 1788. Arabanoo was the first Aboriginal to be captured so that Europeans could learn Aboriginal language. However, he soon died from smallpox and two more men were captured for the same purpose. One of these men, Bennelong, made considerable progress in learning English and was soon utilised as a cultural broker and interpreter (Heiss, 2007). One of the early lessons the Europeans learnt was that there was not one single Aboriginal language since, when Bennelong, who was from the Wangal tribe in Sydney, was taken twenty kilometres inland to Parramatta in 1789, they found him unable to understand the language of the local Burrumattagal.

Unfortunately, there is a long history of reliance on rudimentary English, forms of pidgin English or untrained *ad hoc* interpreters. This is responsible for a notorious record of Anglo/Aboriginal miscommunication often with tragic re-sults (such as the wrongful murder conviction of Dhakiyarr Wirrpanda in 1934[1]). Indeed, the use of interpreters in Aboriginal languages remained sporadic in Australia until the establishment of the Aboriginal Interpreter Service by the NT Government in 2000 – a service restricted to the NT. A few Aboriginal language centres in the NT and WA (set up in the 1970s and 1980s) have also been provid-ing some limited interpreting services.

The need to provide interpreters for many Aboriginal witnesses and defen-dants from a non-English speaking background has been increasingly recognised through a series of judgements, inquiries and reports since the 1970s, with the Royal Commission into Aboriginal Deaths in Custody (1987–1991) being the most wide ranging and exhaustive. Unfortunately, many recommendations have yet to be implemented and consistent outcomes have yet to be achieved. For example, a recommendation that arose from the Commonwealth Attorney-General's 1991 report, *Access to Interpreters in the Australian Legal System* (1991, pp. 82–85), was that a *professional* level of interpreter accreditation be the minimum standard for legal interpreters in any language. Yet, while this is generally followed in respect to non-Aboriginal languages, there are only three Aboriginal language interpret-ers accredited at the professional level. Interestingly, no judge has forced the is-sue by stopping a trial because a *professionally* accredited Aboriginal language interpreter was not available. Meanwhile, formal training of interpreters at the paraprofessional level in Aboriginal languages is now at least regularly offered by several educational institutions and language centres in the Northern Territory, South Australia and Western Australia.

3.   The interpreter code of ethics

The interpreter code of ethics is the foundation upon which a client's trust in the integrity, reliability and competence of an interpreting service is built. In order to achieve interpreter accreditation in Australia – even at the paraprofessional

---

1.   Tuckiar (now written Dhakiyarr) appealed and was released but then disappeared with foul play suspected. His conviction was obtained partly on the basis of hearsay evidence from fellow prisoners elicited through an interpreter in an Aboriginal pidgin which was not the language of these witnesses. This case was extensively analysed by Elkin (1947, pp. 182–204).

level – candidates must be able to demonstrate their familiarity with it. The code of the Australian Institute of Interpreters and Translators (AUSIT, 1996) is the industry standard in Australia. It was developed around eight general principles: professional conduct, confidentiality, competence, impartiality, accuracy, employment, professional development and professional solidarity. Here, I will focus on the three central principles of impartiality, accuracy and confidentiality that are variously and sometimes inevitably compromised through the effects of Aboriginal customary law.

4.   Aboriginal customary law

It is, of course, very difficult to give the sense of a culture and its law in a few words. And the first thing to be said about Aboriginal culture and law is that while there are central themes, there is also wide variation among the many Aboriginal nations across Australia. However, what can be safely said is that Aboriginal society, culture and law are based in kinship and that Aboriginal kinship systems encompass not only family relationships between individuals, but also individual and group kinship with other groups, with land, with languages and with the natural and spiritual worlds. Kinship is the basis of Aboriginal philosophy, social structure, social behaviour, interpersonal behaviour and law.

Within any language group every individual is related to every other individual in one or other of twenty or more different rule-governed kinship categories (the number and characteristics vary across tribal groups). For example, a man's brothers-in-law include not only the husbands of his sisters, but any of scores of men or boys who are in the right kinship category to marry someone in his sister's kinship category.

The identity of a relationship between two people sets the rules for how they are to speak to one another and behave with one another. For example, a man should not face his sister when speaking to her, nor be alone with her. This applies whether she is a blood sister or a categorical sister whom he barely knows. He can't speak or listen to conversation about her dress, her appearance, her relationships with men, her health or any other personal matters at all. A man's avoidance of anything personal about his actual or categorical sisters also carries over to restrict his interaction with their actual or categorical male partners (i.e. brothers-in-law) who *are* able to communicate intimately with these same girls and women.

The presence or operation of Aboriginal customary law is not nullified when a community member becomes subject to Australian criminal law, especially when the offence is also a serious offence under customary law. There are some instances where the offender may be dealt with by each system. In others, elders might wait to see first how the offender is dealt with by the courts. The legal interpreter is seen as having a significant role and this is reflected in the consensus among Aboriginal language interpreters that mature individuals who are respected as individuals in their community are more readily accepted as interpreters than young people (and particularly young women).

The respect given to law by Aboriginal elders is reflected in the expectation that the legal interpreter will be educated not only in two languages but in two laws. In this sense the bar is perhaps set higher for legal interpreters by Aboriginal communities than by the mainstream agencies who use them. Indigenous people do not see legal interpreters as mere language technicians or linguistic conduits as interpreters are often likened to in legal circles. Aboriginal perspectives are encapsulated in these comments by a senior female interpreter:

> The other thing that is peculiar to our traditional customary practice is that older people are to be utilised rather than the younger people ... as interpreters. ...
> Lately, ... the old people felt I had to be put through a ceremony to receive my shield, my *coolamon*, with my story and the poison story as well: the story that gives me real authority to be able to speak. ... [So] my uncles put me through ceremony. ...
> If I am younger, I would not be able to do some of the rape cases. If I was younger, I would not be able to do the murder cases, the homicides. I would have to keep it [to] just petty things: drink driving and things like that. ...
> [Even] if I was a brilliant interpreter, I would not have respect from those back there [in my community] if I was doing that kind of thing. Unlike, I guess, the dominant culture which is the European culture here. With age [for us] comes respect and protection as well. ...
> I do very well because, at my age, I am considered by my traditional group to be almost genderless. I am no longer a young woman. I have had men who have committed rape. I have had men who have violated their own daughter who was under aged. And I've talked to them. And I've talked to them in such a way that they did not feel uncomfortable. (Cooke, 2006, pp. 89–90)

5. The principle of impartiality

The development of interpreter codes of conduct in Australia has proceeded largely without input from Aboriginal languages interpreters or particular consideration of their situation. For example, in 1986 the Standing Committee of Attorneys-General set guidelines governing the use of interpreters in the Australian legal system. They required each jurisdiction to ensure, amongst other things, that interpreters "be independent of litigants" (Commonwealth Attorney-General's Department, 1991, paragraph 2.1.2). Yet this is generally an impossible stipulation for Aboriginal interpreters who would personally know most, and be related to all, members of their speech community – with consequent rights and obligations under customary law according to the kinship category. It is obviously unsatisfactory that the situation of Aboriginal interpreting was neither recognised nor addressed in this determination.

A further complication arises in criminal justice contexts where the perpetrator and victim come from the same community. Serious offences polarise communities, often along kinship lines, and the interpreter may be caught up in this. As a result, Aboriginal interpreters may experience a conflict of interest between their interpreting role and their kinship or other obligations towards their Aboriginal client, or they may not be able to maintain objectivity and professional detachment in the face of community feeling or indeed their own feelings in relation to the situation at hand. As one senior interpreter has put it:

> The hardest thing for me ... has been to stay objective and detached where, say, you came from a clan of a thousand people or eight hundred people. Every one of those are involved with your day-to-day life ... because you are a cog in that wheel, the whole of that wheel that's the community. ... The pains are great, the emotional stress is great and one of the things that we [need] ... is a place where we can debrief ... and it really is difficult because emotionally, you are involved.
> (Cooke, 2006, p. 89)

Trained and experienced interpreters often *can* interpret impartially for their Aboriginal relations in legal situations provided that they are not emotionally affected by the case or by the interviewee. They are assisted by a strategy of discussing the kinship situation with the non-Aboriginal interviewer and carefully explaining to the Aboriginal client their role as interpreter:

> I've actually done that with my very close cousin, very close family of mine [who] was involved but then I had to let the police know, and I have to tell the interpreter service this is very close family of mine. But then they couldn't get another interpreter ... so they used me and I said, ... 'I'll just interpret whatever questions you give and I'm not here to help her'. And I told my sister, 'I'm not here to help you. I'll just interpret *nhungu matha* (your speech), and for the police. And that's it'.
> (Cooke, 2006, p. 102)

Nevertheless, even when interpreters are confident of their own impartiality, their Aboriginal clients or community members may not be. As a consequence, many interpreters refuse to work where conflict is strong:

...the role of the interpreter is just not understood widely by Aboriginal people. ... That's why you get a lot of people, community people, too scared to do that kind of stuff, and especially court. You know, if you approach them they'll say 'No way! I don't want to be blamed for something.' I know I gave up interpreting because of all that stuff. ... Police station [is all] right, you know, when they taking kids in, they just go and pick up family and stuff to help them. That's all right but, you know, court, ... important things like murder or rape or something: too big! ... I stopped doing court interpreting years ago. ... Just time after time you know ... like going back and people saying, 'What happened?' They just didn't really understand what the interpreter's role was, and I just got sick of sort of being blamed, you know, for allowing people to go free or putting people in.

(Cooke, 2006, p. 85)

Some potential difficulties can be avoided by attending carefully to the choice of interpreter. Agencies who wish to book an interpreter need to provide the interpreter service with adequate information including the interviewee's name, language, community and the nature of the interview. This information allows an interpreter service to anticipate potential complications when selecting an interpreter.

There are other strategies that can help avert or minimise potential conflicts of interest or challenges to objectivity:

- For each language, establishing a pool of male and female interpreters from different family groups and from different communities;
- Use of non-Aboriginal interpreters, where available, may sometimes be necessary. (However, with so very few non-Aboriginal people fluent in Aboriginal languages this is usually not a real option.)
- Police, lawyers and members of the judiciary require sufficient cultural awareness training to anticipate, enquire about and deal with potential compromising factors facing an Aboriginal interpreter in respect of their impending assignment.
- Community education about the role of an interpreter and providing people with the opportunity to see interpreters at work will help Aboriginal clients become familiar with the principle that interpreters must not attempt to influence the direction or outcome of an interview.
- Interpreters may require debriefing or access to counselling following upsetting or traumatic assignments (e.g. interviews concerning extreme violence to relatives or about recently deceased relatives). They need training to develop strategies for minimising or otherwise dealing with the emotional impact of traumatic and upsetting interviews and to learn to recognise when they are losing objectivity during an assignment (and therefore to withdraw).

6.   The principle of confidentiality

Interpreters gain access to highly sensitive and confidential information about family and community members in the course of their work. While trained interpreters are clear that they must not share information learnt during an assignment (with legally defined exceptions), they may sometimes be heavily pressured by elders or other family members for information as these two excerpts from interviews with interpreters reveal:

> Some [information] can be pushed outside through the family way: [Aboriginal] politics. Like we were saying the other day: policeman can't get information – I zip up my mouth – not say anything, and then the police will probably try another one ... and makes the person talk. ... Same on the Yolngu side [to] force it out of my mouth!...
> And even old stories will be forced out! Even if you stamp on the story with your foot it will still come out.   (Cooke, 2006, p. 96)

To counter this, community education is again critical so that people come to understand that the interpreter is not allowed to share information. The exclusive use of trained interpreters also assists by ensuring that this principle is observed to be consistently applied (untrained *ad hoc* interpreters are under no such constraint).

One strategy suggested by an interpreter is to assert her restriction from sharing information by proclaiming the information to be secret/sacred under customary law, thus making it unutterable:

> [I would say]: 'I'm under oath and I won't tell anyone.' – a [sacred] proclamation – through this path we can be assisted. Same like swearing on the Bible, that we won't tell. Like it's a [sacred/secret] story.   (Cooke, 2006, p. 96)

Yet one can imagine circumstances in which elders may require information urgently where, for example, their clan or community is in turmoil after being grossly offended on behalf of a victim who is their member, and where the interpreter is the only person whom they are able to access who knows the details of the offence through having interpreted for the suspect at the police station. The interpreter may experience a serious ethical dilemma in circumstances where sharing the information might assist elders in diffusing a tense and possibly violent community situation.

In this scenario (if the interpreter is willing to step outside of the interpreter's role to assist), police could enable the interpreter to report on what transpired at interview by seeking the consent of the suspect. But this presumes a level of cultural awareness and sensitivity on the part of police and lawyers that is not always present. Nevertheless, the point to be made here is that ethical issues and dilemmas facing interpreters arising from the operation of customary law may often be discussed and resolved if the quality of intercultural communication is high, channels of communication are open and cultural awareness is well developed.

7.   The principle of accuracy

AUSIT's annotations concerning accuracy in their Code of Ethics (1996) include:

- Interpreters shall convey the whole message, including derogatory or vulgar remarks, as well as non-verbal cues.
- Interpreters and translators shall not alter, make additions to, or omit anything from their assigned work.

While customary law in respect of language use may vary from tribe to tribe, there are some common examples that may affect Aboriginal interpreters in their work:

- Respectful language is used when interpreting for an elder.
- Some relatives must be addressed in the plural form (just as respect is signified in French by addressing people using *vous* instead of *tu* for *you*).
- Vulgar speech must not be used in many circumstances (as one interpreter said, "you put it another way").
- During periods of ceremony people may be further constrained in who they talk to and how they talk.

An interpreter must not only tailor their speaking style according to whom they are addressing, but also according to whom they are referring. Thus, a man cannot be asked personal questions about a female categorised as his sister without causing great offence which then introduces a significant unintended dynamic into the interview. Another common constraint is to avoid talking about recently deceased people, to avoid using their name (and even any words sounding like their name), and instead to refer to them indirectly or obliquely, or by using the plural pronoun *they* instead of *he* or *she*.

The consequence of these factors is that the course of police and courtroom interviews may be affected in ways that are not recognised or appreciated by the interviewer. On the other hand, if an Aboriginal interpreter insisted on putting their customary law aside and always interpreted questions in the form and manner in which they were asked, then the course of the interview would still be impacted by dynamics of embarrassment, hostility or even a reluctance to proceed on the part of the interviewee. Such unintended communicative effects then also compromise accuracy.

So what are possible responses to this? First, it is important to recognise that these are legitimate constraints which need to be understood and accommodated. It is imperative, for example, for cross-examining counsel to realise that, in circumstances where respectful language is required of interpreter to witness, attempting to unsettle the witness through aggressive questioning uttered in challenging tones might necessarily fall flat.

Again, education and training are indicated. Police, lawyers, magistrates and judges who deal with Aboriginal people need training in intercultural communication and cross-cultural awareness so that they can anticipate the impact of their style of speaking, adjust their style according to the circumstances, and seek and be receptive to advice from the interpreter about the cultural dynamics which may be affecting communication during an interview. This training should not be seen as an added burden but as an extra tool. For example, the advocate who wishes to "vigorously" cross-examine an elder would then know to begin by locating a mature interpreter.

Both counsel and witness would also be assisted by the witness being advised beforehand – through the interpreter – of the process they are about to undergo and to be alerted to its key characteristics (bear in mind that English-speaking Australians absorb this information through the mass media). Community education about these matters, including the role of a witness, would also promote greater acceptance of courtroom questioning as an essential component of justice rather than being feared as a terrifying ordeal of white-man's law.

For the Aboriginal witness who knows the interpreter as a relative and as an individual there is an additional essentially perplexing aspect of the interpreter's role that many might not appreciate. This is the provision that the interpreter should not interpret counsel's utterances in the manner of *reporting* to the witness what counsel has said, but must adopt the persona of counsel and, in effect, play the role of counsel by speaking their words (in the other language) and even adopting their tone. Confusion arises when counsel says something like: "That's not true, is it?" because, when the witness hears the interpreter uttering this in their own language, the witness may assume that the interpreter is speaking person-to-person rather than as an actor. This reinforces the critical importance of providing the interpreter with adequate opportunity to fully explain this aspect of their role (The alternative is for the interpreter to preface all questions addressed by advocates with: "That lawyer is speaking to you like this: ... (*the interpreter then speaks as the lawyer*).").

Finally, there is another challenge to accuracy: the need for an interpreter to sometimes *explain* what cannot be simply translated. One interpreter put the issue in these terms:

> When we do interpreting there's sometimes words, these legal words, that may
> mean nothing to us in our language. So we've got to tell it like a story, so that
> people understand or get the gist of ... what this business is all about. So some-
> times it's really hard to use legal words too when we're interpreting; so we've got
> to tell it like a story, to get the story right and to do it right. (Cooke, 2006, p. 89)

Whether or not interpreters are permitted to explain what cannot be simply translated is questionable. While this is not so much an issue of customary law, it is nevertheless important that courts more readily acknowledge and accommodate the reality that straightforward translation is not always possible because of the fact that explication, or even explanation, of some terms and concepts may be required if a witness is to understand the lawyer's intended meaning or, indeed, if the lawyer is to understand the witness's intended meaning.[2]

8.   Quality and compromise – a shared responsibility

There are some remarkable Aboriginal interpreters who have found ways, through experience, intelligence and training, to successfully negotiate the minefield I have been exposing here. Yet their pursuit of quality in community interpreting may entail compromises.

Take one example, of the female interpreter who is able to deal with direct police questioning on intimate sexual details of a male suspect's actions in a sexual assault, by "putting it another way". And, incidentally, this is not just restricted to female interpreters. The seniority or kinship position of a suspect in relation to a male interpreter may also demand this. The use of euphemism may allow precise communication. Without it the interview may not be possible. Yet it carries the consequence that a defence lawyer can argue that semantic ambiguity inherent in the use of euphemism destroys the interview's evidentiary value as a confession.

I am not making the point that interpreters must be permitted to use euphemism, but that this compromise allows communication to proceed where it would not proceed otherwise. On the other hand, the principle of accuracy requires the interpreter to say it as it is. This may be so, but with the consequence that the interview would often halt with the first explicit question. And while this is not the interpreter's problem, it would mean that many sexual assaults could not be properly investigated through questioning the suspect or, indeed, the victim. In this way, the criminal justice process might be considered compromised.

---

2.   This position is set out by the writer in Cooke (1995, pp. 37–66).

Alternatively, the interpreter may play the role of cultural broker, explaining to the police officer the inherent difficulty of asking utterly explicit questions of every facet of a sexual act and the likely consequence of doing so. And then the interpreter would need to explain to the suspect how, under Australian law, police and lawyers aren't satisfied with him confessing to what he did, but that they want to know the whole story, step-by-step, in explicit sexual detail. The interpreter is then acting as a go-between, helping police and suspect to negotiate the ground rules of the impending conversation.

I am not taking one position or another here in this, or other examples. Rather, I have been explaining some of the ways in which Aboriginal customary law impacts upon the practice of interpreting in Aboriginal contexts. It is up to the main players – the interpreting profession, interpreting services, police, courts, legislators and Aboriginal and non-Aboriginal communities – to address our shared responsibility for quality in Aboriginal interpreting by acknowledging and addressing the impacts of customary law.

I am pleased to note that in some jurisdictions this conversation is progressing. For example, the Law Reform Commission of Western Australia (2006) recently concluded a six-year inquiry into the interaction of Western Australian law with Aboriginal law and culture. The report includes recommendations for: community education about the role of interpreters (Recommendation #123); establishing guidelines for using Aboriginal language interpreters in court (#124); more training for Aboriginal interpreters (#119); cultural awareness training for police (#56) and judicial officers (#128); and establishment of a state-wide Aboriginal languages interpreter service (#117). We now await their implementation.

It is particularly important for the interpreting profession to continue to play its part and I trust that the interpreting industry in Australia will also examine these issues of customary law and interpreting ethics in respect of the interpreting profession's Aboriginal constituency.

References

Australian Institute of Interpreters and Translators. (1996). *AUSIT Code of Ethics*. Retrieved 1 April, 2007 from http://server.dream-fusion.net/ausit2/pics/ethics.pdf
Commonwealth Attorney-General's Department. (1991). *Access to Interpreters in the Australian Legal System*. Canberra: Australian Government Printing Service.
Cooke, M. (1995). Understood by All Concerned? Anglo/Aboriginal Legal Translation. In M. Morris (Ed.), *Translation and the Law* (pp. 37–66). Amsterdam/Philadelphia: John Benjamins.

Cooke, M. (2006). Caught in the Middle: Indigenous Interpreters and Customary Law. In *AboriginalCustomary Laws: Background papers* (pp. 77–120) Law Reform Commission of Western Australia. Perth: Government of Western Australia. (Paper accessible from http://www.lrc.justice.wa.gov.au/094-BP.html)

Elkin, A. P. (1947). Aboriginal Evidence and Justice in North Australia. *Oceania, XVIII*(3), 182–204.

Heiss, A. (2007) *Significant Aboriginal People in Sydney*. Retrieved 1 April, 2007 from http://www.cityofsydney.nsw.gov.au/barani/themes/theme7.htm

Law Reform Commission of Western Australia. (2006). *Project No. 94*: *Aboriginal Customary Laws – Final Report*. Perth: Government of Western Australia.

Royal Commission into Aboriginal Deaths in Custody. (1991). *National Report: Overview and Recommendations,* Commissioner Elliot Johnston QC, (Chairperson). Canberra: Australian Government Printing Service.

CHAPTER 7

A shared responsibility
in the administration of justice

A pilot study of signed language
interpretation access for deaf jurors

Jemina Napier, David Spencer and Joe Sabolcec
Macquarie University, Australia

To date, no research has been conducted on interpreting for deaf jurors, as people are not typically eligible to serve as jurors if they cannot understand the language of the court. This chapter reports one aspect of a pioneering pilot study in Australia, which sought to investigate the capacity for deaf people to serve as jurors in criminal court by accessing courtroom discourse via signed language interpreters. Results of an experimental comprehension test administered to six deaf and six hearing mock "jurors" revealed that levels of comprehension between deaf and hearing participants were similar. Thus it appears that the deaf participants were not disadvantaged by accessing information indirectly via interpreting, and could legitimately serve as jurors, although this needs to be further investigated.

1. Introduction

In many developed countries, the administration of justice in criminal courts is based on a shared responsibility between legal professionals (such as judges, barristers, lawyers), legal administrative support workers (such as clerks, court reporters, etc.), witnesses to crimes, and members of the community being called upon to serve on a jury.

The judge's key responsibilities are: (1) to preside over the proceedings and see that order is maintained; (2) to determine whether any of the evidence that the legal teams want to use is illegal or improper; (3) to give the jury instructions about the law that applies to the case and the standards it must use in deciding the case; (4) to sentence convicted criminal defendants when the jury has presented its verdict.

Each lawyer's task is to bring out the facts using approved legal procedures, in order to convince the jury of the innocence or guilt of the defendant. In criminal cases, one of the lawyers works for the executive branch of the government, which is the branch that prosecutes cases on behalf of society.

Witnesses give testimony about the facts in the case that are in dispute. During their testimony, they sit on the witness stand, facing the courtroom. Because the witnesses are asked to testify by one party or the other, they are often referred to as plaintiff's witnesses, government's witnesses, or defence witnesses.

Courtroom administrators help the judge to keep the trial running smoothly, by calling for witnesses, administering the oaths to the witnesses, marking the exhibits; and court reporters type the official record of the trial.[1]

Members of the community are selected at random to represent the lay view on the facts of the case and ensure that defendants are tried and convicted fairly based on evidence. Jurors should "understand and weigh up the evidence presented, assess the credibility of witnesses and decide on the likelihood of certain events having occurred in the light of the jurors' personal experiences" (Findlay, 1994; cited in NSWLRC 2004, p. 13).

Other people that share in the responsibility of the administration of justice are interpreters. Interpreters are called upon to interpret for defendants, victims or witnesses who do not speak the language of the court. The central role of the court interpreter is to ensure that the witness can access the questions being asked in English, and that all personnel in the courtroom can understand the account of witness statement.

Very little consideration has been given to the need for jurors to use interpreters, as people are not eligible to serve as jurors if they cannot understand the language of the court. However, in some states in the USA it has now been recognized that deaf people can serve as jurors as they are prohibited from accessing the language of the court due to hearing loss, rather than the fact that they cannot use English; and a deaf person recently served on the jury of a tax fraud case in New Zealand. Therefore, we are now seeing cases of deaf people serving on a jury with the provision of signed language interpreters.

Currently, deaf persons cannot serve as jurors in the state of New South Wales in Australia. Nor do they do so in other parts of Australia or in most other countries in the world. The New South Wales Law Reform Commission, acting at the request of the NSW Attorney General, commissioned a pilot study to investigate whether deaf persons ought to be able to serve on juries, in order to perform their civic duty. The aims of the project were: (1) To investigate the accuracy of English

---

1.   http://www.flnd.uscourts.gov/jurors/courtParticipants.cfm

to Auslan interpretations of legal transcripts taken from court proceedings; (2) To determine the level of comprehension of interpretation of potential deaf jurors as compared to a control group of hearing jurors; and (3) To assess the ability for deaf jurors to access court proceedings via signed language interpreters. Given the scope of the study, this chapter focuses only on the comprehension test results. Discussion of the accuracy and translatability of legal concepts can be found in an alternative publication (see Napier & Spencer, 2008).

The pilot study involved a comprehension test of six deaf jurors who had watched an Auslan interpretation of an excerpt of a judge's summation through an Auslan/ English interpreter, and six hearing jurors who had received the same information directly from spoken English; followed by participant interviews concerning perceptions of difficulty.

This chapter reports on the outcome of the comprehension test, in relation to whether deaf jurors can effectively understand court proceedings through a signed language interpreter, and thus effectively share in the responsibility of the administration of justice as a juror. The findings of this project have national and international impact in demonstrating the extent to which deaf people can serve as jurors, and the issues for interpreters to consider when interpreting with some-one in this role.

2.   Literature review

The majority of research and discussion on legal interpreting in the spoken language interpreting literature focuses on court interpreting, with discussions of courtroom interpreting practice, linguistic and pragmatic aspects of court interpreting, the role of the court interpreter, and ethical dilemmas faced by court interpreters (e.g., Berk-Seligson, 1990; Colin & Morris, 1996; Edwards, 1995; Gonzalez, Vasquez, & Mikkelson, 1992; Hale, 2004; Mikkelson, 2000). There has been some discussion of other aspects of legal interpreting, such as solicitor-client interviews, police interviews, police interrogations and confessions, tribunals or immigration/ refugee hearings (e.g., Barsky, 1996; Fowler, 2003; Krouglov, 1999). In Australia, there have been several publications which explore the cultural barriers for Aboriginal people in accessing court proceedings (Cooke, 2002; Eades, 2003; Fryer-Smith, 2002; Goldflam, 1995; Howard, Quinn, Blokland, & Flynn, 1993).[2]

---

2.   See Hale (2006) for a thorough survey of court interpreting research literature.

In all aspects of legal interpreting, the person typically requiring the interpreter is the victim, witness, defendant or complainant. With respect to deaf people's involvement in the legal system, there have been a number of publications that specifically discuss deaf people's access to justice via signed language interpreters (e.g., Brennan, 1999; Mathers, 2006; Russell, 2002) with significant discussions of the potential linguistic barriers that deaf people face in the legal system (e.g., McCay & Miller, 2001, 2005; Miller, 2003).

All of these discussions have focused on the deaf person as a member of a minority group being disadvantaged in accessing the legal system. In all of these publications, the role of the interpreter has been considered in light of the position of the client as a participant in the legal system as a defendant, witness, or complainant. None have considered what the role of an interpreter might be in working with a juror. This is more than likely due to the fact that non-English speaking people (including deaf people) have not historically been allowed to serve on juries.

Although incredibly informative in terms of signed language interpretation in court, yet again these studies have focused on interpreting for people who are accessing the justice system, in the form of witnesses, defendants or complainants. Thus this pilot study is seminal, in that it is the first linguistic study to examine interpretation for deaf jurors in the court system.

2.1   Interpreting for jurors

The few discussions of interpreting for jurors have highlighted the fact that there are different challenges for interpreters working with jurors: because the role of the client is different, the goal of the interpretation is also different (Mather & Mather, 2003; Montalvo, 2001). As opposed to witnesses, defendants or complainants who typically report their version of events, a juror has to make decisions based on the understanding and interpretation of information received. Therefore their information access needs are different.

Mather and Mather (2003) explored the needs of deaf jurors in receiving information via English-American Sign Language (ASL) interpreters, and evaluate whether this should occur through meaningful interpretations or through the verbatim transmission of information. In effect, they revisit the point raised in Brennan and Brown's (2004) work, acknowledging that interpreters need to borrow from English in order to convey legal concepts, terminology, and key facts of the case so that jurors can sufficiently access information for deliberation purposes. To date, no linguistic studies have been carried out on the efficacy of interpreting for the purposes of a deaf juror; confirming that this study is pioneering a new aspect of research on courtroom interpreting

In addition to the analysis of interpretation accuracy and the evaluation of the effectiveness of English to Auslan interpretations in conveying information to deaf jurors, this study also focuses on juror comprehension. Key questions to be considered include: What do deaf jurors understand in court? How does that compare to hearing jurors? Is comprehension influenced by receiving the information directly or indirectly (via an interpreter)?

2.2 Juror and legal text comprehension

The seminal study on juror comprehension was conducted by Charrow and Charrow (1979a, 1979b), which tested and proved the hypothesis that standard jury instructions are not well understood by most jurors. Firstly, they identified a series of complex linguistic constructions in fourteen standard jury instructions, which they hypothesized would be difficult to understand. Then they measured the comprehensibility of these instructions by administering a test, whereby jurors listened to these instructions and paraphrased their understanding of what the instructions meant. Charrow and Charrow then re-wrote the instructions, eliminating the problematic constructions, and re-tested the jurors. They found that the re-written instructions were better understood. Subsequent related studies have also confirmed that jury instructions fail to communicate central points of the law (Elwork, Sales, & Alfini, 1982; Hansen, Dirksen, Kuchler, Kunz, & Neumann, 2006; Luginbuhl, 1992; Steele & Thornburg, 1988).

A particularly interesting study is that of Judith Levi (1993), who conducted a linguistic evaluation of jury comprehension of instructions in her role as a linguistic expert witness. Levi analysed and discussed the language of the Illinois Pattern Instructions (IPI), which are used in the sentencing phase of a murder trial, in order to assess how well the language used in these instructions served in its purpose to clearly communicate the legal concepts to the jury that they needed to understand for sentencing. The study served as a follow up to a survey conducted by Zeisel (1990, cited in Levi, 1993), which concluded that a consistent majority of jurors misunderstood central points of law concerning deliberations on the death penalty, resulting in an increased likelihood that the jurors will impose the death penalty. Levi's linguistic analysis of the IPI also found:

- A consistent theme of presumption of death at all levels of the text (syntax, semantics, pragmatics and discourse organisation);[3]
- Syntactical challenges, for example, use of multiple negatives, covert negatives, and embedded clauses;
- Semantic ambiguity, for instance, use of the words "you" and "your finding" and whether this should be interpreted as a singular or group reference;
- Incohesive discourse organization, that is, confusing sequencing of points, discontinuity, and needless interruptions to the flow with unrelated information;
- Pragmatic problems in that "jurors were given wholly insufficient information from which they had to deduce, or infer, a number of highly significant but regrettably obscured components of both federal and state law".

(Levi, 1993, p. 31)

These studies present interesting findings for us to consider when assessing whether there are any differences in the comprehension of deaf and hearing jurors.

3. Research questions

One aspect of this research project sought to investigate deaf jurors' comprehension of an extract from a courtroom trial via signed language interpretation. The key research questions were as follows:

1. How much do hearing jurors comprehend of a judge's summation?
2. How much do deaf jurors comprehend of a judge's summation?
3. Is there a significant difference between levels of comprehension between deaf and hearing jurors?

4. Methodology

An experimental study was designed to utilize real data from a courtroom trial. It was decided to test twelve "jurors", six deaf and six hearing, in order to compare their level of understanding of a legal text. The jurors were briefed with

---

3. For example, "At one point… the judge first tells the jurors how to sentence the defendant to death and then how to give him a sentence that preserves his life – and then inexplicably restates how to sentence him to death. This death-life-death sequence clearly emphasizes the option of death, not only by repeating it twice but also by presenting it in the two most salient positions within a list, first and last" (Levi, 1993, p. 47).

information as if they had been present throughout a trial, so they knew what evidence had been presented, how long the trial had taken place, etc; then were asked to respond to questions concerning two excerpts from a judge's summation taken from the end of the court case. The goal of the study was to evaluate the accuracy of the interpretation from English into Auslan in relation to legal concepts, and to assess levels of comprehension of information received directly or indirectly through an interpreter. This chapter reports only on the latter goal – the assessment of comprehension.[4] Given the small number of participants in the study, it should be emphasized that this study should only be considered as a pilot in preparation for a larger study.

4.1   Source text

A judge's summation from a case that had been tried in the Supreme Court of New South Wales, Criminal Division, was chosen for this pilot project by the NSWLRC. The case was *Regina v Rodney Ivan Kerr,* which took place between 27 October and 6 November 2003. Rodney Ivan Kerr was charged with the manslaughter of William Christopher Harris at Redfern Station in New South Wales. He was also charged with affray and endangering the safety of a person on the railway. Two excerpts were selected by representatives of the NSWLRC which incorporated sufficient legal terminology and important facts of the case.

4.2   Participants

Deaf and hearing participants for the comprehension test were recruited through the dissemination of a flyer and contacts of the research team. The final group of "jurors" were selected to provide a broad representation across the following variables: age, gender, highest educational attainment, employment category, and first language, as per the directions from the New South Wales Office of the Director for Public Prosecutions regarding jury selection (DPP, 2003). An overview of the background of each participant can be seen in Tables 1 and 2.

---

4.   See Napier & Spencer (2008) for a detailed overview of the whole study, including the discussion of interpretation accuracy.

Table 1. Characteristics of hearing juror participants

Variables		Participant					
		1	2	3	4	5	6
	Gender	M	M	M	F	F	F
	Age range	18–30	31–49	50+	18–30	31–49	50+
	Highest educational attainment	Tertiary (Community college)	High School Certificate	Tertiary (Community college)	Tertiary (Community college)	Tertiary (University)	School certificate
	Employment category	Manual/ Trade/ Paraprofessional	White collar/professional	White collar/professional	White collar/professional	White collar/professional	White collar/professional
	First language	English	Italian	English	English	Korean	English

Table 2. Characteristics of deaf juror participants

Variables		Participant					
		1	2	3	4	5	6
	Gender	M	M	M	F	F	F
	Age range	18–30	31–49	50+	18–30	31–49	50+
	Highest educational attainment	Tertiary (University)	Tertiary (Community college)	Tertiary (Community college)	Tertiary (University)	High School Certificate	School [5]Certificate
	Employment category	White collar/professional	Manual/ Trade/ Paraprofessional	Manual/ Trade/ Paraprofessional	White collar/professional	Not in workforce (student)	Manual/ Trade/ Paraprofessional
	First language	English	Auslan	Auslan	English	Auslan	Auslan

4.3 Procedure of comprehension test

Six hearing jurors listened to/watched a pre-recorded version of the source text in spoken English, and were asked twelve questions (four true/false questions, four multiple-choice questions and four open-ended questions) in English, which they responded to in English. Six deaf jurors watched a pre-recorded Auslan interpretation of the source text, and were asked the same twelve questions in Auslan, which they responded to in Auslan. The test results were analysed for accuracy,

---

5.   In NSW school leavers completing year 10 receive a School Certificate; school leavers completing Year 12 receive a High School Certificate.

and post-test interviews were carried out to determine participant perceptions of jury service, and complexity of the text.

The Auslan interpretation of the source text was carried out by a profession-ally accredited interpreter with extensive legal interpreting experience. Deaf and hearing participants for the comprehension test were recruited through the dis-semination of a flyer throughout the university campus, and to contacts of the research team. The final group of "jurors" were twelve people (six deaf, six hear-ing) selected to provide a broad representation across the following variables: age, gender, highest educational attainment, employment category, and first language. An attempt was made to include non-native users of Auslan and similarly non-native users of English in order to include the additional challenge experienced by such jurors. Although the participants represented a range of social variables, the variable being investigated in this study was deafness; therefore no attempt was made to investigate other social groups.

5.   Results & discussion

The results of the comprehension test show that both hearing and deaf "jurors" misunderstood some concepts. In relation to the closed/multiple-choice ques-tions, approximately 10.5% of the questions were answered incorrectly by all par-ticipants. Of the open-ended questions, some responses were problematic from both deaf and hearing participants. A copy of the questions can be seen in the Appendix. Table 3 summarises the correct responses by participants undertaking the comprehension task.

It can be seen that percentage-wise, there is a minor difference between the number of correct responses from deaf and hearing participants (2.8% difference). Of all the errors in responses to true/false and multiple-choice questions, almost half (five of nine errors made) related to Question 5, a multiple-choice question which was also the longest of all questions asked. Due to the small number of participants, however, this difference cannot be analysed in terms of statistical significance.

A number of similarities can be seen in the responses made by deaf and hear-ing participants and in the errors seen in Questions 4, 5, 10 and 12 in particu-lar, suggesting that these items may have been challenging regardless of language used or whether the information was received directly or mediated through an interpreter. Table 4 provides the different open-ended responses to Question 9 (the majority of which were correct), and Question 10 (the majority of which were incorrect).

Table 3. Summary of correct responses

Questions		Correct responses		
		Deaf participants (n = 6)	Hearing participants (n = 6)	TOTAL (n = 12)
True/ false	Q1	6	6	12
	Q2	6	6	12
	Q3	6	6	12
	Q4	3	5	8
Multiple choice	Q5	3	5	8
	Q6	6	6	12
	Q7	6	5	11
	Q8	6	6	12
Open ended	Q9	6	4	10
	Q10	1	0	1
	Q11	5	6	11
	Q12	0	1	1
TOTAL		54/72 75%	56/72 77.8%	110/144 76.4%

Table 4. Responses to Q9 and Q10

TABLE 4: Responses to Q9 and Q10	Question 9: Explain what witnesses said the two women with Mr Kerr did.	Question 10: Explain the legal rule of 'causation'
Participant	Correct answer: One or both women physically restrained Mr Kerr. When Mr Kerr broke free they again grabbed him and held him back.	Correct answer: Did the accused's conduct cause the victim to die? It doesn't have to be the sole or effective cause but did the act or acts of the acts of the accused significantly or substantially contribute to the death of the victim.
	Participant responses (correct/ incorrect)	
Deaf 1	Both women tried to restrain the man, to stop him from fighting with the other man. The man resisted and broke free, going for the other man. Both women again tried to hold the man but he went for the other man. What happened after that I don't know. (✓)	Sorry, I can't give an answer. (X)

Table 4. (*continued*)

Deaf 2	Witnesses saw the two women get off the train with Mr Kerr. When Mr Kerr became aggressive and approached the other man, the women pulled him back to stop him approaching him. Also, when Mr Harris escaped by jumping onto the tracks, one women yelled 'look train coming'. That's what happened. (✓)	Causation. Two things, A and B happen. If A happens, then eventually B will happen. If A doesn't happen, maybe B would never happen. But if A happens B will definitely happen. (X)
Deaf 3	The two women tried to hold Mr Kerr, then he broke free and ran up to the other man. The two women again grabbed him and held onto him. (✓)	What the accused made the victim do. (X)
Deaf 4	Witnesses said that the two women tried to restrain the man but he broke free so they grabbed him a second time to stop him approaching the victim. (✓)	Sorry, I don't know. (X)
Deaf 5	When the man got off the train the man started to yell at him. The two women tried to stop him but he continued so the women held him but he was determined and resisted. (✓)	Causation. The cause. The man was yelling and that made the other man fearful and run away. This was caused by his yelling at the victim. (X)
Deaf 6	The two women tried to help and keep the men separated, to hold onto the accused. (✓)	That means that the death happened because of the behaviour of the accused, causing the victim to die. There was a link. (X)
Hearing 1	They went over to the victim and pinned him down. Held him down for a little while. (✓)	It goes back to the cause and effect. Was what the accused did, it's hard to put into words, was what the accused, did it cause the victim's action . . . what the accused did is the cause to the victim's action. And it has to be proved beyond reasonable doubt that one affected the other. (X)
Hearing 2	The two women got off the train with Mr Kerr and as Mr Kerr shouted at Mr Harris they attempted to restrain him and hold him back. (✓)	Causation is cause and effect. If there is a consequence of an action and it can be proven that it is a reasonable response to the action of the accused, and the accused is said to have caused that response in the victim. If that victim is of firm mind and sound judgment then that is reasonable cause to say that the action of the accused caused that response in the victim. And it must be continuous. (X)

Table 4. (*continued*)

Hearing 3	They tried to stop Mr Kerr. (X)	It's like cause and affect. A causes B there is causation there if A's act or saying causes B, there is a rule of causation in that incident. (X)
Hearing 4	The two women held Mr Kerr back. (✓)	I was listening but causation and everything else... Cause of something that has happened but being able to prove that you intended something to happen and you were the reason for why it happened. (X)
Hearing 5	Mmmm nothing. They didn't do anything. Failed! (Laughs) Looking at my notes but . . . got off the train . . . yelled . . sorry. (X)	Hmm. It's the actual cause of it? I didn't write it all down but I understood there the question of cause in a common sense non-technical way. Determining criminal responsibility for serious criminal offences. That's what I would take it as. (X)
Hearing 6	When Mr Kerr started yelling and saying 'what the f**k are you doing' or 'what the f**k are you looking at', witnesses said the two women restrained Mr Kerr. He escaped from their restraint, obviously it didn't appear it was a very strong restraint, they then went to restrain him again and he allowed himself to remain under constraint by the two women. (✓)	From my understanding as described here causation is an unbroken chain of cause and affect. If there is any break in that link between a particular cause and a particular effect, that is not legal causation. There can be several links in that chain but they have to be unbroken and they have to be related to one another. (✓)

Interestingly, it can be seen in response to Question 9, that all the deaf participants answered correctly, whereas two of the hearing respondents' answers were inaccurate or incomplete. For Question 10, the only person that answered one question correctly was a deaf participant. It is also interesting to note that in Question 9, the deaf participants' responses are more detailed, as compared to Question 10 where the hearing participants provided fuller answers. This pattern was reversed for Questions 11 and 12, where the hearing participants had a higher number of correct responses.

An overall pattern that can be seen in the responses to the comprehension test is the difference between responses to questions of fact and questions relating to legal concepts. Overall, most respondents answered questions of fact correctly. In the case of deaf respondents, this means that the facts of the case, as presented in this experiment, had been interpreted clearly and correctly and had been understood by deaf participants. When asked to comment on the comprehension test, four participants specifically mentioned the facts of the case as being one of the easier aspects of the activity.

When factual errors did arise, they sometimes arose in respondents who otherwise provided correct answers to more complex questions. An example of this can be seen in Question 9. All the deaf respondents provided correct answers as to the accused being physically restrained by the women while only four of the hearing respondents provided a correct answer. One hearing respondent answered the question correctly but drew a conclusion as to the intentions of the accused to free himself from the grasp of the women. Firstly, this response was not asked for by the activity but offered up by the respondent and secondly, it is inconclusive in terms of the accuracy of the conclusion drawn. One hearing respondent failed to answer the question and guessed incorrectly, yet this respondent had previously answered all of the questions about the legal concepts and the factual matrix correctly.

A similar pattern can be found with Question 11, where one deaf respondent answered with "I can't remember what actual words he used but I remember he yelled. What he actually said I missed". This was an interesting response given the colourful language used by the accused and recounted accurately by the judge in his summation. Further, given that eleven other respondents recounted the wording almost verbatim, it is odd that one respondent missed it completely. It is unlikely that modesty is the reason for this respondent missing the words as the words can be changed when recounted so that they are not so offensive.

A possible explanation for this observation is that the facts of the case were sparsely distributed in the body of the text, often arising incidentally within a discussion about a legal concept. These facts were also rarely repeated during the excerpts selected for this study, therefore making them easier to miss. This suggests that in an actual trial, where evidence is presented over a longer period of time and in a more systematic manner, these comprehension errors may decrease as jurors would have had time to absorb evidence and arguments before hearing the judge's summation. However, it should also be noted that information that emerges throughout a trial by examination-in-chief and cross-examination is conflicting, and is altered sometimes in very subtle ways. So this may also present challenges in comprehension of facts.

We will now concentrate on responses to questions where a pattern of misunderstanding was found. Five out of six hearing respondents answered Question 4 correctly with one additional respondent giving the correct answer but being confused by the reference to murder, stating that the summation had been addressing the issue of manslaughter. Only three out of the six deaf respondents answered this question correctly however, with one of the respondents who answered correctly admitting they did not understand the interpretation of the phrase "beyond reasonable doubt". When the researcher simplified this to "without doubt", the respondent confirmed their correct answer. Overall this may indicate a low level understanding of a basic threshold concept in the trial of criminal law cases. If respondents cannot grasp this basic threshold concept then the rest of the evidence may well be lost or misinterpreted by the jury, whether hearing or deaf, in the jury room. However, the level of misunderstanding is comparable between the two sample groups meaning that the concept or the form of the question were difficult for both groups. This issue will be discussed further below.

Turning to responses to Question 5, only one of the hearing respondents answered this question incorrectly compared to three of the deaf respondents. This response is a concern as this question is a threshold question that distinguishes between the two elements of murder that is the *mens rea* (the intention to kill) and the *actus reus* (the act of killing). The prosecution has the burden to prove beyond a reasonable doubt that the accused intended to kill the victim or acted with reckless indifference to human life and did physically kill the victim. If deaf jurors have difficulty understanding the difference between the act and the intention to kill then there is the potential for juries to deliver unsafe verdicts.

It should also be noted that Question 5 was also the longest of the questions asked of the participants. This raises the challenge of modality in the design of comprehension materials (Hughes, 1989). In this study this becomes an issue not only for participants responding to complex verbal information, but also signed multiple-choice items which must also be held in memory as the participant assesses the question, the options and their recollections.

Questions 10 and 12 resulted in the highest number of errors. All of the hearing respondents answered Question 10 incorrectly. Most were close to the correct answer but none of the hearing respondents stated the rule correctly. Whether this is fatal to their ultimate understanding of the concept and would lead to an unsafe verdict is hard to tell. The following elements of the responses of hearing respondents show how close the responses were to the correct answer:

- "Did what the accused do cause the victim's action?"
- "The accused is said to have caused the response in the victim."
- "If A's act or saying causes B."
- "Cause of something happening."
- "It's the actual cause of it."
- "An unbroken chain of cause and effect."

In a result that is arguably better than the hearing respondents, one deaf respondent correctly answered the question. This respondent stated, "the death happened because of the behaviour of the accused, causing the victim to die. There was a link". While this response is not perfect in relation to the events establishing an unbroken chain of events, it is the best and most accurate response from the entire sample. The other five deaf respondents made the following responses in part:

- "Sorry I can't give an answer."
- "If A happens, then eventually B will happen."
- "What the accused caused the victim to do."
- "Sorry I don't know."
- "The man was yelling and that made the other man fearful and run away."

Turning to Question 12, only one hearing respondent gave a correct account of the "reasonable and proportionate response". Three respondents correctly pointed out that the victim's response needed to be reasonable compared to the risk posed by the accused for causation to be made out. The remaining two hearing respondents totally missed the point and answered the question by talking about irrelevant facts.

All of the deaf respondents answered the question incorrectly. The closest deaf respondent stated, "we need to think about what is fair and proportionate". The respondent in question did not go on to explain what they meant by "fair" and "proportionate". We may assume that "proportionate" meant whether the victim's response was proportionate to the threat by the accused. However, "fair" probably does not mean invoking the objective test. It is too easy for a respondent to not understand the difference between the subjective test ("fair" as judged by the victim's demeanour) and the objective test ("fair" as judged by the reasonable person). It is the lack of adequate explanation that makes even this response an incorrect answer. Only two of the deaf respondents raised the element of reasonableness. The other three deaf respondents totally missed the point and talked about the facts as did the two above-mentioned hearing respondents.

Again, this is a complex legal concept that is difficult to grasp but an important concept that effectively proves the causation issue so central to a successful manslaughter charge. The high level of misunderstanding by both hearing and deaf respondents is a concern.

In sum, results show that both the deaf and hearing "jurors" in this study equally misunderstood some terms and concepts. Nonetheless, all the findings show that legal facts and concepts can be conveyed via signed language interpretation effectively enough for deaf people to comprehend court proceedings to the same extent as hearing people, and therefore share in the responsibility of jury service.

6.   Conclusion

Regardless of the information provided to participants prior to undertaking the various stages of this study, the source text was still de-contextualised from an actual court case and the gradual introduction of material that would have occurred in a real life case. The material was also challenging as hearing "jurors" equally misunderstood some aspects of the summation even though they were receiving the information directly in English. In a real life courtroom, jurors would have had time to absorb evidence and arguments before hearing judge's summation. Even with these limitations, and the fact that the study had a small sample size, this research has demonstrated that levels of comprehension between deaf and hearing jurors were similar. Hearing jurors answered almost 78% of the comprehension test questions correctly, implying a relatively high level of comprehension of the judge's summation. Deaf jurors answered 75% of the comprehension test questions correctly, also implying a relatively high level of comprehension of the judge's summation. Thus, it appears that deaf jurors in this study were not disadvantaged by relying on signed language interpreters to access information in court. The findings of this pilot study suggest that the small number of deaf jurors involved could effectively comprehend courtroom proceedings via sign language interpreting. Post-test interviews with the deaf participants (see Napier & Spencer, in press) indicated that they are keen to share in the responsibility of administering justices, and would be willing to serve as jurors if the opportunity were presented to them.

This research can only be considered as a pilot due to the small number of participants. Nonetheless, this study has demonstrated that a small number of deaf people can understand excerpts from a judge's summation through English to Auslan interpretation. It does not, however, provide evidence for how deaf people can participate in, and make a significant contribution to, jury deliberations. Neither does it explore the potential impact of deaf jurors on the administration of justice from the perspective of the legal professionals, other jurors, the accused and witnesses. Therefore further research is needed to investigate deaf juror participation in court proceedings.

6.1   Impact of this study

Based on the findings of this project and their own consultation process, the New South Wales Law Reform Commission have recommended to the New South Wales Attorney General that deaf people be permitted to serve as jurors in New South Wales criminal courts. It is envisaged that the findings of this pilot study and the resulting recommendation will also influence considerations of Law Reform Commissions in other states in Australia, and will have national and international impact in demonstrating the extent to which deaf people can access courtroom proceedings and make a contribution to a jury.

6.2   Suggestions for further research

-   Administration of the comprehension test on a larger scale throughout Australia, in order to collect data with statistical significance.
-   Following on from Berk-Seligson's (1990), Hale's (2004) and Russell's (2002) research which used mock trials to assess aspects of interpreting, conduct a mock trial over several days, filming the proceedings and jury deliberations and sentencing; and conduct interviews, comprehension tests and discourse analyses of all participant utterances.
-   Following on from Brennan and Brown's (1997) research in the UK, when deaf people are permitted to serve as jurors, carry out courtroom observations of real deaf juror experiences wherever possible.
-   A collaborative study between the USA and Australia to compare comprehension and participation of jurors relying on signed and spoken language interpreters (i.e., Spanish, ASL and Auslan).
-   Interviews with interpreters working with jurors to gauge their perceptions of any difference in their role when working with this client group.

Acknowledgments

This project was made possible with funding from the Macquarie University External Collaborative Grant Scheme, in collaboration with the NSW Law Reform Commission. The original title of this presentation at the Critical Link 5 conference was: *"We find the defendant not guilty"*. *An investigation of deaf jurors' access to court proceedings via sign language interpreting.*

References

Barsky, R. (1996). The interpreter as intercultural agent in convention refugee hearings. *The Translator, 2*(1), 45–63.

Berk-Seligson, S. (1990). *The Bilingual Courtroom: Court Interpreters in the Judicial Process.* Chicago: University of Chicago Press.

Brennan, M. (1999). Signs of injustice. *The Translator, 5*(2), 221–246.

Charrow, V. R., & Charrow, R. P. (1979a). Characteristics of the language of jury instruction. In J. E. Alatis & G. R. Tucker (Eds.), *Language in public life* (pp. 163–185). Washington, DC: Georgetown University Press.

Charrow, V. R., & Charrow, R. P. (1979b). Making legal language understandable: A psycholinguistic study of jury instructions. *Colombia Law Review, 79*, 1306–1374.

Colin, J., & Morris, R. (1996). *Interpreters and the Legal Process*. Winchester: Waterside Press.

Cooke, M. (2002). *Indigenous Interpreting Issue for Courts*. Australian Institute of Judicial Administration Incorporated: Australia. From http://www.aija.org.au/ac01/Cooke.pdf

Eades, D. (2003). Participation of second language and second dialect speakers in the legal system. *Annual Review of Applied Linguistics, 23*, 113–133.

Edwards, A. B. (1995). *The practice of court interpreting*. Amsterdam: John Benjamins.

Elwork, A., Sales, B. D., & Alfini, J. J. (1982). *Making jury instructions comprehensible*. Charlottesville, VA: Michie.

Fowler, Y. (2003). Taking an interpreted witness statement at the police station: What did the witness actually say? In L. Brunette, G. Bastin, I. Hemlin & H. Clarke (Eds.), *The Critical Link 3: Interpreters in the community* (pp. 195– 210). Philadelphia: John Benjamins.

Fryer-Smith, S. (2002). *AIJA Aboriginal Cultural Awareness Benchbook for Western Australian Courts* (AIJA Model Indigenous Benchbook Project). From http://www.aija.org.au/online/ICABenchbook.htm

Goldflam, R. (1995). Silence in court! Problems and prospects in Aboriginal legal interpreting. In D. Eades (Ed.), *Language in evidence: Issues confronting aboriginal and multicultural Australia* (pp. 28–54). Sydney: University of New South Wales Press.

Gonzalez, R. D., Vasquez, V. F., & Mikkelson, H. (1992). *Fundamentals of Court Interpretation: Theory, Policy, and Practice*: Institute for Court Interpretation, University of Arizona.

Hale, S. (2004). *The discourse of court interpreting: Discourse practices of the law, the witness and the interpreter*. Philadelphia: John Benjamins.

Hale, S. (2006). Themes and methodological issues in court interpreting research. In E. Hertog & B. v. d. Veer (Eds.), *Taking stock: research and methodology in community interpreting* (5th ed., pp. 205–228). Antwerp: Hoger Instituut voor Vertalers & Tolken.

Hansen, S., Dirksen, R., Kuchler, M., Kunz, K., & Neumann, S. (2006). Comprehensible legal texts: Utopia or a question of wording? On processing rephrased German court decisions. *Hermes, 36*, 15–40.

Howard, D., Quinn, S., Blokland, J., & Flynn, M. (1993). *Aboriginal hearing loss and the criminal justice system*. From http://www.austlii.edu.au/au/journals/AboriginalLB/1993/58.html

Krouglov, A. (1999). Police interpreting: Politeness and sociocultural context. *The Translator, 5*(2), 285–302.

Levi, J. N. (1993). Evaluating jury comprehension of Illinois Capital-Sentencing Instructions. *American Speech, 68*(1), 20–49.

Luginbuhl, J. (1992). Comprehension of a judge's instructions in the penalty phase of a capital trial. *Law & Human Behaviour, 16*, 203–218.

Mather, S., & Mather, R. (2003). Court interpreting for signing jurors: Just transmitting or interpreting? In C. Lucas (Ed.), *Language and the law in deaf communities* (pp. 60–81). Washington, DC: Gallaudet University Press.

Mathers, C. (2006). *Sign language interpreters in court: Understanding best practice*. Bloomington, IN: Authorhouse.

McCay, V., & Miller, K. (2001). Linguistic incompetence to stand trial: A unique condition in some deaf defendants. *Journal of Interpretation*, 99–120.

McCay, V., & Miller, K. (2005). Obstacles faced by deaf people in the criminal justice system. *American Annals of the Deaf, 150*(3), 283–291.

Mikkelson, H. (2000). *Introduction to court interpreting.* Manchester, UK: St Jerome Publishing.

Miller, K. (2003). Signs of prison life: Linguistic adaptations of deaf inmates. *Journal of Interpretation*, 129–142.

Montalvo, M. B. (2001). *Interpreting for non-English speaking jurors: Analysis of a new and complex responsibility.* Paper presented at the American Translators' Association.

Napier, J., & Spencer, D. (2008). Guilty or not guilty? An investigation of deaf jurors' access to court proceedings via sign language interpreting. In D. Russell & S. Hale (Eds.), *Interpreting in legal settings* (pp. 72–122). Washington, DC: Gallaudet University Press.

Russell, D. (2002). *Interpreting in legal contexts: Consecutive and simultaneous interpretation.* Burtonsville, MD: Sign Media.

Steele, W. W., & Thornburg, E. G. (1988). Jury instructions: A persistent failure to communicate. *North Carolina Law Review, 67*, 77–119.

Appendix: Comprehension test questions

1. Mr Harris was hit by a train at Redfern. True or false?
2. The Crown or the solicitor for the prosecution has to prove the accused was guilty of the offence. True or false?
3. There were no witnesses to what happened when Mr Harris died. True or false?
4. The offence of murder has to be proved beyond reasonable doubt. True or false?
5. To prove murder it must be established:
   a. only that the accused caused the death of the victim
   b. that the accused caused and intended to cause the death of the victim
   c. that the accused caused the death of the victim without intention
   d. that the accused only intended to cause the death of the victim but death did not actually occur.
6. Mr Harris and Mr Kerr:
   a. went to school together
   b. were brothers
   c. were work colleagues
   d. were strangers to each other
7. Manslaughter is:
   a. killing without the intention to kill
   b. recklessly killing
   c. killing recklessly with intention to kill
   d. only committing grievous bodily harm
8. When Mr Kerr got off the train he:
   a. hit Mr Harris
   b. pushed Mr Harris off the platform
   c. yelled but did not touch Mr Harris
   d. told Mr Harris to run away
9. Explain what witnesses said the two women with Mr Kerr did.

10. Explain the legal rule of 'causation'.
11. Explain what witnesses said Mr Kerr yelled at Mr Harris when he saw Mr Harris.
12. In assessing the actions of Mr Harris in response to the actions of Mr Kerr, explain what you, as a juror, must take into consideration.

CHAPTER 8

Interpreting for the record

A case study of asylum review hearings

Franz Pöchhacker and Waltraud Kolb

Center for Translation Studies, University of Vienna, Austria

This paper addresses a specific aspect of interpreting in Austrian asylum review hearings, i.e., the interpreter's role as a co-producer of the written record. The interpreter-mediated encounter is viewed as a joint, co-constructed activity, with responsibility for its content, progression and outcome shared by all the interacting parties. This includes the production of the written record of the interview, which is typed by a recording clerk under the supervision of the adjudicator. The discourse-based analysis of fourteen hearings with English-speaking asylum seekers from African countries shows that most interpreters tend to adjust to a striking degree to the needs of record production. This perceived need to interpret "for the record" not only entails an increased cognitive task load but also a significant degree of shared responsibility on the interpreter's part for the legally relevant manifestation of the interview.

1.   Introduction

Over the past decade, interpreter-mediated communication in asylum proceedings has increasingly come to the attention of researchers in various disciplines, including communication studies, sociolinguistics, sociology, and translation studies. Aside from legal and organizational aspects, research so far has reflected a focus on role issues and power relations (e.g. Barsky, 1996; Fenton, 2004; Pöllabauer, 2004, 2005, 2007) as well as specific institutional constraints (e.g. Barsky, 1994; Inghilleri, 2005; Maryns, 2006).

One feature of asylum hearings that has received little attention to date is the role of the record that is kept, in one form or another, of the interview. As part of a larger study on asylum review hearings in Austria, our paper addresses this specific aspect of the interpreter-mediated interaction between adjudicators and asylum-seekers.

As highlighted by the work of Wadensjö (1998), an interpreter-mediated interview is best viewed as a joint activity rather than a sequence of text production and translation moves by participants with clearly delineated speaker and listener roles. Naturally, then, the content, progression and outcome of the interpreter-mediated encounter are the joint responsibility of all the interacting parties, including the interpreter, and so is the quality of the communicative interaction. What is less obvious, in our particular case, is where the responsibility lies for the written record of the interview. As we will show, this too, contrary to what one might expect from the provisions governing this administrative procedure, is co-produced by all participants, with the interpreter assuming a role and responsibility far beyond normative precepts. The fact that interpreters in the asylum hearings under study thus share responsibility for the quality of the written record has significant implications in terms of both cognitive task load and interactional dynamics, and certainly with regard to the interpreter's role and professional ethics.

2.   Legal and institutional context

As a particular setting of what is most generally called community-based interpreting (Chesher et al., 2003), asylum proceedings are, characteristically, defined by a given national and institutional context. While relating to a single set of international legal provisions (i.e., the 1951 Geneva Convention and 1967 Protocol on the status of refugees), there is no uniform procedure for determining refugee status – and no standard code for interpreters working in this setting. It is therefore necessary to say a few words about the institutional context in which our case study is set.

2.1 The IFARB

As recommended by international bodies such as the UNHCR and the Council of Europe, Austria has a two-tier system for refugee status determination, with a single central authority (Federal Asylum Office) conducting the initial evaluation of asylum applications and a review board hearing appeals against a negative decision. It is the second-instance authority, the Independent Federal Asylum Review Board (IFARB), which constitutes the institutional setting of our study.[1]

---

1. In July 2008, after completion of our study, the IFARB was reconstituted as the Asylum Court. All IFARB adjudicators became judges of the Asylum Court, which is still not part of the judiciary and follows many of the same practices as its predecessor, particularly as far as interpreter use and record keeping are concerned.

The IFARB was set up in 1997 after the country's (Supreme) Administrative Court had been overwhelmed by appeals against decisions of the Federal Asylum Office. Though the IFARB is not a judicial authority but an administrative review panel reporting to the Interior Minister, its forty-some individual "Members" are appointed for life by the Austrian President and enjoy the same degree of independence and irremovability from office as judges.

Cases brought before the IFARB are heard by individual Members, with sole responsibility for scheduling a hearing (and booking a qualified interpreter), conducting the interview, and issuing a written decision (hence our use of the term "adjudicator" in the remainder of this paper). Though the Federal Asylum Office, as the institution whose negative decision is being appealed against, is legally a party to the proceedings, it normally remains unrepresented on the appellate level. For all practical purposes, therefore, the appeal hearings under study take the form of yet another interview in which the asylum seeker is asked to present his or her claim to an adjudicating official.

2.2   The written record

Like the refugee status determination process in general, procedures for documenting the oral proceedings vary widely. Barsky (1994), for instance, offers a scathing description of a tape-recording and transcribing method that was used in the late 1980s in Canada, and Maryns (2006) mentions various reporting styles in the Belgian asylum procedure and generally characterizes the written account of the hearing as "the product of a tangled network of discursive processes" (2006, p. 1). In some institutions, like the Australian Refugee Review Tribunal, all proceedings are audio-recorded while the adjudicator essentially relies on handwritten notes taken during the hearing. In others, no audio recording is permitted, but the adjudicator works with a clerical assistant to produce a written record during the hearing. This is the case in Austria's first- and second-instance asylum authorities (and in most of the country's judicial institutions). The relevant provisions of the Code of Administrative Procedure do not specify the record-keeping technique to be used, nor the level of detail required. Even so, the written record, signed by all participants at the end of the hearing, constitutes the prime evidence of the case and therefore plays an essential role in backing up the adjudicator's decision. This evidentiary function tends to increase the weight given to the written record, not least in documenting vagueness or contradictions in an applicant's account in the event of a negative decision. The written record thus is closer in nature to a verbatim standard, with far-reaching implications for the work of the interpreter in such hearings, as our analysis will show.

3.   Method, participants and corpus

Similar to Pöllabauer's (2004, 2005) study on interpreting practices in first-in-stance hearings, our research approach was based mainly on audio recordings of hearings, supplemented by field notes from participant observation and informal interviews. Given our own linguistic qualifications, we focused our study on English-speaking appellants. Thus, while the case under study is, in principle, the nature of interpreter-mediated hearings at the IFARB, our case study is limited to a set of hearings involving English.

Five IFARB Members (three women, two men) agreed to have some of their hearings recorded. Following advance notice of the date and time of hearings, we participated as observers, equipped with a digital tape recorder (Sony TCD-D8) fitted with an external stereo microphone. Whereas the interpreters in most cases were informed about the recording in advance by the official, the asylum seekers were approached before the hearing in the waiting area and asked for their permission after a brief explanation of the aims and methods of the study. They were told, in particular, that all personal data would be anonymized and that the study had no bearing whatsoever on the outcome of their cases. Having agreed to the recording, they received detailed information about the project in writing (in English) and were expressly advised that they could revoke their permission at any time during or after the hearing.

A total of fourteen hearings conducted by the five adjudicators were taped between October 2005 and October 2006, amounting to a corpus of twenty-five hours of recordings. On average, hearings lasted about 100 minutes, ranging from twenty-six minutes to three-and-a-half hours. While the sample of seven interpreters (five women, two men) exhibits a range of professional qualifications and experience, all but a few have a Masters-level degree in interpreting and/or court certification.

The sample of asylum seekers in the study includes twelve men and two women. Most of them came from Nigeria, with one each from Gambia and Zimbabwe.

Figure 1 illustrates the typical seating arrangement in these (rather informal) proceedings and also indicates the position of the observers (OBS) and the recording equipment. The main interactants are labelled as follows: ADJ = adjudicating official, APP = appellant (i.e. asylum seeker), INT = interpreter, REC = recording clerk. The interpreter's position in most cases is such that he or she can see the screen in front of the record-keeping clerk.

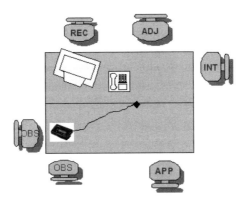

Figure 1. Seating arrangement and technical set-up

4.   Analysis

Though not explicitly included in the original design of our research project, the role of the written record emerged so forcefully from our observations that it became a crucial point of interest, alongside and as part of such fundamental topics as role boundaries, neutrality and fidelity. The present paper reports our findings on this particular issue, based on a range of examples drawn from our corpus. The excerpts are taken from different hearings (coded by interpreter, e.g. T1H1, T4H2) and illustrate phenomena such as linguistic adjustments and various initiatives by the interpreter for the benefit of the recording clerk.

4.1   Co-producing the record

In the first excerpt,[2] from an early stage of the hearing, the adjudicator (ADJ) is inquiring about the circumstances of the applicant's life before she left the country.

---

2.   Transcription conventions were applied as follows:

underlining	overlapping speech (e.g.: APP word <u>word word</u>
	INT <u>word word</u> word)
(→INT)	addressee of (part of) utterance
ə	voiced hesitation ("uh")
..	short pause (.. = approx. 1 sec.)
oo	pause filled with keyboard noise (oo = approx. 1 sec.)
wo-, word-	false start or interruption
(?word)	uncertain
(? ?)	unrecoverable speech

Our translations of German utterances appear in italics.

Having established the place, ADJ asks with whom the appellant (APP) had been living (1).

Ex. 1: T4H2 (06:08–06:16)

1   ADJ   Mit wem haben Sie dort gelebt?
          With whom did you live there?
2   INT   You were living there together with whom?
3   APP   With my father.
4   INT   Dort hab ich mi- habe ich mit meinem Vater gelebt.
          There I was wi- was living with my father.

APP's short answer (3) could easily have been rendered in similar terms in German ("Mit meinem Vater"). However, INT expands the answer and, repairing the elliptic colloquial form of the auxiliary verb ("habe"), turns it into a full sentence. Adding the adverb of place ("there") that occurred in ADJ's question (and has been recorded as such) ensures a perfect fit between question and answer in the written record. By such explicitation the interpreter adjusts his rendering to the more literate (written-like) style of the record.

A more extreme form of explicitation can be seen in the following example, in which the interpreter teams up with the recording clerk to ensure the correct spelling of a proper name in the record (end of turn 3).

Ex. 2: T6H3 (44:10–45:46)

1   APP   [...]
          My wife called me on the DD of MM 2003. She told me the- the
          ZANU-PF militants they've come to my place, they've raided my
          p- my my house where I sa- where I stay, so she suggested it
          wouldn't be safe for you to return to Zimbabwe.
2   ADJ   Mhm.
3   INT   [...]
          Am TT. MM 2003 ᵒᵒ ᵒᵒ hatte ich mit meiner Frau . telefoniert. ᵒᵒ ᵒᵒ
          In diesem Gespräch hatte sie mich informiert, ᵒᵒ ᵒᵒ ᵒᵒ ᵒᵒ dass Militanten
          der Zanu ᵒᵒ Z A N U
          On the DD of MM 2003 I had spoken on the phone with my wife.
          In that conversation she had informed me   that militants
          of the Zanu Z A N U
4   ADJ   (→REC) Zanu, ja.
          Zanu, yes.
5   INT   Bindestri- Bindestrich P F ᵒᵒ ᵒᵒ   ᵒᵒ unser Haus angegriffen
          hatten ᵒᵒ ᵒᵒ ᵒᵒ ᵒᵒ und sie sagte mir, ᵒᵒ ᵒᵒ ᵒᵒ ᵒᵒ dass es wahrscheinlich
          für mich nicht sicher ist, ᵒᵒ ᵒᵒ ᵒᵒ ᵒᵒ zurück nach Simbabwe zu reisen.

> *hyph- hyphen P F   had attacked our house*
> *and she told me   that it was probably not safe for me*
> *to travel back to Zimbabwe.*

While it is not possible to establish whether the interpreter received a nonverbal prompt (such as a questioning look) from the recording clerk, she evidently makes sure that the acronym (for Zimbabwe African National Union – Patriotic Front) is recorded correctly. She spells it, complete with punctuation, whereas the adjudicator (turn 4) limits himself to checking the writing on the computer screen and acknowledging that it is correct.

Punctuation also features in the following excerpt, which provides some revealing insights into the complex linguistic and educational constellation in these appeal hearings, many of which take place several years after an asylum seeker's first interview, that is, after an extended stay in the host country.

Ex. 3: T2H1 (17:42–18:11)

1 ADJ   Können Sie lesen und schreiben?
         Can you read and write?
2 INT   You know how to read and write?
3 APP   In Nigeria I don't know but when I came to Austria I go to school here, so
         this is- I can read Deutsch and write in Deutsch, not in English.
4 INT   In In Nigeria hatte ich nicht lesen und schreiben gelernt, °° °° °° °° °° Punkt.
         Hier in Österreich habe ich aber ə lesen und schreiben- also auf Deutsch
         lesen und schreiben gelernt. Auf Englisch kann ich nicht lesen und schreiben.
         In in Nigeria I had not learned to read and write,   Full stop.
         Here in Austria, though, I have ə learned to read and write – that is,
         to read and write in German. In English I cannot read and write.

The applicant states that he was illiterate before coming to Austria, where he received his schooling in German. The interpreter renders this rather freely, again expanding utterances into complete and grammatically correct sentences. APP's present tense predicates ("I don't know", "I go to school"), which are typical of many African speakers of English, thus appear in their correct German tense, even including the past perfect ("had not learned"). Curiously, the interpreter ends the first part of her translation (4), followed by a five-second pause, with an explicit indication of the punctuation mark to be used ("full stop") – an instruction to REC which, incidentally, remains unheeded by the recording clerk, who typed a comma after the sentence in question.

An even more striking example of the interpreter dictating punctuation marks can be seen in Excerpt 4, which is taken from a crucial scene of the applicant's story and reflects considerable agitation.

Ex. 4: T1H1 (19:21–19:46)

1   APP   So when he rushed to me I I- when he rushed to the office I
            w- I was sur- surprised a- what happened? What happened?
            He said-

2   INT   Ich war sehr überrascht, °° als er hereingestürmt kam °° °° °°
            °° °° °° °° und fragte °° °° °° Doppelpunkt, Anführungszeichen
            °° °° Was ist denn passiert? Was ist passiert?
            I was very surprised,   when he came storming in
            and asked   colon, quotation mark
                But what happened? What happened?

The asylum seeker's hurried narrative is interrupted rather soon by the interpreter, who proceeds to dictate her translation in calmly uttered, well-formed sentences, pausing extensively (up to seven seconds) to allow REC to catch up with her typing. Opting for a verbatim rendering of the unmarked direct speech in the original ("what happened?"), she provides explicit instructions to the clerk on how to represent this in the record.

Whereas the previous examples reflect record-oriented initiatives on the part of the interpreter (indeed of four different interpreters in the sample), the following two excerpts show that the interaction between the interpreter and the recording clerk is in fact mutual, that is, that the typist views the interpreter rather than the adjudicating official as the prime interlocutor in matters of record keeping. The discursive event in question here is an interruption of the interpreter's delivery by the typist (end of turn 2, 3).

Ex. 5: T5H1 (71:04–72:13)

1   APP   I told how how- but- is two shrine, the one is the stronger shrine which is
            NAME, I said it earlier. .. .. I drunk from my own community, but the
            neighbouring con- con- the neighbouring community said no that I
            should once swear the stronger shrine, which is which is in central city,
            which is Benin City, I said it earlier.

2   INT   Ich habe das schon vorher gesagt, dass es zwei Schreine gibt,
            einen in meiner Gemeinschaft und einen in Benin City, dass ich-
            I have said that earlier that there are two shrines, one in my
            community and one in Benin City, that I-

3   REC   Moment! °° °° °° °° °° °° °° °° Ja. Dass ich -?
            One moment!   Yes. That I -?

4   INT   dass ich in meiner Gemeinschaft °° den Eid abgelegt habe, °° °° °° aber dass
            die Nachbargemeinschaft darauf bestanden hat,°° °° °° °° °° °° °° dass ich
            ein- dass ich noch einen Eid in Benin City ablege.

that I swore the oath in my community, but that the neighbouring community
insisted that I swear another oath in Benin City.

Unlike the interpreters in previous examples, INT does not leave extended pauses
for the recording clerk to catch up with her typing (2). She is therefore interrupted
by REC (3), who forces an eight-second pause in the interpreter's delivery before
indicating that she is ready for more. Conveniently, she reminds the interpreter of
the last words before the interruption, helping her to pick up the thread.

In the next excerpt, this collaborative relationship, or mutual co-orientation,
can be observed for a different interpreter (and clerk). The clerk's initiative, albeit
not an interruption, takes place after the interpreter's rendition (2).

Ex. 6: T6H1 (65:30–66:41)

1   APP   Yah, I've I've I've tried to make you understand that .. they were just
            haunting for my life and in several occasions maybe I narrowly escaped
            their wrath and .. I wish anybody here will understand how dangerous
            and how my life was jeopardized and made me to flee away from the country.
2   INT   Ich weiß nicht, wie ich es Ihnen verständlich machen soll. ºº ºº ºº
            ºº Ich habe alles gesagt ºº ºº und .. dass man nach ºº nach
            meinem Leben ºº ºº dass man mein Leben bedroht hat,
            Entschuldigung. ºº ºº ºº ºº ºº ºº Es ist mir mehrmals gelungen,
            wegzukommen, ºº ºº ºº ºº ºº ºº aber mein Leben war in Gefahr
            und deshalb verließ ich mein Land.
            I don't know how I can make you understand.
                I have told everything   and   that they were   were after
                my life   that my life was threatened,
                sorry.   I managed several times to get away,
                                          but my life was in danger
            and therefore I left my country.
3   REC   Und deshalb?
            And therefore?
4   INT   Verließ ich mein Land.
            I left my country.
5   REC   Danke.
            Thanks.

The interpreter manages to take in a relatively long utterance by the appellant (1)
and renders it with a typically pausing rhythm for the benefit of the typist. Even
so, her delivery proves too dense, and REC fails to record the last clause ("and
therefore I left my country"). REC asks the interpreter to repeat (3), and then
thanks her for doing so (5).

In the same excerpt, this polite move by the clerk also has a counterpart of sorts in the opposite direction: When the interpreter decides to repair a clause that she has already uttered (2), she explicitly apologizes – ostensibly to the recording clerk, who may have had to backspace and correct what she had already typed.

The next, and last, example of the interpreters' active involvement in the (co-)production of the written record highlights the extent to which an interpreter may assume this responsibility.

Though not a subject of the present analysis, it might be pointed out that the initial turns in Excerpt 7 also exemplify some of the other role-related and translational phenomena studied in our project (see Kolb and Pöchhacker, 2008). The adjudicator's question about specific "acts of persecution" (1), for instance, is rendered by a set of explanatory paraphrases (2), in which the interpreter adopts the interviewer's perspective ("we need to understand"), thus forming a verbal alliance with the adjudicator. When her prompting for a detailed answer proves ineffective and the applicant repeats his previous, vague description ("he came after me") (3), the interpreter does not give a translation at all but directly asks two more follow-up questions to elicit more concrete information (4).

Ex. 7: T1H2 (29:31–30:11)

1   ADJ   Welche Verfolgungshandlungen hat dieser Mann konkret gegen
Sie als Person gesetzt?
*What acts of persecution specifically did this man commit against
you personally?*

2   INT   Now, what exactly did this man do to you? I mean you said he came
you, (APP: Yea.) but we need to understand what- how did he come
after you?

3   APP   Yea, he came after me .. you know, before we w- that is why we you know
the man took me to Lagos, (INT: Mhm.) he came after me while I was still
in PLACE

4   INT   But what happened? How did he come after you?

5   APP   Yea, əm. Er hat ən unser Haus geschossen. Und an- o-
angegriffen.
        He ən shot our house.   And at- o-
attacked it.

6   INT   Der Mann °° °° hat unser Haus beschossen . und angegriffen.
        The man   shot at our house   and attacked it.

The interpreter's initiatives finally prove successful as the appellant describes an attack on the house where he was staying (5). However, he does so in German, the language of record. Even so, the interpreter proceeds to give a "rendition" (in

German), correcting the appellant's minor phrasing error ("unser Haus geschossen" instead of "beschossen") for the record. Unless one wishes to view this as an example of "sense-based interpreting" in which the interpreter is completely oblivious to words and languages, INT's restatement of APP's utterance is yet another illustration of the collaborative arrangement in which it is the interpreter – rather than the interviewee or, as one would expect, the adjudicating official conducting the hearing – who supplies the input for the written record.

There is no doubt that interpreters who assume responsibility for the correctness and completeness of the record – e.g. by spelling out names, indicating punctuation, pausing for the typist or repeating parts of their delivery – enhance the efficiency of the interviewing process. Nevertheless, their additional role as co-producers of the record may also come with added liability in case of inconsistencies or outright errors in the written outcome of the hearing. This – and indeed the crucial role of the written record – is highlighted in the following section, in which a particular passage in the appellant's account is studied from three sources: the oral interview, the German record, and the oral back-translation of the record into English before its authentication at the end of the hearing.

4.2   Lack of coherence as a joint responsibility

The excerpt is taken from the latter stages of a ninety-minute hearing in which the appellant states that the reason for leaving his country was a political incident in which the adjacent house of a politician was burned down, and the arson falsely imputed to his family. The adjudicator seeks to establish (or confirm, in relation to the record of the first-instance hearing) when the appellant's father, allegedly responsible for the arson, was arrested. In a complicated exchange before the excerpt, the appellant indicated that the arrest had taken place in the morning: "five o'clock, we were sleeping" (69:10–69:12).

Ex. 8a: T6H2 (79:37–80:23)

1   ADJ   Wie viele Tage nach der Brandstiftung wurde Ihr Vater festgenommen?
          How many days after the arson was your father arrested?
2   INT   How many days after the burning of the house was your father arrested?
3   APP   .. How many days?
4   ADJ   Days, weeks, or months.
5   INT   The house of the neighbour was burned down, and how many days later, or weeks, or months, was your father arrested?
6   APP   Was arrested? (INT: Mhm) Before the election, the day, that night, they arrest him before in the morning, to the prison and -

7 ADJ   Also am Ta- am- in- nach der Nacht, oder nach dem Tag, an dem
        die Brandstiftung stattgefunden hat?
        So, on the da- on- in- after the night, or after the day on which the
        arson had occurred?
8 INT   So, after the house was burned (APP: Yea, yeah), on this same day
        (APP: Yeah), the night and the following morning.
9 APP   Five o'clock, you know, that is morning.
10 ADJ   Ja, um fünf Uhr in der Früh.
        Yes, at five o'clock in the morning.
11 INT   Ja.
        Yes.

Although the interpreter renders the technical term Brandstiftung (arson) used
by ADJ (1) with a more transparent paraphrase (2), APP repeats the question as
if seeking clarification (3). The latter is forthcoming, both from the adjudicator,
who offers various (increasingly improbable) response options directly in English (4), and from the interpreter, who takes up ADJ's utterance but expands it
to an explanatory restatement and paraphrase (5). The appellant's response, after
another confirmation-seeking question (6), is rather unclear, prompting ADJ to
respond to it directly (without relying on a translation) in an attempt to elicit a
clear-cut answer. His hopelessly garbled question (7), rendered more understandable by the interpreter (8), finally elicits a response (9), albeit one that merely
repeats what APP had said before and fits the question only indirectly, in conjunction with the interpreter's prompt (8).

Unlike the actual exchange during the interview, the written record reflects a
clear and explicit answer to the interviewer's question, as seen in the first two lines
of Excerpt 8b, which is taken from the (German) record. The subsequent lines,
however, reveal a striking incoherence.

Ex. 8b: T6H2 (Excerpt from written record, pp. 9–10)

1 VL: Wie viele Tage nach der Brandstiftung wurde Ihr Vater festgenommen?
        ADJ: How many days after the arson was your father arrested?
2 BW: Nach dem Tag, an dem die Brandstiftung stattgefunden hat, um 5
        Uhr in der Früh.
        APP: After the day on which the arson took place, at 5 o'clock in the
        morning.
3 VL: Warum haben Sie vor dem BAA angegeben, dass die Polizei
        2 Tage nach der Brandstiftung zu Ihrem Haus gekommen ist?
        ADJ: Why did you say before the Federal Asylum Office that the police
        came to your house 2 days after the arson?

4   BW: Ich habe gesagt, er wurde nach dem Tag des Brandes festgenommen?
       APP: I said he was arrested after the day of the fire? [sic]

5   VL: Zu welcher Tageszeit?
       ADJ: At what time of day?

6   BW: Es war am Abend.
       APP: It was in the evening.

The adjudicator confronts the appellant with an apparently different response taken down during the first-instance interview (3); APP reaffirms his previous answer (4), only to be seen contradicting himself (6) in response to the adjudicator's question about the "time of day".

The three adjacency pairs excerpted from the written record (Ex. 8b) could easily be seen as evidence of inconsistency in the appellant's account, clearly undermining his credibility. It is only the exceptional opportunity, in this case, to check the written record against the audio-recorded interview that allows for introducing an explanation. Excerpt 8c below is the direct continuation of Excerpt 8a.

Ex. 8c: T6H2 (80:23–81:16)

1   ADJ   Warum haben Sie vor dem Bundesasylamt angegeben, dass die Polizei
              zwei Tage nach der Brandstiftung zu Ihrem Haus gekommen sei?
              Why did you state before the Federal Asylum Office that the police
              had come to your house two days after the arson?

2   INT   And why did you say at your first interview that the police came two days
              after the house was burned?

3   APP   No, I tell them that, the d- after the, after the day of the burn (INT: Mhm)
              they catch him.

4   INT   Ich hab gesagt, er wurde <u>nach dem Tag des Brandes festgenommen.</u>
              I told them he was arrested after the day of the fire.

5   APP   <u>Maybe they made a mistake. This I</u> don't know.

6   ADJ   Zu welcher Tageszeit fanden diese Kundgebungen statt beziehungsweise
              wurde das Haus niedergebrannt?
              At what time of day did these rallies take place and was the house burned
              down, respectively?

7   INT   And at- at what time of the day did it all happen? When was the house
              burned down?

8   ADJ   (→REC) Zu welcher Tageszeit
                   At what time of day

9   APP   In the evening.

10   INT   Es war am Abend.
              It was in the evening.

The first four turns in Excerpt 8c match the corresponding parts of the written record (Ex. 8b, 3–4). However, after the subsequent turn – APP's overlapping statement that remains off the record (5) – the adjudicator formulates a new question, regarding the time of the rally and the ensuing burning down of the house (6). After the question has been translated (7), the adjudicator instructs the typist to enter it in the record (8), apparently failing to check that the entire question is written down. With no trace in the record that the question asked by ADJ and rendered correctly by INT (turns 6 and 7 in Ex. 8c) was about the fire set to the house, the juxtaposition of lines 4 and 5 in Excerpt 8b from the written document erroneously relates the question – and the answer – to the time of the arrest.

Ironically, then, the appellant's doubt (5) about the accuracy of the record produced during the first-instance hearing ("Maybe they made a mistake.") receives fresh justification. The mistake in this case seems to have been caused by the clerk's failure to type the question, and type all of it, in conjunction with the adjudicator's failure to monitor that his question is written down in full. Whereas the interpreter here can be absolved of any error of commission or omission, it should be noted that the abovementioned tasks of REC and ADJ are ones that most of the interpreters, in other parts of the hearings, were seen to take responsibility for – directly, by supplying the input for typing, or indirectly, by facilitating the clerk's work in various ways.

Even where the interpreter's performance during the interview is not at fault (and there are indeed numerous instances of misunderstanding and distortion in the corpus), responsibility for the correctness of the record emerges with a vengeance at the end of the hearing, when the interpreter performs an oral back-translation (at sight) of the record which the appellant is then asked to sign and thus authenticate as an accurate and faithful representation of the interview.

In the example of incoherence discussed in this section, the interpreter's back-translation of the record, performed in indirect speech and with rather monotonous intonation, fails to function as a safety net. As shown in Excerpt 8d below, the interpreter skips the (incomplete) question (line 5 in Ex. 8b) and by latching the response onto the previous clause, makes it impossible for the asylum seeker to detect the contradiction in the record.

Ex. 8d: T6H2 (98:35–99:00)

1   INT   You were asked how many days after the house was burned your father was arrested, you said it was on the morning following the day of the burning down of the house, around five o'clock in the morning they came, and you said əm you were asked why last time you said it was two days after the burning of the house, and you said, no, I told them the same thing, I told them it was on the day after the burning down of the house, in th- in the evening.

5.   Discussion and conclusion

As illustrated in a range of examples, most of the interpreters in our study were seen to assume a degree of responsibility for the written record, the production of which should, in principle, be the sole task of the recording clerk working under the guidance of – and from dictation by – the adjudicating official conducting the hearing. Over and above the often very demanding task of rendering questions and statements for the two (highly unequal) principal interactants, the interpreters observed in the asylum review hearings at the IFARB are also involved in co-producing the record, which is what remains on file of the applicant's account and serves as crucial evidence in the decision-making process.

The fact that the interpreters are frequently "interpreting for the record" implies an increased cognitive task load resulting from, inter alia, adapting the interpreted utterance to the written register; tailoring the answer to the recorded question; adjusting delivery to typing speed; dictating punctuation and spelling foreign terms; and repeating passages the typist has failed to record.

As regards adaptation to the written medium, this is an expectation widely held among IFARB Members, as demonstrated by the results of a survey on interpreter use (Maurer-Kober, 2004). Asked about the relative importance of various re-hiring criteria, none of the thirty-three respondents thought that a "rendering that is fit to type" was "irrelevant", whereas nearly three quarters regarded this as an important feature of an interpreter's performance (see Figure 2).

However clear this expression of institutional norms may be, it challenges established principles of professional ethics, whereby the interpreter essentially renders what was said rather than what is to be written. Nevertheless, a more functionalist perspective that envisages interpreter-mediated interaction as a process

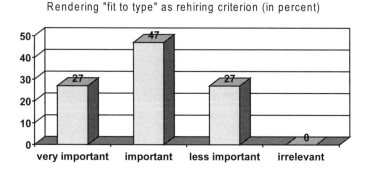

Figure 2. Rendering "fit to type" as a rehiring criterion (n = 30)

of co-construction and teamwork shaped by a given situational and institutional context should have room for a more actively involved and less invisible interpreter – on condition that the additional task load and responsibility are matched by appropriate training and professional status, and that all interacting parties, not least the representatives of the institution, are aware of their mutual and shared responsibility for the quality of the interaction and its outcome.

References

Barsky, R. F. (1994). Constructing a Productive Other. Discourse Theory and the Convention Refugee Hearing. Amsterdam/Philadelphia: John Benjamins.

Barsky, R. F. (1996). The interpreter as intercultural agent in Convention refugee hearings. The Translator, 2(1), 45–63.

Chesher, T., Slatyer, H., Doubine, V., Jaric, L. and Lazzari, R. (2003). Community-based interpreting: The interpreters' perspective. In L. Brunette, G. Bastin, I. Hemlin and H. Clarke (Eds.) The Critical Link 3. Interpreters in the Community (pp. 273–292). Amsterdam/Philadelphia: John Benjamins.

Fenton, S. (2004). Expressing a well-founded fear: Interpreting in convention refugee hearings. In G. Hansen, K. Malmkjær and D. Gile (Eds.) Claims, Changes and Challenges in Translation Studies (pp. 265–269). Amsterdam/Philadelphia: John Benjamins.

Inghilleri, M. (2005). Mediating zones of uncertainty: Interpreter agency, the interpreting habitus and political asylum adjudication. The Translator, 11(1), 69–85.

Kolb, W. and Pöchhacker, F. (2008). Interpreting in asylum appeal hearings: Roles and norms revisited. In D. Russell and S. Hale (Eds.) Interpreting in Legal Settings (pp. 26–50). Washington, DC: Gallaudet University Press.

Maryns, K. (2006). The Asylum Speaker. Language in the Belgian Asylum Procedure. Manchester: St. Jerome.

Maurer-Kober, B. (2004). Die aktuelle Praxis des Dolmetschens in Asylverfahren vor dem UBAS: Eine Bestandsaufnahme. MA thesis, University of Vienna.

Pöllabauer, S. (2004). Interpreting in asylum hearings: Issues of role, responsibility and power. Interpreting, 6(2), 143–180.

Pöllabauer, S. (2005). "I don't understand your English, Miss." Dolmetschen bei Asylanhörungen. Tübingen: Gunter Narr.

Pöllabauer, S. (2007). Interpreting in asylum hearings: Issues of saving face. In C. Wadensjö, B. Englund Dimitrova and A.-L. Nilsson (Eds.) The Critical Link 4: Professionalisation of Interpreting in the Community (pp. 39–52). Amsterdam/Philadelphia: John Benjamins.

Wadensjö, C. (1998). Interpreting as Interaction. London/New York: Longman.

CHAPTER 9

Court interpreting in Basque

Mainstreaming and quality:
The challenges of court interpreting in Basque

Erika González and Lurdes Auzmendi
University of Western Sydney and University of the Basque Country

Basque is one of the official languages of the Basque Country, a region in Northern Spain. Within the legal system, translators and interpreters are mandatory, in order to guarantee the linguistic rights of citizens in their dealings with that system.

Because of the nature of the Basque language itself and because of the delicate political situation in the Basque Country, the interpreter's job is extremely arduous. This chapter will report on the results of an analysis of court cases compiled over the last decade. The cases were classified according to the nature of the trials and hearings in which Basque was used. The strategies developed by Basque interpreters in order to meet the quality criteria which the profession requires are also part of the analysis.

1.   Introduction

Sometimes court interpreting in the Basque language turns out to be a truly complex type of interpreting, not only because of the nature of the Basque language itself but also because of the delicate political situation the Basque Country is currently undergoing. Both of these factors make the job of interpreters especially difficult. Over the last few decades there has been a noticeable improvement in the quality of the services offered. However, there are many steps that still need to be taken and many areas that call for improvement.

In order to analyse the level of difficulty and complexity involved in trials where Basque is required, we created a small corpus composed of court cases compiled by Basque interpreters from 2003 to 2005. A review of the literature showed that most of the articles published on court interpreting in Basque, and which describe the situation of the discipline, are written in Basque and published in *Senez*, the journal of the Association of Translators, Correctors and Interpreters of the Basque Language (EIZIE). For this reason, these papers have had a limited readership. We consider it of the greatest interest to share the experiences of Basque interpreters with other colleagues who work under similar circumstances, especially since efforts here and the search for quality have led to an interesting career development program.

2.   The nature of the Basque language

Basque (*Euskera*) is one of the most ancient languages in Europe. Its origin is still unknown. It is a non-Indo-European language, and shows no resemblance to languages in neighbouring countries. Unlike Spanish, which has a subject, verb, object (SVO) structure, it has a subject, object, verb structure (SOV). It is also an ergative-absolutive language. It has some similarities with Georgian, and that has led some linguists to believe there is a relationship with the languages of the Caucasus. Others relate the language to non-Arabic languages from Northern Africa. The most widely believed hypothesis holds that the Basque language developed *in situ*, in the land of the primitive Basques (*Euskera, the Language of the Basque People*, n.d.).

The Basque language has six main dialects, comprising Biscayan, Guipuzcoan, and High Navarrese (in Spain), and Low Navarrese, Labourdin, and Souletin (in France). The dialectal boundaries are not, however congruent with political boundaries. Currently, there is a unified version of the Basque language called *Batua* ("unified" in Basque). It is also referred to as Standard Basque. It is the dialect taught at school and the one used by the media, as well as by official institutions. This proliferation of dialects makes the job of interpreters more difficult since it is a vital prerequisite to have a wide knowledge of all dialects, or at least, of those spoken in the area/province where they carry out their work as interpreters.

Barambones & González described (2002), quoting Urrutia (1989, pp. 19–21), a number of difficulties which have arisen due to the nature of the language itself, as well as the lack of standardization and lack of tradition in the use of Basque in court settings:

1.   Basque has no legal administrative tradition.
2.   The lack of a fixed Basque standard is readily apparent.
3.   The serious sociolinguistic problem that Basque labours under.
4.   The fact that legal content published in Basque legal documents is translated from Spanish.
5.   The legal framework is not the most suitable.

6.   The problem of Basque dialects.
7.   The lack of language registers in Basque.

Barambones & González (2002) describe the process which the language had to go through in these settings until the first documents were translated:

> As a result of the long silence imposed by the post-war dictatorship, the process that had begun ever so humbly during the Spanish Civil War came to an abrupt halt and had to wait for the new Spanish Constitution to be proclaimed. Indeed, it was that fundamental body of law that gave the language of the autonomous communities official status. As soon as the government, provincial government and municipalities were set up, work on the translation of laws, decrees, orders, decisions, and various kinds of regulations issued by those institutions was begun. In any case, the first working attempt directly related to law was very late in coming, in 1987 to be exact, when the terminological think tank, UZEI, published two volumes.

3.   The political situation in the Basque Country

It is nearly impossible to talk about court interpreting in Basque without having a look at the political situation in the region. Basque politics and Basque society are influenced by a series of factors that have a direct impact on the judicial process. There are four obvious dividing lines and four "axes" on which these lines are based:

1.   The French/Spanish border: The map axis.
2.   Nationalist/State opposition: The national axis.
3.   Pro-armed struggle/non-violent: The violence axis.
4.   Basque-speaking/Non Basque-speaking: The language axis.
     (*Euskal Herria:Politics*, n.d.)

While some people consider themselves Spanish citizens, others claim the independence of the Basque Country. They consider that the Basque Country includes the three provinces which belong to the French department of the *Pyrinees Atlantiques* (Lapurdi, Nafarroa Beherea and Zuberoa) and the four provinces which belong to Spain (Araba, Biscay and Guipuzcoa, and Navarre). Officially, however, only Araba, Biscay and Guipuzcoa are considered part of the Autonomous Community of the Basque Country (see Graph 1).

The claim for independence has led to an armed struggle. ETA, the nationalist paramilitary group was created in 1959, while the country was under Franco's dictatorship. A group advocating traditional culture and customs, which were totally

Graph 1. Map of the territory the Basque independent movement claims.
(Euskal Herriko mapa, n.d.)

suppressed under Franco's dictatorship, it was transformed into a terrorist group fighting for Basque independence (*ETA,* n.d.).

Not all the trials where Basque is spoken have political implications, but a high percentage of them are directly related to different sorts of activities related to the struggle for independence.

4.   The beginnings of court interpreting in Basque

Nowadays, the law as such protects the use of the Basque language in dealings between citizens and the Judicial System (see the Appendix). As a result, a citizen has the right to use either Spanish or Basque when communicating with any branch of this system.

When translation started within this system, in relation to trials, statements, and other such legal matters, interpreters had no preparation whatsoever, because up till then they had simply carried out their work as translators rather than interpreters. These translators lacked the necessary preparation for interpreting and were totally unacquainted with the environment in which they had to work. As a result, some serious mistakes were made in these early stages, but pro-Basque language militancy tended to excuse or cover up these mistakes as a kind of goodwill gesture. This goodwill, however, proved in time to be a double-edged sword.

Over time, certain militant and political sectors also started to demand the use of the Basque language in the different police and justice departments, claiming that Basque speakers were defenceless due to the fact that there were no law enforcement officers capable of dealing with Basque speakers who chose to express themselves in that language. Under these circumstances, pro-Basque language militants started to doubt the efficiency of the interpreting services, joining their cause with that of a few judges who, due to differences of opinion or out of contempt for the criteria applied to the use of Basque, relegated the role of the interpreter to insignificance.

In 1987, the central government in Madrid granted more autonomy to the Basque Country and justice started to be administered and ruled from the Basque Country itself. Basque language interpreters were no longer employed by Madrid, but by the Basque Government's Justice Department. A training and career development policy was implemented for those interpreters, and since then training courses have been run dealing with the various issues experienced by court interpreters in the Basque Country. However, this policy has never been applicable in the Community of Navarre, nor in Madrid, where citizens also enjoy the right to speak Basque in courts.

These interpreters working in the Autonomous Community of the Basque Country were very much aware of the importance of providing a high quality interpreting service, with the result that they have been organising career development courses for themselves since the aforementioned policy was implemented. They have the freedom to arrange the courses which they consider most interesting for their job, and they also recruit experts/lecturers for these courses. Basque interpreters currently working in the Basque Country's Judicial System receive solid training in consecutive interpreting. Furthermore, they are trained in the various legal procedures in which they become involved and in which they must often participate. In addition, current interpreters are also well prepared psychologically, as emotional strain is a major issue for them.

5.   Types and categories of interpreters working with the Basque language

There are three different types of Basque language interpreters in the judicial system:

1.   Full time interpreters who work in the Autonomous Community of the Basque Country. Most of these hold a degree in Basque Philology. However, the new degree course in Translation and Interpreting offered by the University of

the Basque Country has trained many graduates who are filling some of the new positions that have been advertised lately. The interpreters who work in this environment have received solid training and are well prepared to face their job. All their training courses are funded by The Department of Justice of the Basque Country. Interpreters are entitled to join a career development program, and thus, they organise courses focused on the improvement of interpreting skills, and other related issues. New interpreters do not have to go through an internship period and there is no mentorship system either so, as soon as they are employed, they become full time interpreters.

2. Interpreters who work in the same geographical area, on a casual, part-time basis, that is, interpreters who work on processes held outside the normal working hours a full-time interpreter would cover. They are hired by an agency, and the remuneration they receive is poor.[1] According to González (2004, p. 99), the agency does not follow a rigorous selection process when hiring these interpreters.

3. Interpreters who work in Navarre (on a casual, part-time basis). In Navarre there is no pool of full-time interpreters in any court of the region. Interpreters are hired by an agency too, but their working conditions are better than those of the freelance interpreters in the Basque Country. The use of Basque in this autonomous community is considerably lower than in the Autonomous Community of the Basque Country.

4. Interpreters who work in Madrid, mainly at the *Audiencia Nacional*,[2] in cases that carry strong political implications. The sole requirement for this job is to have studied through secondary level education and to have passed a Basque language examination. Remuneration is poor, and over the past few years there has been much controversy because of the quality of their services, to the extent that their performance has been criticised by the local and national press. In one particularly long case, which started in November 2006 (the

---

1. Freelance interpreters in the Basque Country earn on average 15€/h. Weekends and nights are paid 50% more. In Navarre the situation is slightly better. The agency which manages the interpreting services in court settings recruits its interpreters taking into account criteria such as their qualifications and experience. The remuneration is higher (around 50%) and working conditions for these interpreters are more decent.

2. The *Audiencia Nacional* has its seat in Madrid. It is the tribunal where serious crimes are filed. Appeals against its decisions go to the Spanish Supreme Court. It consists of 5 different courts: (1) Criminal (for cases related to terrorism, organised crime, mafia, genocide, etc.); (2) Appeals (to appeal cases filed in the criminal court); (3) Administrative; (4) Industrial, and (5) civil.

so-called 18/98+[3]) and was still open at the time this paper was written, there were more than fifty defendants being sued, which resulted in great media attention as a result of bad translations. The authorities in Madrid decided to employ interpreters working in the Basque Country, but their efforts were unsuccessful.

6.   The study

All previous papers and articles have a descriptive nature, and thus, we considered it interesting to carry out some quantitative/qualitative research in order to:

1.   Define and classify the difficulties interpreters find in the court cases where Basque is involved.
2.   Be able to extract some conclusions that could help to improve the current situation of court interpreting in the Basque language.

6.1   Data collection

Out of the nine full-time interpreters in the Basque Country, this study is based on data collected from seven with more than five years experience (see Table 1). These were selected to take part in this study precisely because they were the most experienced and had worked as interpreters for more than five years.

The corpus on which this study is based contains reports about trials that occurred between 2003 and 2005. The interpreters had to write a report about each court case which they considered complicated and which posed a special difficulty for them. We decided there was no point in describing cases which were not interesting for the research community or other colleagues, so they just reported those cases which had a real impact on their job and which had affected them as interpreters.

The interpreters were supplied with a checklist (see Table 2), and had to fill in all the fields specified.

---

3.   The famous 18/98+ case had a huge impact on Basque society. More than fifty people who belonged to different social and political groups were accused of financing ETA. The case was covered by the national as well as the local press, and interpreting inaccuracies occurred far too often, with the result that they became a real scandal in the media and in Basque society, as well. One of the interpreters had to quit as she could not stand the pressure. She has been on depression leave ever since.

Table 1. Profile of the interpreters who took part in the study
(data updated in July 2007).

Interpreter	Qualifications	Years of experience	Career development courses
1	BA in Basque Philology	10	Note taking Consecutive/simultaneous interpreting Register Introduction to civil law Judicial terminology
2	BA in Pedagogy	10	Note taking Consecutive/simultaneous interpreting Register Introduction to civil law Judicial terminology Public speaking
3	BA in Basque Philology Translation and Interpreting Studies[4]	14.5	None
4	BA in Basque Philology	10	Consecutive/simultaneous interpreting
5	Translation and Interpreting Studies	16	Note taking Consecutive/simultaneous interpreting Introduction to civil law Judicial terminology
6	BA in Basque Philology	10	Note taking Consecutive/simultaneous interpreting Courses related to new laws
7	BA in Law MA in Translation and Interpreting	6	Note taking Consecutive/simultaneous interpreting Courses related to new laws

Most of the cases were reported immediately after the trial/hearing was over, but others were reported from memory (some cases which took place between 1992 and 2000), as they were old cases which had had a real impact on the interpreter's professional life, and they considered it important to report them.

---

4. The Translation and Interpreting studies mentioned by two of the interpreters were carried out at the Civil Service and Law Translation School, which was administered by the Basque Institute of the Civil Service. The School offered a non-university three-year degree course in translation and interpreting. The School was set up in 1986 and was closed in 1991. The studies were focused on translation, but an interpreting course was offered in the third year.

Table 2. Guideline to fill in the reports

a.	Geographic location of the trial:
b.	Date:
c.	Time:
d.	Brief description of the case:
f.	Explanation of why the case created enough interest to be reported (main difficulties found-terminology, political pressure, etc.-):
g.	Attitude of the interpreter (explanation of how you felt, what kind of impact the case had on your job):
h.	Conclusions/additional comments:

Twenty-one reports of court cases were received. These consisted of fifteen cases from 2003 to 2005, and six from 1992 to 2000. Some of the reports were written together by two or three interpreters in those cases where the performance of more than one interpreter was required (trials with political implications that were longer in duration). Before we focused on the group of cases reported in real time, we analysed the nature of the oldest cases, so that we could understand why they were reported so many years later (which meant that they must have had a real impact on the interpreters). Two of these cases were held in Madrid at the *Audiencia Nacional,* and had to do with Basque political prisoners; two had to do with the pressure and poor working conditions interpreters have to face (due to lack of recognition by judges and defendants); two were related to the use of dialects and terminology that the interpreters were not familiar with (in both cases the terminology was related to agriculture).

Among the court cases reported from 2003 to 2005, eight cases had strong political implications; five were found difficult for the kind of terminology used by the Basque-speakers (unusual agricultural terminology was combined with the use of a very specific sub-dialect, and in one particular case, the interaction of the Basque speaker was full of local references and nicknames) and; two were found difficult because the Basque-speakers tried to pay the interpreters somehow (in one case a farmer became angry because the interpreter refused to go for a drink with her – Reported by Interpreter 7).

6.2   Qualitative results

The classification of the court cases and the additional comments/explanations provided by the informants allowed us to extract the following qualitative information:

1. In cases with strong political implications interpreters become an instrument that each side tries to bend to their own interests. The social/political pressure during these cases is enormous and all the informants have experiences such situations several times over the years. According to the responses given by the seven interpreters the difficulties that arise from these cases can be categorised as follows:

    1.1 Interpreters have to interpret (in the consecutive mode) passages read at a high speed and are sometimes requested to interpret for video recordings without technical equipment – reported twice by Interpreter 1. There were even two cases in which the defendants answered a question posed by the judge/prosecutor by singing a *bertso* (verse), a poetic form belonging to the Basque oral tradition – Reported by Interpreters 7 and 3. A *bertso* is a type of oral poem created spontaneously and sung according to specific metrics and rhyme. These poems are very typical of Basque folklore. It is very difficult to render these poems accurately, and the only possible solution is to give an approximate translation of the content of the verse.

    1.2 Interpreters have to cope with the pressure exerted by both sides of the conflict in different ways:

        1.2.1 Many Basque-speaking defendants consider Basque interpreters part of an unfair system, since they believe there should not be an interpreting service, but a fully bilingual Judicial System and so, they tend to treat interpreters with contempt – Reported by Interpreters 1 and 6.

        1.2.2 Judges and prosecutors do not know how to work with interpreters and thus, are ignorant of the role/code of ethics of the interpreters (they are suspicious of the interpreters, and sometimes think that they may act in benefit of the defendants), nor do they realize the difficulties posed by the lack of adequate technical equipment in the courtroom – Reported by Interpreters 1, 2, 3, 4 and 6.

        1.2.3 The defendant's lawyers frequently try to hinder the interpreters' work: they pay no attention to speed of delivery nor to the necessary intervention periods which would permit a proper consecutive translation. These same lawyers, during trials, when giving their final reports, often read them in Basque (though these are pre-prepared translations from a Spanish text) filling them with all kinds of legal references, jurisprudence reference quotes, etc., and delivering them at a speed that makes it impossible to translate if not provided in written form – Reported by Interpreter 6.

2. The people assisted by interpreters are in most cases bilingual (Basque–
    Spanish), who demand interpreters just for political reasons or because they
    have the right to speak in the language they choose. It is a highly unusual
    situation rarely found elsewhere. Interpreters are not interpreting to over-
    come language barriers, but to allow defendants/witnesses who speak both
    languages to use the language they prefer in their dealings with the Judicial
    System. In cases where the person giving testimony is supposedly involved
    in matters directly or indirectly related to political issues, the interpreting is
    often questioned: "I did not say that", "I did not mean that", etc. – Reported
    by Interpreters 1, 4 and 5.
3. Interpreters' work is not appreciated, with the result that they are often sum-
    moned but then not required to do anything; or, on the other hand, at the last
    moment it is decided that they are needed and they have to suddenly rush to
    court – Reported by Interpreters 1, 2, 3 and 7.
4. The Basque language has seven dialects and sometimes, mainly when the
    people concerned are elderly, live in rural areas and cannot speak fluent
    Spanish, interpreting becomes an arduous task. As we have mentioned above,
    these clients often offer money to the interpreters and the interpreters find it
    very difficult to explain their role, as none of the parties involved has any real
    awareness of what this is – Reported by Interpreters 1, 2, 4, 5 and 7.

6.3   Lack of adequate equipment

We realised that there was a factor that made it even more difficult for interpreters to carry out their job professionally: the lack of booths in the courtrooms. In
the Basque Country there is one single courtroom with booths, but they have not
been used yet.[5]

The lack of technical equipment is a problem which should be overcome in
the future, especially concerning the trials where there are political implications.
Some situations are so delicate and have such an impact on the Basque political
scene that it is not uncommon for interpreters to become the focus of the media,
who hang on every word to get a headline, and make the news. After analysing the

---

5.   In the history of Basque interpreting the simultaneous mode was used only once in Navarre,
in a long trial of a somewhat passionate crime. The booths were hired and two highly qualified
freelance conference interpreters did the job.
In Spain the use of the simultaneous mode is not common practice. The only exception was the
interpreting for the trials of the attacks of 11 March 2004. The interpreters were AIIC members.
In the trial problems arouse due to the poor installation of the technical equipment for simultaneous interpreting.

corpus, we think that the use of booths will contribute to improve the interpreters' performance in different ways:

1. It would save time.
2. Interpreters would not be so exposed to the media and the different parties, allowing them to focus on their work and minimising the pressure they face.
3. The interpreted version would be more accurate, ensuring a higher quality end product.

7.   Conclusions

This chapter has attempted to describe the situation endured by legal interpreters who work with the Basque language through the presentation of the results of a small study. The main results found by the study were that:

1. The different parties involved (judges, prosecutors, lawyers and defendants) have no awareness of the role of interpreters, and thus, there is a great lack of consideration shown to them.
2. Quality is not a shared responsibility, as the only ones who are aware of its importance are the interpreters themselves.
3. Technical equipment must be made essential in courtrooms if a quality interpreting service is to be provided.

Interpreters themselves have taken responsibility for their own professional development so as to maintain high standards in their everyday performance. We believe it crucial that the authorities get involved in the development of this profession, and though it may be difficult, we must keep struggling in order to achieve the objectives outlined below and so ensure that all future vacancies are covered by true professionals. To make this happen we consider the following steps to be vital:

1. New vacancies should be filled taking into account criteria such as the training and experience of the candidates (a minimum requirement should be to hold a degree in Translation and Interpreting).
2. Solid training in legal matters should be considered essential. Third or post-graduate level education in Legal Studies would be desirable.
3. Psychological preparation is required in order to resist bullying by lawyers and judges, an all too common occurrence.
4. Agencies which hire freelance interpreters should set rigorous standards to ensure that the people they hire are adequately trained and well prepared to face their task.

5.   Courtrooms should be equipped with adequate booths for simultaneous interpreting.

The achievement of these goals would go a long way towards raising the professionalism of court interpreting in the Basque language, and the work carried out by interpreters would improve considerably. The responsibility for offering quality services, therefore, not only lies with the interpreters, but also with the authorities and with the organisations that are responsible for procuring interpreting services.

Acknowledgements

We would like to thank all the interpreters who shared with us their experience and expertise, and who compiled the case studies for this article. Special thanks to Aitziber Eizagirre, Jon Goikoetxea, Oscar González, Irene Zubizarreta, Itziar Labaka, Asier Sanz and Jon Andoni Sayago.

Last but not least, very special thanks to Associate Professor Sandra Hale for encouraging us to publish the article and for her attentive proofreading, as well as corrections.

References

Auzmendi, L. (1997). Administrazio eta justiziako euskal itzultzaileak: egoera eta estatus profesionala. *Senez, 19.* [Electronic version]. Retrieved 15 May 2007 from http://www.eizie. org/Argitalpenak/Senez/19970101/Auzmendi
Barambones, J. and González, O. (2002). Euskerazko zuzenbidea: printzipio orokorrak eta orain arteko ibilbidea itzultzailearen ikuspegitik. *Senez, 24 (special issue).* [Electronic English version]. Retrieved 15 May 2007 from http://www.eizie.org/Argitalpenak/Senez/20021001/ Barambones
Euskal Herria: politics (n.d.). Retrieved 10 March 2007, from http://www.geocities.com/ Athens/9479/ehpol.html
Euskal Herriko mapa (n.d). Retrieved 27 May 2007, from http://www.euskosare.org
Euskera, the language of the Basque people (n.d.). Retrieved 9 March 2007, from http://simr02. si.ehu.es/DOCS/book.SS-G/v2/Euskera.html
ETA (n.d.). Retrieved 9 March 2007, from http://en.wikipedia.org/wiki/ETA
González, E. (2005). Interpretación social: una necesidad que emerge día a día. Aproximación al contexto guipuzcoano. *Sendebar, 15,* 97–113.
Urrutia, A. (1989). Administrazioko euskararen hizkera-mailak eta terminologi arazoak. In *HAEE/IVAP* (Ed.), *Administrazioko Hizkera eta Terminologiaz Jardunaldiak* (pp. 19–21). Vitoria-Gasteiz: HAEE/IVAP.

Viceconsejería de Justicia (2005). *Memoria año 2005*. Retrieved 20 May 2007, from http://www.justizia.net/docuteca/ficheros.asp?intcodigo=3247&IdDoc=sp

Appendix

Act 10/1982 of 24 November – On Standardisation of the Use of Euskera

Section 5

1. All citizens of the Basque Country have the right to know and use both official languages, orally and in writing.
2. The fundamental linguistic rights of citizens of the Basque Country as defined by law are as follows:
    The right to communicate with the Administration and with any body or organisation based in the Autonomous Community in Basque or in Spanish, orally and/or in writing.
    The right to be educated in both official languages.
    The right to receive periodicals, and radio, television and other mass media programs in Basque.
    The right to develop professional, political and trade union activities in Basque.
    The right to address any meeting in Basque.

Section 6

1. All citizens have the right to use both Basque and Spanish in their interactions with the Public Administration in the area covered by the Autonomous Community and to be assisted in the language of their choice.
    Therefore, the appropriate measures shall be taken and the necessary means provided to progressively guarantee the exercise of this right.

Section 9

1. All citizens shall have the right to use the official language of their choice in their interactions with the Justice Administration without having to provide a translation.
2. Papers and documents, as well as court files, in the Basque language shall be fully valid and effective.
3. The Basque Government, in conjunction with the relevant bodies, shall promote the standardisation of the use of Euskera in the Justice Administration.

CHAPTER 10

Community interpreting in Spain

A comparative study of interpreters' self perception of role in different settings

J. M. Ortega Herráez, M. I. Abril Martí and Anne Martin
University of Alicante, GRETI Research Group / University of Granada,
GRETI Research Group / University of Granada, GRETI Research Group

This paper presents the results of a study aimed at determining how community interpreters in Spain perceive their work. The study involves interpreters in different settings including hospitals, social services, emergency and civil defense organisations, the security forces and the law courts. It has basically been conducted in Andalusia and in the case of the justice system it includes data gathered nationwide. The aim is to explore the interpreters' perception of their role and specifically the limits of that role with regard to adaptation of language register, cultural explanations, expansion and omission of information, the relation with clients, and specialized terminology, amongst other aspects. As in previous studies by the GRETI research group, the methodology is questionnaire-based and has also resorted to a structured interview. The results show that in terms of professionalization there are certain differences between the law courts (where interpreting is explicitly legally provided for), and other settings. However, in both instances interpreters seem to shape their role according to intuition, and the majority would seem to go beyond the function that most codes of ethics stipulate. Moreover, the results reveal a total lack of knowledge regarding interpreting as a specialized professional activity.

1. Introduction

The aim of this chapter is to bring together the results of several different research projects on the role of community interpreters in Spain.[1]

---

1. The original studies were carried out by the GRETI research group based at the University of Granada, Spain, and funded by the Andalusian Regional Authorities (*cf.* Foulquié 2002c;

All the studies were carried out using similar methodology and were all principally conducted in the south of Spain, although in the case of the judicial system data gathered from interpreters nationwide is included. The purpose of all the original studies was to explore the interpreters' perception of their role and responsibilities in the interaction and specifically the limits of that role with regard to issues such as adaptation of language register for clients, explanations of a cultural nature, expansion and omission of information, the use of specialized terminology, and the relation between interpreter and clients, amongst other features. A wider aim was to contribute with solid data to promoting awareness of quality issues and to professionalization of community interpreting in Spain.

2.   Background

Community interpreting as a recognized profession does not exist as such in Spain. Despite the fact that Spain receives more immigrants than any other country in the EU[2] and is one of the world's major tourist destinations, there is little recognition of the need for language mediation to guarantee access to public services for those who do not speak the majority language. This is probably due to a series of factors: lack of economic resources, misunderstandings concerning the nature of work done by translators/interpreters and the fact that official policy has evolved – albeit implicitly – along "assimilationist" lines. Such a policy tends to place responsibility for communication with ethnic communities themselves and NGOs are given or assume an important role, similar to the situation in Italy (Díez, 2003; Russo, 2004, p. 2). *Ad hoc* solutions are the order of the day and (inter)cultural mediation is given priority over interpreting (or translation, as it is usually mistakenly called) which is seen as being somehow narrowly literal and inadequate for community settings. This can be clearly seen in the few cases in which public authorities have become involved in service provision: if any professional profile for those involved in communication is stipulated it is that of (inter)cultural mediator, with no requirements regarding translator/interpreter training, despite the fact that the majority of these posts mainly involve translation and interpreting work and that degree courses in translation and interpreting are offered at no less than 24 Spanish universities (*cf.* Aguessim, 2004; Abril, 2006; Martin, 2006; Ortega Herráez, 2006; Taibi and Martin, 2006).

Martin and Abril, 2008; Martin and Ortega, 2006; Ortega, 2006). GRETI's homepage: http://www.ugr.es/~greti/.

2.   Net migration data from Eurostat (2006) at http://epp.eurostat.ec.europa.eu. (Accessed July 21, 2007).

Admittedly, court interpreting is afforded a slightly higher official status and involves a certain degree of regulation, in the sense that both national legislation and international conventions guarantee the right to an interpreter in court although with few stipulations regarding who can practise as such. The need to guarantee this right led to the hiring of a small number of permanent staff interpreters, some of whom have a degree in translation and interpreting, although this was not one of the requirements for the post. However, such interpreters are a minority and much court interpreting work is done by poorly paid freelance staff who are not required to accredit any training or qualifications.[3] Likewise, police authorities have hired staff interpreters, although specific qualifications are not required for the post and interpreting is also done mainly by unqualified freelancers who claim to speak the working languages and who are not required to hold any academic qualifications. As for the health and social services sector, until recently there has not even been a recognition of the need for interpreters, and communication barriers are mainly overcome with the help of friends or family members, untrained volunteers or medical staff using English or French as vehicular languages.

The figure of the interpreter is thus largely ignored or sidelined by the institutions, and there are no specific accreditation systems for those who interpret for the administration or public services. There is growing interest from universities in community interpreter training with several community interpreter training courses now on offer but they are uncoordinated and generally of an introductory nature, which in turn is logical considering the lack of employment prospects for students who complete them (Taibi and Martin, 2006). As training and accreditation are considered vital elements for professionalization, Spain is clearly in a pre-professional phase.

The studies collated in this chapter were motivated by the desire to explore the techniques and mechanisms used by people involved in interpreting activities, as part of a larger project to describe the *status quaestionis* of community interpreting in Spain and highlight inequities, all with the hope of furthering professionalization. In countries where "community interpreting is not a generally accepted reality" (Pöchhacker, 1997, p. 216) any contribution to improving quality must start at the initial phases of the process, and one of the purposes of research can be to increase the visibility of interpreting *vis-à-vis* the authorities. Thus it

---

3. The hiring of professional conference interpreters for the 11th March 2004 Madrid train bombing trial points to heightened awareness of interpreting issues and a desire to improve professional standards at least in this instance. Generally increased visibility of interpreting has been the result.

was our aim to determine what exactly those involved were doing and why they believed they were doing it.

Although literature on the subject abounds with theoretical considerations on role or position (Mason, 2009), the degree of interpreter intervention and similar considerations, we hypothesized that non-professional interpreters, not subject to a code of ethics or mechanisms for professionalization, would be largely unaware of such issues. When referring to a similar situation in Austria, Pöchhacker (2000, p. 50) points out that: "These interpreters presumably shape their task according to some implicit norms of translational behaviour as well as expectations on the part of their (professional) clients".

We were interested in finding out what these norms and expectations were, and whether there was a difference between settings. Other authors (eg. Pöchhacker, 2004, pp. 162–163) have pointed out the multiple fragmentation that afflicts community interpreting, partly as a result of it being carried out in a variety of different settings, which detracts from the sense of belonging to a "profession", even in countries where a professional service has developed.

Although translation and interpreting studies have long since left behind the notion that translation is a mechanical operation based on a series of previously internalised rules, such views are still widely held in society at large. It is therefore particularly interesting to explore the translator/interpreters' own view of their activity (and analyse its subsequent effect on professionalization and quality) in a country where such a simplistic and naïve view of what translating and interpreting is has actually led to the avoidance of the terms "translating and interpreting" to refer to this activity in community settings, as pointed out above.

Research has clearly demonstrated that interpreting in public service settings is a highly complex process and that the sociocommunicative, contextual, pragmatic and functional characteristics which make up this complexity often affect the interpreters' role. Thus, tensions arise that may lead to ethical conflicts, which in turn make it difficult to take decisions about the limits to which the "third participant" – that is to say, the interpreter – can legitimately intervene. Mason (1999, p. 155) summarizes the pressure that may result from this complexity in the following way: "[…] interpreters are influenced in their interpreting behaviour by situational constraints: role conflict (*cf.* Anderson, 1976), in-group loyalties, stress in a sensitive situation, perceptions of power and distance, and so on."

In this sense, Angelelli's (2003, p. 16) notion of the interpreter being "opaque" rather than transparent and invisible is very apt, as is the idea put forward by Wadensjö (1998, p. 12) that interpreter-mediated encounters are not comparable with monolingual ones but rather form a different genre subject to different considerations. The interpreter's presence conditions the interaction and it will be affected in different ways depending on how the interpreter behaves.

This view of the interpreter as having the power to influence the interaction has been supported by different observational studies giving rise to a new independent research paradigm applied to community interpreting which Pöchhacker (2004, p. 79) refers to as "dialogic discourse-based interaction (DI)". The starting point of this paradigm is attributed to Berk-Seligson (1988, 1990), Wadensjö (1992, 1998), Roy (1996) and Hale (2004), whose work coincided in demonstrating that the community interpreter is far from being a sanitised, invisible figure with no influence on the interactive encounter.

These theoretical considerations form the backdrop against which the studies collated in this chapter were carried out. Our studies aimed at continuing the trend of other similar studies which have explored the opinions of interpreters with regard to their role (Lang, 1978; Mesa, 2000; Pöchhacker, 2000; Tomassini, 2002; Angelelli, 2003; Chesher et al., 2003), and were partly inspired by such studies. In general, all these studies show that the interpreter's role and the limits of intervention are complex questions on which different speakers and the same interpreter have different and occasionally conflicting expectations and views.

3.   Methodology

All the studies reflected in this chapter are based on a common methodology aimed at permitting comparison and cross-analysis of the results obtained with different target populations in order to gain insight into community interpreting practices and the role of interpreters in Spain. The survey and questionnaire research carried out by the GRETI group can be divided into two phases. During the first stage (2000–2003) the status quo of community interpreting in Spain was explored through fieldwork (Martin, 2000; Morera, 2000; Delgado, 2001; Foulquié, 2002a and b; Perez, 2003; Calvo, 2004; Ortega, 2004; Martin and Abril, 2006) and structured interviews based on open-ended questions were used in order to obtain qualitative answers. The interviews were conducted among various public, private and third sector institutions which are in close contact with non-Spanish speakers.

During the second stage of the group's work, the main aim was to explore the interpreters' perspective on their role, given the pre-professional nature of community interpreting provision in Spain. To this end, various independent studies were carried out through questionnaires based on closed questions in order to obtain quantitative answers. The questionnaire design followed the model described by Oppenheim (1996) and Fink (1995) and also applied by other researchers at the University of Granada (Calvo, 2001; Way, 2004) and was inspired by other surveys described in the literature on community interpreting, as has already been mentioned (particularly Pöchhacker, 2000; Mesa, 2000).

The first questionnaire was that used by Ortega (2004 and 2006) in large-scale research into court interpreters' role and court interpreting service provision. This same questionnaire was subsequently adapted for use in smaller-scale surveys (Martin and Abril, 2008; Ortega and Foulquié, 2008). The adaptation process consisted of limiting questions to those focusing on the interpreters' role and adaptations to different settings. In order to facilitate cross-analysis of the results all adaptations were slight and aimed at taking account of the specificities of the different settings involved.

Prior to the final administration, all questionnaires were thoroughly peer reviewed and subsequently piloted and/or submitted to external expert review, depending on the scope of the survey concerned.

Although the methodology was the same in each case, the number of subjects surveyed in the different settings varied. This was due to the relative difficulty encountered by the researchers in accessing certain target population groups. Questionnaires were originally designed to be self-administered, but time and logistic constraints, together with problems gaining access to certain groups, meant that a few of the questionnaires were administered in the form of a structured interview. In some instances (notably police settings) even this approach was not successful in obtaining a substantial body of replies. This means that results obtained for some settings can be considered representative to a certain degree, whereas for others, so few responses were forthcoming that the same can hardly be said.

The surveys carried out included interpreters working in court, police settings, healthcare and social services. In Table 1, a brief description of each particular research project is presented.

Table 1. Studies carried out in different settings

Population	Scope	No. respondents	Languages (in combination with Spanish)
Court	National	83	English, French, Arabic, Italian, Portuguese, Russian, Basque, Galician, Polish, Rumanian, Berber, Catalan, Chinese, Czech, Greek, Dutch, Albanian, Bulgarian, Slovak, Japanese, Macedonian, Moldavian, Serbian-Croatian, Ukrainian.
Health/ Social	Southern Spain	25	English, German, Arabic, French, Dutch, English, Lithuanian, Rumanian, Russian, Wolof
Police	National	7	French, English, Rumanian, Russian, Urdu, Punjabi and Hindi

The analysis of the results was carried out using SPSS software package. In order to compare the results of the different studies, it was necessary to slightly adjust and combine some categories, but we do not believe that such adjustments alter the final trends observed.

4.   Results

First of all, the questions about the profile of the subjects reveal that in the case of the court and police interpreters, the majority (60% and 71.5% respectively) received payment for their services, either as staff or as freelance interpreters, and 42% of court interpreters actually had a degree in Translation and Interpreting; most of the others also had a degree although in another discipline, whereas the health and social services interpreters were mainly volunteers (56%), and in fact 70% were self-taught. Finally, police and court interpreters were mostly Spanish whereas most of the health and social services interpreters were foreign born.

When asked whether they modified language register (see Chart 1), the majority of interviewees answered affirmatively. If we look at the *yes* and *sometimes* answers, we can see that an overwhelming majority of subjects do so. The difference between the interpreters in different settings is one of degree and is perhaps predictable: health/social services interpreters are more likely to change register whereas police interpreters are less likely to do so, with court interpreters somewhere in between.

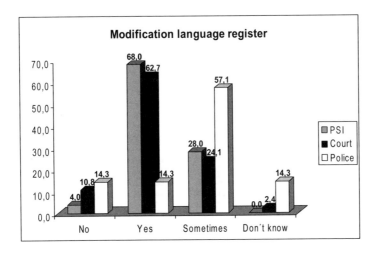

Chart 1. Modification of language register

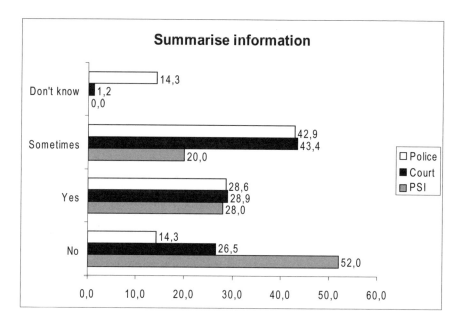

Chart 2. Summarise information

The same proportion of interpreters from each setting state they do summarise information (approximately 28%) (See Chart 2). The difference between inter-preters working in different settings that become apparent here is that the court and police interpreters give less categorical responses: they give roughly the same proportion of *sometimes* responses, which could be construed as recognition of the fact that not every situation that they work in is the same. As for the health/ social services interpreters, 52% of them state that they do *not* summarise in-formation, which we consider to be curious because this is slightly incongruent with some of the results that we obtained for other questions regarding "editing" speakers' utterances. For example, answers by this group to the previous question (register changing) show readiness to intervene with strategies that modify the speakers' message. As for the omission of information, the incongruence we see lies in the explanations they provide rather than the number of interpreters that state that they do omit elements (see following question).

When asked whether they omitted information (see Chart 3), the majority of interpreters for all three settings stated that they do not omit information, thus establishing the general trend. However, here the most interesting and perhaps most revealing aspect was the comments made by those who do omit: in general court interpreters stated that when they omit information it is for communicative purposes, whereas the health/social services interpreters stated (quite openly)

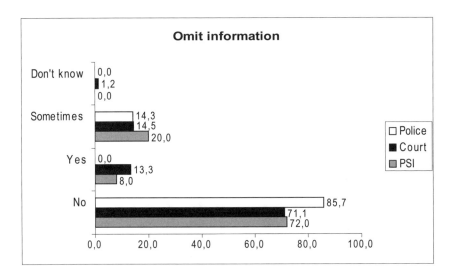

Chart 3. Omit information

that when they omit it is because they have forgotten the information, have not understood it or do not know how to express it in the target language. In other words, they referred quite openly to their own lack of competence. Some of the comments by interpreters from this group expressed a particular view of what their role is: "I only have to tell the doctor medical information, not the other things the patient says" or "I don't omit things by lying to the patients but sometimes I dress things up, for example if I have to tell someone that they have a malignant tumour".

Regarding cultural differences (see Chart 4), if the *yes* and *sometimes* answers are combined, it becomes apparent that the vast majority of interviewees do explain cultural differences, although 50% of police interpreters said they did not. On closer examination, it is interesting to note that the police interpreters who said they did not explain cultural differences were those working with English, and in most cases using it as a contact language, so it is quite likely that they did not have access to the cultural background of the speakers in question, since it was not a native English-speaking culture. Those who stated that they did do so, however, were interpreters working with Arabic, Hindi and Russian, cultures which are quite remote from Western European cultures and therefore more likely to require elaboration in order to fully transmit the source language message adequately.

The same pattern is found in the explanation of procedures (See Chart 5). In the vast majority of cases, the health/social services interpreters did explain

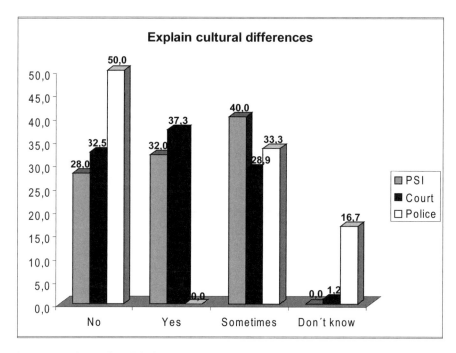

Chart 4. Explain cultural differences

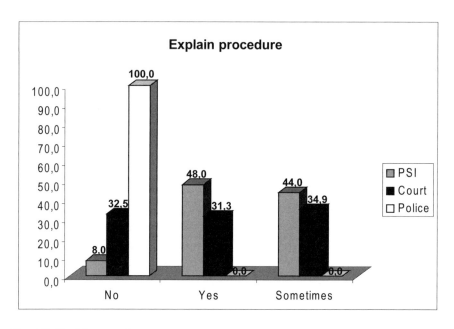

Chart 5. Explain procedures

procedures, which is in keeping with the rest of their answers (in line with the image of themselves as adopting a humanitarian, "helpers" role). In contrast, 100% of police interpreters stated that they never explain questions of procedure, and we would attribute this answer to the fact that in police settings there is more control over the interpreters (they do not have the opportunity to chat to non-Spanish speakers) and the fact that there is less procedure to explain. As far as court interpreters are concerned, if we combine the *yes* and *sometimes* answers two thirds of the respondents do explain procedure at least sometimes. Their comments gave us some insight into why: they stated that the non-Spanish speaking clients asked them for such explanations and, since the solicitors very often are not available to answer questions, the interpreters felt obliged to help. In other cases, differences in procedure give rise to misunderstandings that interpreters feel they have to solve, since they are in a better position to understand the root of the problem. One of the interviewees explained:

> Sometimes non-Spanish speaking clients do not understand why the solicitor or the judge does not act in a particular way. For instance, Germans want to know why the prosecutor is not doing more in their favour, and they have to be made aware of the fact that in Spain it is the judge's duty, not the prosecutor's, to examine the case.

The subjects who stated that they summarised, omitted, and/or explained cultural differences or procedures were asked whether they implemented such strategies discreetly without anyone being aware of this, or whether they alerted the parties concerned, either before or after the intervention (see Chart 6). The majority of those who intervene state that they do in fact ask permission or inform the parties either before or after the intervention takes place. Amongst those who do not inform about their intervention there are a high proportion of health/social services interpreters (a figure which increases if the *don't know* responses are added), which was predictable in the light of their previous answers. Police interpreters would seem to perceive greater risk in acting on their own initiative, probably because they work in a setting where encounters are much more ritualised and restrictive.

Most of the interpreters surveyed stated that they did identify with the non-Spanish speaker (see Chart 7), although to a differing degree depending on the setting, for reasons explained in Chart 8.

The health/social services interpreters who identified with the non-Spanish speakers did so because they were from the same country and shared the same language (in equal proportions), whereas the court interpreters stated that they identified with the non-Spanish client due more to the fact that they shared the same language and less to the fact that they came from the same country. This

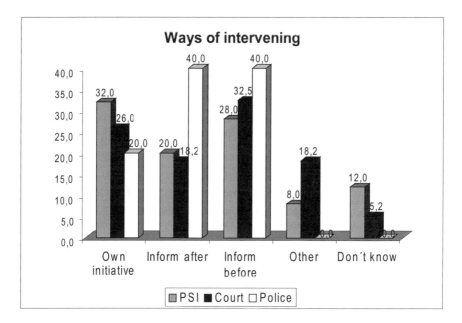

Chart 6. Ways of intervening

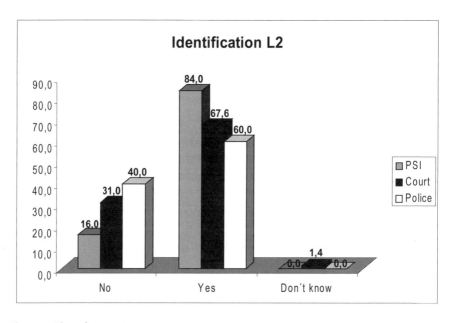

Chart 7. Identification L2

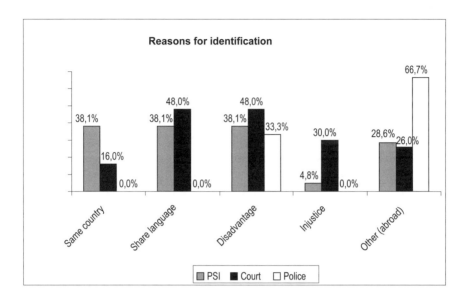

Chart 8. Reasons for identification

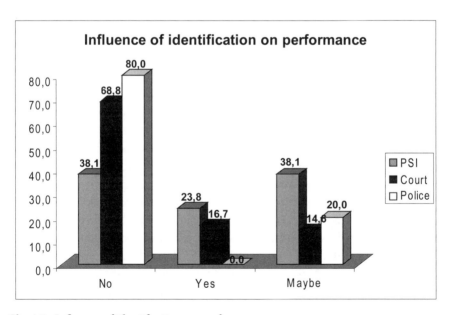

Chart 9. Influence of identification on performance

is due to the fact that most of the health/social services interpreters were foreign born, whereas the court interpreters were mostly Spanish. Also, some of the
comments provided by court interpreters suggest that they identify with the client because they feel others do not care. One of the interviewees stated that he
empathized with the client because "The duty solicitor washes his hands of the
whole affair". Another interesting result was that in the health and social services
settings, very few interpreters suggested they identified because they felt the non-
Spanish-speaking party was the victim of an injustice, whereas approximately one
third of the court interpreters felt that this was the case. As for the police interpreters, the majority of those that identified with the non-Spanish speaker did so
because they had been in a similar situation abroad.

The vast majority of court and police interpreters feel that this identification
with the non-Spanish speaker did not affect their interpreting performance (see
Chart 9). The answers from the health/social services interpreters were less clear
cut, although putting together the *yes* and *maybe* answers (61.9%) we can state
that the majority openly recognised what would normally be classed as non-professional behaviour. Once again this result reinforces the lack of role awareness in
this group as a whole.

5.   Discussion

The results show that in terms of professionalization there are certain differences
between those settings in which interpreting is explicitly legally provided for (law
courts), and other settings which do not benefit from such explicit provisions
(health care and social services). In the courts, timid steps have been taken towards the improvement of quality and service provision (with a combination of
different forms of service provision depending on the region and level of the court:
hiring of staff interpreters, creation of in-house interpreting services and/or out-
sourcing of interpreting services), whereas in health and social services most of
the interpreting is in the hands of untrained volunteers and staff from within the
institutions surveyed (eg. health professionals, administrative staff).

However, in both cases, interpreters seem to shape their role according to intuition and personal criteria, which is no doubt a reflection of the general lack of
professionalization in Spain. The results indicate that the majority apparently go
beyond the functions that would usually be attributed to community interpreters
in countries where this activity has become consolidated as a profession.

The differences that emerge from our study suggest that court and police interpreters would seem to have a narrower, more limited view of their role, and are
subject to certain constraints. The general perception is that the situation seems

to be more controlled by the service provider and perceived as more formal. Neither must we forget that the level of specific qualification and training was higher amongst these interpreters. On the contrary, the health and social services interpreters tended to adopt a broader view of both their role and their responsibilities, or be unaware of them. This again fits in with their profile as being mainly untrained volunteers.

In general there was a lack of awareness about interpreting as a profession involving a specialized cognitive activity requiring competences that are acquired through training. This is definitely the case amongst the health and social services interpreters surveyed, but also to a lesser extent amongst the court and police interpreters. This impression was transmitted in some of the replies given by health and social services interpreters: the fact that they did not know the difference between consecutive and simultaneous, the high number of languages that some respondents claim to speak, and some of the explanations about interpreting strategies reveal a serious lack of knowledge about interpreting as a specialized activity.

6.   Conclusions

The present contrastive study would seem to indicate certain disparities in interpreter self-perception in the different settings surveyed, against a backdrop of general lack of professionalization. These disparities appear to be related to:

1. the profile of the interpreters, their level of training and qualifications and their (lack of) contractual relation with the Administration (the majority are volunteers rather than paid staff).
2. the profile of each setting, depending on how formal the procedures and language used in a particular setting are and the degree to which the interpreter perceives the service provider as wielding control over the situation. In certain cases, the working languages were also decisive in interpreters´ perception of their role, depending on the cultural distance between their working languages/cultures and Spanish.

Indeed, the results of our research show that volunteer, ad hoc interpreters mostly in health and social services, tend to perceive their responsibility as being that of humanitarian workers, and not so much as quality professionals. In fact, it was evident that some respondents only reflected about professional issues for the first time as a result of our questionnaires and, although this is an interesting development, it is not likely to change the situation in the short term.

It is therefore highly improbable that the interpreters will spearhead any movement towards professionalization of community interpreting in Spain, or even assume their part of the responsibility for such professionalization and the improvement of quality. Firstly, many of those working as interpreters are no more aware of interpreting as a specialized activity than the service providers themselves; they are even less aware of the interpreter's responsibilities and the possible implications of over/under intervention. In this sense, the first step towards furthering quality necessarily involves awareness raising, and it is here that the academic community can usefully contribute by promoting research of this nature and sharing the results in order to provoke reflection among ad hoc interpreters, in addition to bringing the situation to the notice of the authorities. Similarly, the role of training and qualification cannot be overlooked, and again the responsibility of the academic community is paramount in designing and providing either formal or ad hoc training, flexible and pragmatic enough to reach all interpreters and convince them of the need to work together for professionalization.

At a later phase, interpreters will presumably be in a position to assume at least part of the responsibility towards professionalization from their central position in the field. Obviously public service providers, non-Spanish speakers and more essentially, the authorities should also be aware of their own responsibilities for communication and mutual understanding. Interpreters can contribute to educating service providers and authorities regarding community interpreting as a service to the community which would best be rendered by offering quality interpreting, instead of volunteer-based ad hoc services conceived as a "humanitarian mission".

Furthermore, reflection upon the nature of interpreting as a specialized activity as well as upon the implications of the interpreter's many potential roles should lead interpreters to demand and take advantage of training, as well as accreditation. Finally, the creation of professional associations would consolidate the organization of interpreters as a group of qualified professionals with a clear sense of their identity and role, which will hopefully promote quality across the board.

References

Abril Martí, I. (2006). *La Interpretación en los Servicios Públicos: Caracterización como Género, Contextualización y Modelos de Formación. Hacia unas Bases para el Diseño Curricular*. Doctoral dissertation. Granada: Editorial de la Universidad de Granada [available online from the homepage of the university library: http://www.ugr.es/~biblio/].

Aguessim, A. (2004). Inmigración, traducción y mediación intercultural. (Ley de Extranjería y su traducción al árabe). *Puentes* (4) (Eds. Anne Martin and Isabel Abril Martí), 55–64.

Angelelli, C. (2003). The interpersonal role of the interpreter in cross-cultural communication: A survey of conference, court and medical interpreters in the US, Canada and Mexico. In L. Brunette, G. Bastin, I. Hemlin and H. Clarke (Eds.) *The Critical Link 3. Interpreters in the Community: The Complexity of the Profession* (pp. 15–26). Amsterdam/Philadelphia: John Benjamins.

Berk-Seligson, S. (1988). The impact of politeness in witness testimony: The influence of the court interpreter. *Multilingua 7*(4), 411–439.

Berk-Seligson, S. (1990). *The Bilingual Courtroom.* Chicago/London: University of Chicago Press.

Calvo Encinas, E. (2001). La evaluación diagnóstica en la didáctica de la traducción jurídica: diseño de un instrumento de medida. Unpublished research dissertation, Department of Translation and Interpreting, University of Granada, Spain.

Calvo Encinas, E. (2004). La Administración Pública ante la interpretación social: Toma de contacto en la provincia de Toledo. *Puentes* (4) (Eds. Anne Martin and Isabel Abril Martí), 7–16.

Chesher et al. (2003). Community-based interpreting: The interpreter's perspective. In L. Brunette, G. Bastin, I. Hemlin, and H. Clarke (Eds.) *The Critical Link 3. Interpreters in the Community: The Complexity of the Profession* (pp. 273–291). Amsterdam/Philadelphia: John Benjamins.

Delgado C. E. (2001). *La interpretación social en los sindicatos.* Final Project. Doctoral Course: Interpretación Social. Doctoral Program: Traducción, Comunicación y Sociedad. Department of Translation and Interpreting, University of Granada, Spain. Unpublished.

Díez, R. (2003). Traducción e interpretación en los servicios públicos en Italia (entrevista a S. Putignano, E. Tomassini, R. Buri y F. Caciagli). In C. Valero (Ed.) *Traducción e Interpretación en los Servicios Públicos. Contextualización, Actualidad y Futuro* (pp. 249–58). Granada: Comares.

Fink, A. (1995). *The Survey Kit.* London: SAGE Publications.

Foulquié Rubio, A. I. (2002a). *El Intérprete en las Dependencias Policiales: Perspectivas de Abogados y Estudiantes de Derecho de Granada.* Unpublished research dissertation, Department of Translation and Interpreting, University of Granada, Spain.

Foulquié Rubio, A. I. (2002b). Interpretación social: La interpretación en la policía en Granada y Málaga. *Puentes* (1) (Eds. Presentación Padilla, Dorothy Kelly and Anne Martin), 107–115.

Foulquié Rubio, A. I. (2002c). La interpretación en la policía: ¿Un derecho o un privilegio? In C. Valero and G. Mancho (Eds.) *Traducción e Interpretación en los Servicios Públicos: Nuevas Necesidades para Nuevas Realidades* (pp. 91–96). Alcalá de Henares: Universidad de Alcalá Publicaciones. [CD-ROM].

Hale, S. (2004). *The Discourse of Court Interpreting: Discourse Practices of the Law, the Witness and the Interpreter.* Amsterdam/Philadelphia: John Benjamins.

Lang, R. (1978). Behavioural aspects of liaison interpreters in Papua New Guinea: Some preliminary observations. In D. Gerver and W. Sinaiko (Eds.) *Language Interpretation and Communication* (pp. 231–244). New York/London: Plenum Press.

Martin, A. (2000). La interpretación social en España. In D. Kelly (Ed.) *La Traducción y la Interpretación en España Hoy: Perspectivas Profesionales* (pp. 207–223). Granada: Comares.

Martin, A. (2006). La realidad de la traducción e interpretación en los servicios públicos en Andalucía. *Revista Española de Lingüística Aplicada (RESLA). Monográfico Retos del Siglo XXI para la Lingüística Aplicada: Nuevo Mapa Lingüístico y Cultural de la Península Ibérica* (Eds. Francisco Raga and Carmen Valero), 129–150.

Martin, A. and Abril Martí, I. (2006). Percepciones de los profesionales de los servicios públicos con respecto a la interpretación para la población inmigrante. In P. Blanco Garcia and P. Martino Alba (Eds.) *Traducción y multiculturalidad* (Actas de "*XI Encuentros Complutenses en Torno a la Traducción*". Madrid, 1–19 de noviembre, 2005). Madrid: Universidad Complutense. Instituto Universitario de Lenguas Modernas y Traductores.

Martin, A. and Abril Martí, I. (2008). Community interpreter self-perception: A Spanish case study. In C. Valero and A. Martin (Eds.) *Crossing Borders in Community Interpreting. Definitions and Dilemmas* (pp. 203–230). Amsterdam/Philadelphia: John Benjamins.

Martin, A. and Ortega Herráez, J. M. (2006). El intérprete judicial ante la encrucijada de su papel profesional: estudio de la realidad española. In N. A. Perdu, F. J. Garcia, E. Ortega and M. A. Garcia (Eds.) *Inmigración, Cultura y Traducción: Reflexiones Interdisciplinares* (pp. 437–446). Almería: Universidad de Almería. [CD-ROM].

Mason, I. (1999). Introduction. *Dialogue Interpreting. The Translator. Studies in Intercultural Communication*, 5(2), 147–160.

Mason, I. (2009). Role, positioning and discourse in face-to-face interpreting. In R. De Pedro Rico (Ed.) *Interpreting and Translating in Public Service Settings: Policy, Practice, Pedagogy* (pp. 52–73). Manchester: St Jerome.

Mesa, A. M. (2000). The cultural interpreter: An appreciated professional. Results of a study on interpreting services: Client, health care worker and interpreter points of view. In R. Roberts, S. E. Carr, D. Abraham and A. Dufour (Eds.) *The Critical Link 2: Interpreters in the Community* (pp. 67–79). Amsterdam/Philadelphia: John Benjamins.

Morera de Paz, I. (2000). *Trabajo de campo: La interpretación social en los hospitales de Granada capital.* Final Project. Doctoral Course: Interpretación Social. Doctoral Program: Traducción, Comunicación y Sociedad. Department of Translation and Interpreting, University of Granada, Spain. Unpublished.

Oppenheim, A. N. (1996). *Questionnaire Design, Interviewing and Attitude Measurement.* London: Pinter Publishers.

Ortega Herráez, J. M. (2004). *Panorámica de la interpretación judicial en España: Un análisis desde la profesión.* Unpublished Research Dissertation, Dpto. de Traducción e Interpretación, University of Granada, Spain.

Ortega Herráez, J. M. (2006). *Análisis de la Práctica de la Interpretación Judicial en España: El Intérprete frente a su Papel Profesional.* Doctoral dissertation. Granada: Editorial de la Universidad de Granada [available online from the homepage of the university library: http://www.ugr.es/~biblio/].

Ortega Herráez, J. M. and Foulquié Rubio, A. I. (2008). Interpreting in police settings in Spain: Service providers' and interpreters' perspectives In C. Valero and A. Martin (Eds.) *Crossing Borders in Community Interpreting. Definitions and Dilemmas* (pp. 123–146). Amsterdam/Philadelphia: John Benjamins.

Pöchhacker, F. (1997). Is there anybody out there? Community Interpreting in Austria. In S. E. Carr, R. Roberts, A. Dufour and D. Steyn (Eds.) *The Critical Link: Interpreters in the Community* (pp. 215–225). Amsterdam/Philadelphia: John Benjamins.

Pöchhacker, F. (2000). The community interpreter's task: Self-perception and provider views. In R. Roberts, S. E. Carr, D. Abraham and A. Dufour (Eds.) *The Critical Link 2: Interpreters in the Community* (pp. 49–65). Amsterdam/Philadelphia: John Benjamins.

Pöchhacker, F. (2004). *Introducing Interpreting Studies.* London/New York: Routledge.

Roy, C. B. (1996). An interactional sociolinguistic analysis of turn-taking in an interpreted event. *Interpreting, 1*(1), 39–67.

Russo, M. (2004). *Community interpreter, liaison interpreter, ad hoc interpreter, intercultural interpreter... What kind of curriculum for such a multifaceted profession?* Paper presented at *The Critical Link 4: Professionalisation of Interpreting in the Community. Fourth International Conference on Interpreting in the Community* (Stockholm, 2p. 23 May, 2004). Retrieved 3 April 2006, from www.criticallink.org/pdfs/Russo%20M.pdf.

Taibi, M. and Martin, A. (2006). Training public service translators and interpreters: Difficulties in an uncharted field. *Translation Ireland. Special Issue on Training Translators and Interpreters in Europe* (Guest Editor: John Kearns) *17*(1), 93–107.

Tomassini, E. (2002). A survey on the role of the community interpreter conducted in the region of Emilia Romagna, Italy. In C. Valero and G. Mancho (Eds.) *Traducción e Interpretación en los Servicios Públicos: Nuevas Necesidades para Nuevas Realidades* (pp. 193–199). Alcalá de Henares: Universidad de Alcalá Publicaciones. [CD-ROM].

Wadensjö, C. (1992). *Interpreting as Interaction: On Dialogue Interpreting in Immigration Hearings and Medical Encounters.* Doctoral dissertation. Department of Communication Studies, University of Linköping, Sweden.

Wadensjö, C. (1998). Interpreting as Interaction. London/New York: Addison Wesley Longman.

Way, C. L. (2004). *La Traducción como Acción Social. El Caso de los Documentos Académicos (Español-Inglés).* Doctoral dissertation. Granada: Editorial de la Universidad de Granada.

PART III

Pedagogy, ethics and responsibility in interpreting

CHAPTER 11

Toward more reliable assessment of interpreting performance

Jieun Lee
Department of Linguistics, Macquarie University

This pilot study examines the use of rating scales in the assessment of interpreting performance quality. The three criteria and descriptors in the band scale were developed *a priori* based on intuitive understanding of different levels of interpreting quality and the rating scale models used in second language assessment. Nine professional Korean interpreters rated five English Korean consecutive interpreting performances using the scales, and provided feedback on the use of rating scales. The results indicate that rating scales may enhance the reliability of assessment of interpreting performance.

1. Background

The genesis of this study was the challenge or problem I have faced as a teacher and examiner in interpreting performance assessment in the Master of Translation and Interpreting Program at Macquarie University in Australia (henceforth T&I Program). The end-of-semester examination for an interpreting practice unit in the T&I Program is tied to professional qualifications in Australia. The examination format is standardised in accordance with the Professional Interpreter Test administered by the National Authority for Accreditation of Translators and Interpreters (NAATI). The examination consists of two sets of dialogue interpreting, four socio-cultural questions and four questions on the professional ethics related to the dialogue interpreting, and consecutive interpreting in two language directions (A-B, B-A).[1] In addition to the examination, there are other components of assessment including class performance, portfolio, and practicum, but the essential requirement for professional interpreter accreditation through the T&I Program is the interpreting performance examination.

---

1. This examination format has been revised in 2008.

More than sixty interpreting students in 3–5 different language streams take this end-of-semester examination every semester. Several raters may be involved in the assessment even within the same language stream. In some language streams where there are fewer numbers of students, rating may be carried out *in situ* in the examination, whereas in other language pairs where there are large numbers of students, rating is done *post situ* based on audio recordings. If the internal marker, namely the teacher, and the external marker agree that the student's performance demonstrated professional interpreting quality, NAATI professional interpreter's accreditation is recommended for the student.

Performance assessment necessarily involves raters' subjective judgements about the quality of performance (McNamara, 1996, p. 117). Therefore, it is very important to apply the same scoring rubric and same interpretation of the criteria of performance assessment across the board. Nevertheless, much has been left to the examiners' intuitive understanding of quality in interpreting and mark-ing, and there has not been sufficient discussion to apply the same standards across different language streams within the program. Given that "a haphazard and impressionistic approach to grading undermines the reliability of interpreter testing" (Sawyer, 2004, p105), the current assessment practice deserves atten-tion, and has started to draw scholarly attention in the interpreter education community (e.g. Hatim and Mason, 1997; Sawyer, 2004).

1.2   Criteria of quality assessment

The fundamental aspect in interpreting quality appears to be the sense consistency between the source text and the target text, which is also referred to in various terms, such as accuracy or fidelity. However, other aspects, such as comprehensibility, clar-ity, style, target language quality in terms of grammatical appropriateness, pub-lic speaking skills, interpersonal skills, ethical and professional behaviour of the interpreter, are also important components of quality in relation to professional interpreting. As Gile (1995, p. 151) pointed out, "quality is a subjectively weighted sum of a number of components". The degree of importance of each component may vary depending on specific interpreting contexts and the perspective of those who assess the quality in interpreting. In fact, various perspectives on quality are held by professional interpreters, service users, and trainers (e.g. Bühler, 1986; Moser-Mercer, 1996; Kurz, 1993; Kopczyński, 1994; Schjoldager, 1996; Kalina, 2002). These professional standards and service users' expectations of quality are essential elements in shaping the criteria of quality to be upheld in interpreter education.

Amidst a growing body of literature on professional standards of quality in in-terpreting, there is a dearth of literature on the formal assessment of interpreting performance in interpreter education. Constructs for interpreting performance assessment in interpreting education have not been precisely defined (Sawyer, 2004, p. 98), and interpreter trainers and researchers have rarely examined the criteria for quality in interpreting performance assessment. Schjoldager (1996) and Riccardi (2002) discussed criteria for interpreting quality in the teaching environment, namely classroom feedback. Schjoldager (1996) suggested four criteria for simultaneous interpreting quality: comprehensibility and delivery, target language, coherence and plausibility, and loyalty. Riccardi (2002, pp. 121–123) provides seventeen microcriteria for interpreting assessment, which include phonological deviations, prosody deviations, production deviations, pauses, eye contact, posture, lexical deviations of common words and lexical deviations of technical words. The list of criteria may be exhaustive, but the practical use of so many criteria in test settings is a moot point. However, both of their approaches to criteria do not appear to be applicable or practical enough in formal assessment and both lack specific scoring rubrics.

The gap in the literature on the examination of interpreting skills suggests that there has been little theoretical discussion or reflection on the nature of assessment in interpreter education. Sawyer (2004) shed light on assessment practices which lacked sufficient validity and reliability and stressed the importance of assessment integrated in the curriculum. He mentioned three criteria, namely meaning and clarity, style, and presentation, for interpreting examination in the interpreting program with which he is involved, but the information on definitions and weighting for each criterion and raters' perception was not provided.

The only literature I found that contained weighting for quality criteria in interpreting assessment was in the work of Roberts (2000). According to Roberts (2000, p. 115), the Canadian community interpreter's qualification test scoring system has four criteria of assessment, namely understanding, accurate rendition of ideas, handling of names and numbers, and appropriate target language usage. The test also suggests weighting for each criterion, and a point deduction system for errors. This test scoring system is as follows. (See Table 1)

Table 1. Canadian community interpreter's qualification test scoring system

Criteria	Weighting	Point deduction
Understanding	30%	6 points
Accurate rendition of ideas in the target language (excluding names and numbers)	30%	6 points
Handling of names and numbers	10%	2 points
Appropriate target language quality	30%	6 points

However, these criteria appear to be ambiguous: it is not clear how understanding and accurate rendition of ideas could be distinct criteria in performance assessment, and how accurate rendition of ideas in the target language differs from appropriate target language quality. Since interpreting performance assessment tends to rely on the demonstration of skills rather than on tasks that test comprehension of the source speech, understanding may have to be assessed only through the message rendition.

Criteria should be the only basis for the judgment of quality in criterion-referenced assessment, and that is why criteria should be distinct and clear. Norm-referenced assessment is concerned with test takers' relative ranking in a given group (Hatim and Mason, 1997), and thus the outcome of norm-referenced assessment cannot provide information on the interpreting skill level of test takers. Therefore, criterion-referenced assessment is a more suitable method in interpreting performance assessment since performance quality is assessed on the basis of absolute criteria.

1.3   Rating scales

Rating scales, which are widely used in standardised language proficiency assessment, are believed to enhance reliability in assessment and produce more transparent test results (Alderson, 1991; Hudson, 2005, p. 205). Scales allow an indication of each level of competence to be described, and rating scales refer to an ordered series of such descriptions (McNamara, 2000, p. 40). There are scales that are nominal (e.g. pass/fail) or ordinal (e.g. high pass, pass, borderline fail, fail) or interval scales, where categories of a given attribute are equidistant from one another on a scale (e.g. 100 point multiple choice test). However, as North (1993, p. 32) cautioned, data from language proficiency scales are ordinal at best. The differences of quality between scales are not exactly the same. Performance assessment is by no means an exact science.

Rating scales may be divided into two types: holistic scales and analytic scales. Holistic scales examine several components of qualities globally, whereas analytic scales examine different components of qualities separately (Bachman and Palmer, 1996, p. 211). Though criteria may be considered in holistic scales and they are not entirely impressionistic, holistic scales may pose difficulties in determining the level of performance quality when the aspects of performance exhibit mixed levels of quality. By contrast, analytic scales enable identification of each criterion of quality, and are a more appropriate method of criterion-referenced assessment.

The rating scales to be pilot-tested in this study were designed using most of the existing criteria utilised in the T&I Program's current marking sheet, but with different labels. The criteria for the rating in the study are *Accuracy* (which refers to accuracy in content), *Target Language Quality* (which refers to accuracy in language, grammar, syntax, and register), and *Delivery* (which refers to delivery speed in the existing marking sheet). This study also drew on the interpreting quality standards suggested by Pöchhacker (2001), namely accurate rendition, adequate target language expression, equivalent intended effect and successful communicative interaction, which aptly illustrate the multiple dimensions of quality in interpreting from lexico-semantic core to the socio-pragmatic sphere of interaction. A brief discussion of the criteria to be included in the rating scales follows.

1.4   Accuracy

Based on accurate understanding of the source speech, the interpreter should reproduce the meaning and intention of the speech, achieving the same effect on the target language listener as on the source language listener. Given that accuracy should take communication effect into account, the Accuracy in the rating scales also contained an element of equivalent effect on the target text audience. The interpreted rendition should achieve equivalence across languages and cultures. Accuracy can be defined as the quality of faithfully conveying the message of the original speech with semantic and pragmatic equivalence (e.g. Baker, 1992, p. 217; Hale, 1995, 2004). Accuracy may also be measured in terms of deviations, such as omissions, additions, unjustifiable changes or misinterpretations of the meaning and intention of the speaker, the gravity of which should be considered in terms of the effect on the coherent and faithful rendering of the message.

1.5   Target Language Quality

Target Language (TL) Quality refers to the rendition in linguistically accurate, natural, and contextually appropriate language. In other words, it is related to comprehensibility, and listener-oriented product quality in interpreting. The sub-criteria for the TL Quality are features of grammaticality, phonology, morphology, syntax, naturalness, register, and style. This quality is also measured by deviations from the language norms, including inaccurate pronunciation, accent, stress; and grammar/morphosyntactics, unnatural or unidiomatic language (i.e. interference from the source language, inappropriate language in the target culture and for the target audience).

1.6 Delivery

While Accuracy and TL Quality relate to the content of the interpretation, Delivery is the package that delivers the content. Unlike the other two criteria, the quality of delivery can be assessed without reference to the source text. Quality in delivery may be defined in terms of good public speaking or presentation skills, namely effective communication. This criterion is similar to Pöchhacker's criterion of "successful communicative interaction". This quality is measured by deviations, including inarticulate speech, long pauses, hesitation, false starts, fillers, noise, excessive repairs or frequent self-corrections, monotonous intonation and unconvincing voice quality, and irritatingly slow speech rate. Though eye contact and postures are important public speaking skills, such kinesic information is not available in audiotaped performance, and thus has been excluded as components of quality in the rating scales used in this study.

1.7 Band scales

There are several things that should be determined in developing scales, such as the number of bands and graduation within each scale. The greater the number of scales, the harder it becomes to write distinct band descriptors and the harder for raters to use scales with precision consistently, because of the increased cognitive load (North, 1993, p. 49). On the other hand, if the number of scales is too small, distinguishing different performance qualities may become difficult. Practical utility is an important matter to consider in addition to theoretical validity. According to North (1993), the optimal number of scales for the maximum reliability of band scales is around six.

The term "band" usually implies a range of possible scores and, therefore, band scores may be converted into test scores (Alderson, 1991, p. 73). The mark for consecutive interpreting in one language direction in the T&I Program is worth 15 points in the interpreting examination. The number of bands in each criterion was determined on the basis of the existing weighting, namely 6 points for Accuracy in content, 6 points for Target Language Quality, and 3 points for Delivery. (See Table 2.)

Based on the weightings, six band scales were written for Accuracy and the Target Language (TL) Quality respectively from zero to six, and four bands for Delivery, from zero to three. All of the bands have no half point scales. The band equals a score in this study, thus eliminating further interpretation of the quality resulting from band-score conversion. The difference between the number of scales for accuracy and TL Quality and Delivery was simply due to a decision to

Table 2. Criteria and weighting

Criteria	Weighting
Accuracy	40%
Target Language Quality	40%
Delivery	20%

maintain the same interval scales instead of the same number of band scales for the three criteria.

Given that continuous numerical scales offer no advantages in terms of reliability or validity (North, 1993, p. 48), each band in this rating scale has descriptors for different levels of performance quality. Otherwise, various interpretations of the performance quality are possible. Descriptors can be brief and general, or detailed and specific, depending on the context of the use of the band scales and the expertise of the raters (Bachman and Palmer, 1996, p. 213). Descriptions that are too general or too brief may leave room for imprecision and ambiguity but, on the other hand, descriptions that are too specific or too long may be time-consuming and ineffective.

The graduation within the band scales may depend on the range of the students' abilities. Interpreting is a complex linguistic behaviour that takes mastery of essential skills, such as source language processing competence, language transfer competence, and target language processing competence (Hatim and Mason, 1997, p. 205). However, the level of the language skills required for interpreters has not been well documented in the literature (Valdés and Angelelli, 2003).

This study turned to the models of rating scales in second language assessment (e.g. Hughes, 2003, pp. 131–133), but there are differences between the assessment of second language and interpreting performance. In second language speaking assessment, test takers demonstrate their speaking skills, but there is no expectation that the target language production should be based on the source speech. An interpreter must deliver the source language message accurately based on comprehension of the original message. The descriptions about listening ability at each level were also provided in italics in addition to the extent of faithfulness in the delivery of the message in the rating scale. (See Appendix.) The bands for TL Quality contained descriptions about the extent of target language usage in terms of expressions and target language proficiency. Since consecutive interpreting is rendered in either the interpreter's A language or B language, the deviations in each case may vary slightly. Deviations in the course of interpreting into B language may contain grammatical and syntactic problems whereas grammatical issues may not be so prominent during interpreting into A language. The bands for Delivery contained descriptions about communication ability as well as the extent of delivery/public speaking skill to accommodate interactive aspects in communication. The bands used in this study are shown in Appendix.

The top level of quality, demonstrating the mastery of skill in language proficiency tests, is usually termed "native proficiency", but in this rating scale the TL Quality for interpreting assessment for Band 6 used a description, "excellent target language production". The descriptors for the lowest quality may differ depending on the level of the skills of the group of test takers. Second language proficiency assessment usually used "zero proficiency" for the rock bottom level. In this paper, the band descriptor for the lowest quality used the description, "test abandoned", considering a possibility that the test taker may give up or abandon the test. This quality represents Band 0. Compared with descriptors for the lowest and highest quality, it was difficult to write discrete descriptors for each level between the two extreme levels. The level of quality was differentiated by the following adjectives, namely "excellent", "very good", "good", "adequate", "inadequate" and "poor", while the gravity of deviations are differentiated by such quantifiers as "many", "some", "a few" and "few". This makes the rating scale ordinal rather than interval, despite the numbering from zero to 6. The difference in quality expressed by qualifiers or quantifiers is somewhat vague and relativistic. The criteria and scales were developed based on the literature review only, which needs to be evaluated empirically.

2.   The study

The aim of this research was to pilot-test *a priori* developed rating scales. By examining the results of sample assessment by raters and their feedback on the scales, this study attempted to determine whether or not the rating scales in criterion-referenced assessment could serve as a reliable and consistent method of assessment of interpreting performance.

2.1   Participants

Nine professional Korean interpreters participated in this study as raters and they rated five students' consecutive interpreting performances. Since assessment of interpreting into different languages raises another variable, this pilot study was limited to one language pair only (namely English to Korean). Six of them were experienced practitioners and teachers, and the other three were professional interpreters with no teaching experiences as interpreting teachers. Their age ranged between mid-thirties to early forties. There was one male rater and eight female raters. The following table (Table 3) displays the profile of the raters.

Table 3. Rater profiles

Features	Sex	Age	Title	Residence	Interpreting exp (years)	Teaching exp (years)
Rater 1	F	30s	P	K	9	0
Rater 2	M	30s	P	K	9	0
Rater 3	F	30s	P	K	9	0
Rater 4	F	40s	PT	K	17	14
Rater 5	F	30s	PT	K	9	4
Rater 6	F	30s	PT	A	5	2
Rater 7	F	30s	PT	A	9	2
Rater 8	F	40s	PT	A	18	7
Rater 9	F	30s	PT	K	9	5

Note: F = female   M = male
         P = practitioner   PT = teaching practitioner
         A = Australia   K = South Korea

The research design was affected by the time constraints on the professional interpreters, so double marking was not feasible and the number of sample interpreting performances was limited to five. Geographic distance was another challenge. Because of difficulty in recruiting qualified professional interpreters who would participate in this research, both Australian-based Korean interpreters and Korean-based Korean interpreters were invited. Therefore, it was impossible to hold a face-to-face rater training session with the raters, since they were located in different countries and cities.

2.2   Procedures and materials

The sample consecutive interpreting performances were provided by five student interpreters who had been enrolled in the interpreting course in the T&I program for two semesters. The test takers were in their late twenties to early thirties, with Korean being their mother tongue, and English their second language. Four of the students were female and one male. The students were given two weeks preparation time before the examination date. The samples were taken at the end-of-semester exam for the interpreting unit, which is usually audiotaped for marking purposes. With the students' permission, the segments of consecutive interpreting from English to Korean were used for this study.

The English source text was adapted from a speech delivered by an Australian government official on demographic changes in Australia. The 300-word English source text was recorded by a native Australian English speaker at an average speed of 110 words per minute at a recording studio, and the source speech transcript was provided to the raters for reference. The target text transcripts and the information on the duration of interpreting was provided to the raters, so that they would assess the performance quality based only on audio, not on transcripts or any other supplementary information. The original speech was 160 seconds long and the duration of interpreting varied from 140 seconds to 301 seconds.

Since rating sessions could not be held because of logistical constraints, written instructions were provided to the raters. A package containing information on the procedures, consent forms, rating scales, an audiotape containing the source speech followed by five different interpretations, the English source speech transcript, a score sheet, and a feedback sheet were mailed to the raters with self-addressed envelopes. To help the raters understand the procedure, contacts by email and phone were made after the package was sent out. The raters were asked to assess five consecutive interpreting performances at their convenience, and provide their feedback on the adequacy or usefulness of the rating scales on the feedback sheet provided. The whole procedure was estimated to take about forty minutes, but the raters reported that it took over an hour largely because they were not familiar with the rating scales.

3.   Results and discussion

3.1   Raters' feedback on the rating scales

Most raters assumed that analytic assessment was more accurate than holistic assessment. Eight out of nine raters responded that holistic assessment would not have rendered more accurate measurement. All of them responded that the criteria were easy to understand and were distinct, and that the examples of criteria were useful to understand the concept of the criteria. When asked if paired criteria were distinct from each other (i.e. Accuracy and TL Quality; TL Quality and Delivery), seven out of the nine raters responded that the criteria of Accuracy and TL Quality were separable. However, the raters were clearly divided about the distinction between TL Quality and Delivery. While the majority responded that they were distinguishable, three raters (Raters 5, 6 and 7) acknowledged that they experienced more difficulty in distinguishing these two than in distinguishing Accuracy and TL Quality because they seemed interrelated. Despite the raters' reservations, their scores on each criterion quality did not reflect decisions that suggested that they were linked, which may be interpreted in the following way. They seem to have distinguished the two qualities during the assessment, despite the fact that they were of the view that there were some interconnected features. This issue deserves further investigation in relation to the extent that these components of quality are correlated. This seems crucial if a valid and reliable criterion-referenced assessment is to be achieved.

In relation to the weightings for each criterion, there was a consensus. However, as for Accuracy, five raters wanted to increase the weighting from 40% to 50%, but they disagreed on the weightings for TL Quality and Delivery. (See Table 4.) The majority agreed to the predetermined weighting for Delivery quality. Revision was not possible because some participants did not specify their preferences.

As for band scales, seven raters found the band scales helpful for consistent rating, and were satisfied with the information on the level of performance quality described in the scales. Only two raters were somewhat sceptical about the usefulness of the band scales, stating that these scales were already in experienced raters' minds. In fact, these responses, as much as the responses of those who were satisfied with the band scales, indicated that the band scales appropriately described the level of qualities the raters unconsciously or consciously expected in interpreting performance. Given that the purpose of these band scales was to externalise the perceived quality across levels for consistent assessment, instead of making guesses with numerical scales, this was a positive sign.

As for the number of band scales, different opinions were found with regard to Accuracy and Delivery, whereas there was 100% agreement on the number of band scales in TL Quality. (See Table 5.) While 78% of the raters thought the degrees of band scales were adequate for the other two quality criteria, two raters

Table 4. Weightings suggested by the raters

Criteria	Weighting	Number of respondents	Remark
Accuracy	50%	5	
	40%	4	
TL Quality	40%	4	1 rater did not specify.
	30%	2	
	20%	2	
Delivery	20%	6	1 rater did not specify.
	30%	2	

Table 5. Number of scales suggested by the raters

Criteria	% of raters	Number of band scales
Accuracy	78%	Adequate
	11%	More band scales needed
	11%	Fewer band scales needed
TL Quality	100%	Adequate
Delivery	78%	Adequate
	22%	More band scales needed

preferred more band scales for Delivery. Among those who did not agree with the suggested number of scales for Accuracy, one rater responded that more band scales were needed for Accuracy, while the other preferred fewer band scales.

3.2   Inter-rater reliability

One of the typical indicators of reliability of assessment is inter-rater reliability, which refers to the level of rater agreement (Smith, 2000, p. 160). To measure the consistency of marking across raters, I calculated the correlations between all pairs of raters, and then calculated the average of the Pearson correlation coefficients, using Fisher's Z-transformation for each category. The average correlation coefficients were then put in this formula to compute interrater reliability for each category (Hatch and Lazaraton, 1991, p. 533).

$R = nr / [1+ (n-1)r]$
R: interrater reliability
N: number of raters
r: the average correlation of raters

Table 6 displays the correlation coefficients for each criterion quality rating.

According to McNamara (2000, p. 580), 0.7 is equivalent to 50% agreement and 50% disagreement between a pair of raters, whereas 0.9 is equivalent to 80% agreement and 20% disagreement. The acceptable level of inter-rater reliability may be different depending on the importance of the assessment, but reliability of about 0.7 and over is generally considered acceptable (Shohamy, 1985, p. 70). Considering that there was virtually no rater training, the consistency in marking appears to be very robust, with over 80% agreement for Accuracy and TL Quality. Rater agreement was lower in the assessment of Delivery than the other qualities, which may be attributable to different perceptions of Delivery quality. The overall inter-rater reliability coefficients were high enough to claim that the use of rating scales resulted in reliable assessment by multiple raters. However, the results do not overrule the likelihood of rater agreement by chance, which may increase with low numbers of scales, and the number of five samples was too small to draw a meaningful conclusion on inter-rater reliability.

Table 6. Inter-rater reliability for each category

Criteria	Inter-rater reliability
Accuracy	0.98
TL Quality	0.93
Delivery	0.77

The second language assessment literature suggests that rater training helps to improve reliability in assessment but has limitations in eliminating the rater bias and rater effects (Weigle, 1994). Raters are encouraged to conform to the common standards of interpretation of quality through training. In the limited scope of this study, there was no way to investigate the rating process in depth, but a rater (Rater 4) showed a noticeable discrepancy from the other raters in ranking each target quality. This rater was not enthusiastic about the advantage of rating scales over holistic scoring according to her feedback on the use of rating scales for interpreting performance. This kind of erratic rating behaviour may be controlled to some extent through rater training.

It was also found after data collection that not all raters referred to the source text consistently. Some relied on their memory of the source text from the start of the assessment and only referred to the source text transcript when they suspected deviations, while others referred to the source text transcript in assessing the first few students and stopped referring to the source text transcript half way through the rating process. This was an oversight on the part of the researcher, but this inconsistent rater behaviour was uncontrollable in this research design constrained by the limited availability of professional interpreters.

4.   Conclusion

Amidst the lack of research to promote theoretical discussion and reflection on the nature of assessment in interpreter education and lack of interface between interpreter education and language learning and testing, this pilot study explored the use of rating scales as a means of improving the reliability of interpreting performance assessment. The majority of raters approved of the rating scales proposed by the researcher, and the rating results also pointed to high inter-rater reliability, even in the absence of rater training. Given the raters' feedback that the rating scales were useful in consistent rating in multiple performance assessment, the provision of rating scales is expected to guide the raters to make conscious efforts to keep the same scoring principles throughout the rating over time. However, this pilot study raised more questions than it answered. Further research needs to be carried out to corroborate the utility of rating scales in broader contexts, and the scales require further rigorous empirical studies with diverse interpreting performance qualities in order to be validated. In addition, the construct of quality, which was labelled "Accuracy", "TL Quality", and "Delivery" respectively, require further examination whether it may be broken down into linguistically meaningful but nonetheless practically manageable components.

References

Alderson, J. C. (1991). Bands and scores. *Language Testing in the 1990s: Communicative Legacy*, *1*(1), 71–94. J. Charles Alderson & Brian North (Eds.) London/Basingstoke: Macmillan Publishers.

Angelelli, C. and Valdés, G. (2003). Interpreters, interpreting, and the study of bilingualism. *Annual Review of Applied Linguistics*, *23*, 58–78.

Bachman, L. and Palmer, A. (1996). *Language Testing in Practice: Designing and Developing Useful Language Tests*. Oxford: Oxford University Press.

Baker, M. (1992). *In Other Words: A Coursebook on Translation*. London/New York: Routledge.

Bühler, H. (1986). Linguistic (semantic) and extralinguistic (pragmatic) criteria for the evaluation of conference interpretation and interpreters. *Multilingua*, *5*(4), 231–235.

Hale, S. (1995). *Pragmatic Equivalence in Court Interpreting: A Study of Accuracy of Interpreting in Spanish-English Proceedings*. Unpublished MA thesis, Macquarie University.

Hale, S. (2004). *The Discourse of Court Interpreting*. Amsterdam/Philadelphia: John Benjamins.

Hatch, E. and Lazaraton, A. (1991). *The Research Manual: Design and Statistics for Applied Linguistics*. Boston: Heinle and Heinle Publishers.

Hatim, B. and Mason, I. (1997). *The Translator as Communicator*. London/New York: Rutledge.

Hudson, T. (2005). Trends in assessment scales and criterion-referenced language assessment. *Annual Review of Applied Linguistics*, *25*, 205–227.

Hughes, A. (2003). *Testing for Language Teachers*. (2nd ed.) Cambridge: Cambridge University Press.

Kalina, S. (2002). Quality in interpreting and its prerequisites: A framework for a comprehensive view. In G. Garzone and M. Viezzi (Eds.) *Interpreting in the 21st Century* (pp. 121–130). Amsterdam/Philadelphia: John Benjamins.

Kopczynński, A. (1994). Quality in conference interpreting: Some pragmatic problems. In M. Snell-Hornby, F. Pöchhacker and K. Kaindl (Eds.) *Translation Studies: An Interdiscipline* (pp. 189–198). Amsterdam/Philadelphia: John Benjamins.

Kurz, I. (1993/2002). Conference interpretation: Expectations of different user groups. In F. Pöchhacker and M. Shlesinger (Eds.) *Interpreting studies reader* (pp. 313–324). New York: Routledge.

McNamara, T. (1996). *Measuring Second Language Performance*. London/New York: Longman.

McNamara, T. (2000). *Language Testing*. Oxford: Oxford University Press.

Moser-Mercer, B. (1996). Quality in interpreting: Some methodological issues. *The Interpreters' Newsletter*, *7*, 43–55.

North, B. (1993). *The Development of Descriptors on Scales of Language Proficiency: Perspectives, Problems, and a Possible Methodology Based on a Theory of Measurement*. Washington D.C.: The National Foreign Language Centre.

Pöchhacker, F. (2001). Quality assessment in conferences and community. *Meta*, *46*(2), 410–425.

Riccardi, A. (2002). Evaluation in interpretation: Macrocriteria and microcriteria. In E. Hung (Ed.) *Teaching Translation and Interpreting 4: Building Bridges* (pp. 115–126). Amsterdam/Philadelphia: John Benjamins.

Roberts, R. P. (2000). Interpreter assessment tools for different settings. In R. P. Roberts, S. E. Carr, D. Abraham and A. Dufour (Eds.) *Critical Link 2* (pp. 103–130). Amsterdam/Philadelphia: John Benjamins.

Sawyer, D. (2004). *Fundamental Aspects of Interpreter Education: Curriculum and Assessment.* Amsterdam/Philadelphia: John Benjamins.

Schjoldager, A. (1996). Assessment of simultaneous interpreting. In C. Dollerup and V. Appel (Eds.) *Teaching Translation and Interpreting 3: New Horizons* (pp. 187–195). Amsterdam/Philadelphia: John Benjamins.

Shohamy, E. (1985). *A Practical Handbook in Language T*esting. Tel Aviv: Tel Aviv University.

Smith, D. (2000). Rater judgements in the direct assessment of competency-based second language writing ability. In G. Brindley (Ed.) *Studies in Immigrant English Language Assessment 1* (pp. 159–189). Sydney: National Centre for English Language Teaching and Research.

Weigle, S. C. (1994). Effects of training on rates of ESL compositions. *Language Testing, 11,* 197–223.

CHAPTER 12

Quality in healthcare interpreter training

Working with norms through recorded interaction

Raffaela Merlini and Roberta Favaron[1]
University of Macerata and University of Vienna / ISMETT, Palermo

This paper presents an interpreter training program recently implemented at an Italo-American healthcare facility and illustrates how the notion of "norm", as developed within Descriptive Translation Studies, successfully shifted the trainees' attention away from externally imposed instructions onto internally generated behavioural patterns. The process of critical rethinking was carried out through guided self-assessment of both authentic and simulated interpreting performances, based on transcript analysis. Exemplification is provided here by the use of first vs. third person. Given the highly specific context of the medical institution in question, the experience described in this study is significant only insofar as it indicates how to make rigid and undifferentiated rules superfluous while, at the same time, assuring quality services and enhancing the professionalisation of healthcare interpreting.

1. Introduction

> Learn, but with reservations. A lifetime does not suffice to unlearn what you, in your naivety and submissiveness, have let into your mind – you, innocent one! – without thinking of the consequences.   (Michaux, 1981, p. 9; our translation)

This quotation appears at the beginning of a recent book on medical education by Gérard Danou (2007). Conceived of as integration to the scientific dimension of medical curricula, Danou's approach focuses on the need for trainees to critically assess the repercussions of traditional healthcare models.[2] This same emphasis

---

1. Although this paper is the outcome of a joint research project, Sections 1, 2 and 5 were written by Raffaela Merlini, and Sections 3 and 4 by Roberta Favaron.

2. Danou suggests refocusing on the doctor-patient relationship and, in particular, on the doctor's ability to "understand not just the illness [...] but the ill human being" (2007, 16; our

on awareness-raising activities is at the core of the interpreting training project discussed in this paper. In encouraging interpreting trainees to challenge received knowledge, we are also adopting Graham Turner's (2007) notion of "expository" interpreting, as a substitute for "defensive" interpreting. In his presentation at the Critical Link 5 conference, Turner defined expository interpreting as "pro-active, self-revealing and collaborative", thus offering a perfect synthesis of the philosophy guiding our training initiative. Equally useful for our purposes was the concept of "norm" as developed within Descriptive Translation Studies (Toury, 1980, 1999, 2004; Hermans, 1996).

The project involves an interpreting scholar from the University of Macerata (Raffaela Merlini), and ISMETT, a transplant centre based in Palermo, which, at the time, employed eight staff interpreters (among whom Roberta Favaron) to enable communication between its Italian- and English-speaking clinical and administrative personnel.[3] The initiative originated from a combination of needs. On the one hand, in scholarly milieus in Italy the lack of authentic interpreting data has been a serious obstacle to theoretical reflection; on the other, institutions employing in-house interpreters find it difficult to provide further training internally. In return for training seminars, ISMETT has authorised the scholar, in her capacity as trainer, to record interpreted events. These recordings have been used both for the trainees' self-assessment and for research purposes. Whereas, to the knowledge of the present authors, on-the-job training in Italy rarely relies on transcripts of interpreting performances, this is precisely the didactic material used in our seminars.

The following sections are meant to illustrate our training methodology and, more specifically, how norms can offer a useful theoretical framework. The exemplification will be provided by a distinctive issue in dialogue interpreting practice, namely the use of first vs. third person, as emerging from interpreted interactions between English- and Italian-speaking nurses.[4] Though yielding interesting clues as to the interpreter's reading of his/her role, the reporting mode will be explored here only insofar as it demonstrates our training practice. No generalizations are intended, or indeed possible, as to which of the two modes should be preferred. This is all the more true given the highly specific context of

translation). For a discussion of a "humane" approach to health care in linguistically mediated doctor-patient interaction, see Merlini and Favaron (2005).

3.   ISMETT (*Istituto Mediterraneo per i Trapianti e Terapie ad Alta Specializzazione*) was established in 1997 as a partnership between the Region of Sicily, Italy, and the University of Pittsburgh Medical Center (UPMC), Pennsylvania.

4.   For an exploration of conversational alignments during interpreter-mediated interactions between healthcare professionals and patients, see Merlini and Favaron (2003; 2005).

peer-to-peer communication in an institution where interpreters interrelate daily with their clients, and where they feel and are perceived by the healthcare staff as part of a team.

2.   Rules vs. norms

The investigation of quality in interpreting has been a predominant concern since the beginning of scholarly research in the field. Evidence of this, as Viezzi (1996, p. 12) observes, has been the development of quality criteria, with the twofold aim of guiding professional practice and training, and establishing a frame of reference for performance evaluation. Concentrating initially on the former objective, we turned to the end products of work on quality, i.e. professional codes of practice, where criteria are explicitly given prescriptive status. Examining the worldwide *Environmental Scan of Standards of Practice for Interpreters* (Bancroft, 2005), we found that codes for healthcare interpreters leave practitioners a wider room for manoeuvre in comparison with conference and court interpreting codes. This flexibility, as Bancroft (2005, p. 25) notes, may be due to the emphasis that all the reviewed healthcare interpreting codes place on the promotion of a "bond" between healthcare practitioners and their patients.

A non-negligible datum, however, emerges from the survey, which seems to contradict this flexibility: the instruction to "use the first person" (Bancroft, 2005, p. 26). The most likely reason for prescribing this as a rule is to be sought in the equation, frequently echoed in the literature, of the use of the first person with professional interpreting (Harris, 1990; Wadensjö, 1998; Pöchhacker, 2004; Hale, 2004; Dubslaff and Martinsen, 2005) and the consequent attempt to push forward the professionalisation of healthcare interpreting, by giving it the same procedural instructions as the ones applying in more established settings, such as conference and court interpreting ones. Besides, the first person presents a number of additional advantages; over and above enhancing clarity, brevity, and impartiality, it is thought to create "the illusion of a direct exchange between the monolingual parties" (Wadensjö, 1997, p. 49). The third person, on the other hand, is explicitly mentioned either as an exception (Shlesinger, 1991; Gentile, Ozolins and Vasilakakos, 1996; Meyer, 2002), or as the norm for non-professional interpreters (Shackman, 1984; Knapp and Knapp-Potthoff, 1985; Harris, 1990; Pöchhacker, 2004).

First-person interpreting is also prescribed to newly hired ISMETT interpreters. In this case, the rule is meant to apply to the whole range of interactional scenarios which characterize cross-lingual communication at ISMETT. These extend beyond asymmetrical, i.e. professional-patient, encounters – the traditional area of concern in medical interpreting codes of practice – to symmetrical dialogue interpreting ones involving healthcare staff members. Our feeling was that this prescription might be an ideal candidate for critical rethinking. We thus looked for a conceptual framework that could accommodate both our training objectives and our theoretical enquiries. This implied taking a step back from prescription to description, i.e. from rules to norms.

Developed within the field of translation studies as "a category for descriptive analysis" (Toury, 1980, p. 57), the concept of "norm" refers to regularities in translational behaviour, resulting from internalised socio-cultural constraints.[5] Lying between absolute rules and subjective idiosyncrasies, norms occupy a large, undefined area, where shifts in binding force are frequently observable, especially in conjunction with changes in the values shared by a social group. In time, "norms can gain so much validity that [...] they become as binding as rules; or the other way round" (Toury, 2004, p. 206). Not yet formalised and institutionalised, as rules are, norms provide a useful frame of reference for a number of reasons.

Firstly, being a historically and socially determined construct, the norm allows for variability of behaviour not only in time but also throughout sectors of activity. In Toury's theorization, norms are precisely an attempt to have "variability in all its facets *introduced into the notion of translation itself*" (1999, p. 12). Closely connected to the intrinsic mutability of norms is the need to study them within a clearly defined "system", which, as Marzocchi (2005, p. 89) observes, "must be conceptualised at the level of the interpreting event or setting".

Secondly, as models of behaviour, norms originate from an inter-subjective negotiation process. This presupposes the existence of a community where norms are formed through socialization processes. Admittedly, the embryonic state of healthcare interpreting in many countries, including Italy, is tantamount to the absence of a sizable and clearly identifiable community. However, smaller-scale communities – such as the one involved in this project – can, in our view, be taken into account as norm-generating environments. As for the actors involved in the negotiation of norms, over and above the interpreters themselves, their clients, and the initiators of the interpreting act (Garzone, 2002, p. 116), our contention is that one more agent should be included, namely the researcher. Traditionally considered an outsider, the researcher has been cast in the role of "external observer" (Viezzi, 1996, p. 12), whose major task "consists in identifying and interpreting the norms" (Hermans, 1996, p. 39). Where, however, the researcher's role comes to coincide with that of trainer, as in our case, s/he is bound to become an integral

---

5.   So far, relatively few scholars have applied the concept of norm to the study of interpreting; among them Shlesinger (1989), Harris (1990), Schjoldager (1995), Gile (1999), Garzone (2002) and Marzocchi (2005).

part of that very socialization process by which norms are produced. As will be presently illustrated, ISMETT may be seen to represent an ideal microcosm for the study of normative models, in that it affords the involvement of all the above-mentioned actors.

The third and final reason for adopting the notion of norm lies in what Marzocchi (2005, p. 105) calls its "undefining potential", which could be exploited to challenge acquired notions about interpreting practice.

3.   The ISMETT training project

The training project started in April 2005 and is still underway. It has developed over a number of phases, which are summarized in Table 1.

Following a theoretical introduction by the scholar/trainer to the concepts of Conversation Analysis as applied to dialogue interpreting in health care (sub-phase 1a), a number of interpreted encounters at ISMETT were observed (sub-phase 1b). On the basis of her field-notes, the trainer identified some critical areas (concerning technical, linguistic, cultural, interpersonal, and ethical issues), which were then discussed during a brainstorming session (sub-phase 1c). Participants in the session were the trainer, who guided the discussion, all ISMETT interpreters, including their coordinator in his double role as interpreter and institutional representative, and a senior American nurse with a limited knowledge

Table 1. Summary description of the ISMETT training project

Phase	Description
One 04/2005	a. Trainer's theoretical introduction
	b. Trainer's shadowing of interpreted sessions
	c. Brainstorming on critical issues
Two 10/2005	Learning needs analysis
Three 01/2006-01/2007	Recording and transcription of 11 nurse-nurse authentic interpreted interactions
Four 02-03/2007	a. Group discussion of transcripts focusing on 1st vs. 3rd person interpreting
	b. Role-play exercise based on transcripts of real interactions
	c. Group discussion of role-play transcripts vs. those of the original sessions
Five (to be started)	a. Further recording of authentic data
	b. Expansion of topics for analysis (face-work, turn-taking and topic control)

of Italian, who usually relies on the interpreting service. During the discussion, the concept of norm was introduced as the basis upon which to reconsider pre-scribed interpreting conduct. Out of the identified issues, the use of direct vs. indirect speech emerged as a priority object of analysis, given the evident clash between the first-person rule and the wide variability of behaviour observed in real practice. This same aspect has been chosen to exemplify our training meth-odology in the present paper.

Eleven authentic interpreted sessions were recorded and transcribed (phase 3).[6] These were instances of interaction between American and Italian nurses during change-of-shift reporting, when the interpreting service is often requested to en-sure flawless communication of vital information concerning patients' conditions and therapeutic prescriptions. Excerpts were then shown to the interpreters and jointly analysed to detect recurrences in the use of direct and indirect speech (sub-phase 4a). More specifically, interpreters were asked to reflect on why they used one form instead of the other, and on the effects of their choices. Although brevity was highlighted as one of the main reasons for using direct speech, the self-effacement entailed by it was judged by most interpreters to be at odds with the informal nature of this kind of interaction. On the contrary, the use of indirect speech was assessed as a more suitable device to create a cooperative climate among colleagues.

A few days later, a new training session was held without prior notice as to its content. Three interpreters were asked to interpret scripted role-plays based on the transcripts of the original interactions in which they had taken part (sub-phase 4b). The role-plays were then transcribed and all the trainees were invited to compare them with the transcripts of the original sessions (sub-phase 4c).[7]

4.   Analysis of transcripts and interpreters' comments

This paragraph will attempt to summarize the most significant results of com-parative transcript analysis. The behaviour of each interpreter will be discussed; however, for reasons of length, only examples concerning two of the three in-terpreters will be shown. Excerpts from the original interactions (T2 and T10) will be followed by the corresponding sequences in the simulated ones (ST2 and

---

6. The recording and transcription was mostly carried out by two post-graduate students, Eleonora Iacono and Simona Orefice. Their precious contribution to this project is here gladly acknowledged.

7. The three real interactions took place respectively on 22.01, 23.01, 07.03.2006 and lasted 18'52", 8'49", 10'43". The three corresponding role-plays took place on 25.02.2007 and lasted 7'44", 6'12", 6'54".

Table 2. Profile of the three interpreters involved in the role-plays

	Intepreter 1	Intepreter 2	Intepreter 3
Sex	Male	Female	Male
Age	35–40	35–40	35–40
Mother tongue	Italian	English/Italian	English/Italian
Years at ISMETT	6.5	6.5	2.5
Education	Conference Interpreting	Marketing and Communication	Conference Interpreting
Stated preference	Direct speech	None	Indirect speech

ST10), and by the interpreter's relevant comments. The examples are indicative of recurrent patterns. Table 2 shows relevant details about the three interpreters.

Interpreter 1
A brief introduction to the context of the original session should be provided. The outgoing American nurse (USn) has not carried out some of the assignments during her shift. Therefore, the incoming Italian nurse (ITn) feels annoyed, since she has to carry them out herself, as the following exchange shows:

[1]
    T2   454–458[8]

454 ITn: […] la devo pesare↑
                shall I weigh her

455 INT: should I also do this↑
456 USn: okay unless you want me to s- I mean

---

8. These numbers refer to the place of the reported lines in the transcript. Idiomatic translations into English of the Italian utterances are in italics, and features of interest in bold. Transcription conventions:

[…]	omitted portions
[ ]	overlap
=	latched utterances
(.)	intra-turn pause
((pause))	inter-turn pause
↑	rising intonation
wo:::rd	lengthened sound
word-word	abrupt cut-off
word	emphasis
WORD	increased volume
°word°	decreased volume
>word<	quicker pace
((word))	contextual information and characterisations of talk

457   ⌈ I can stay and I can do all this ⌉
458 INT: ⌊ oh vabbè **posso** rimanere   ⌋ un po' di più e lo **faccio io**
              okay I can stay   *a bit longer*   *and I will do it*

In [1] and throughout the session, Interpreter 1 consistently uses the first person to render the utterances of both primary parties, in line with his stated preference (see Table 2). The same direct speech mode is adopted in the simulation of similar passages, as exemplified in [2]:

[2]
       ST2   85–89
85   ITn: […] la devo pesare↑
              shall I weigh her
86   INT: should I:: should I weigh the patient
87   USn: u::h oka::y as I said I can do that as well
88   […]
89   INT: **posso** farlo:: **posso** pesarla anch'**io** la paziente se vuoi
              I can do it   *I can weigh the patient myself*   *if you want*

But as the role-play unfolds something happens:

[3]
       ST2   99–104
99   ((the interpreter's mobile starts ringing at a distance))
100 INT: that's my telephone […]
101 USn: do you wanna answer the telephone↑
102 INT: ((low voice)) no no never mind
103 USn: no is it fine↑ ((the interpreter nods)) okay so >what did **she** say<
104 INT: **she** said **she** will take care of everything don't worry you can go home

Significantly, the interruption and the subsequent explanation (lines 99–100) foreground the interpreter as an interlocutor in his own right, and trigger the shift to the indirect style (lines 103–104). This mode is maintained in the subsequent long sequence of one-language turns between the American nurse and the interpreter, where the latter uses the third person to reiterate that the Italian nurse will carry out the outstanding assignments.

Going back to the original interaction, another significant sequence occurs following an exchange of turns where the Italian nurse manifests all her annoyance at having to do extra work, and the American nurse blames the doctor who wrote down the orders only towards the end of her shift. This meant that she did not have the time to carry them out herself:

[4]

	T2	667–673
667	USn:	=but that's=

668 ITn: =ma le credo   dille che le credo
but I believe her   *tell her I believe her*

669 USn: between me and him   that's

670   between me and the doctor
671 INT: ((whispering)) **she** believes you

672 ITn: dille che le credo
tell her   *I believe her*

673 INT: glielo **di:rò:** (.) **io** stessa a questo medico
I will talk   *personally to this physician*

In a nineteen-minute-long session, line 671 shows one of the very few occurrences of the third person in this interaction. As illustrated in the sequence, Interpreter 1 immediately shifts back to the first person (line 673). The indirect mode is much more frequent in the role-play:

[5]

ST2 180

180 USn: °u::h°(.) >okay< this is my final word I'm staying I'm doing this (.) okay↑ °so-°
191–197

191 INT: va bene okay °a posto° **lo fa lei**
all right okay   *it's settled*   **she will do** it

192 USn: how-how-however ((with an irritated tone of voice)) I mean the doctors'd better
193 **write** all the time   they __round__ next time you know you know because=
194 INT: these doctors are I mean sometimes you know the way it
works
195 USn: =this is not   the first time that this happens
196 INT: I know I know there was not enough   time
197 comunque LO **FA LEI** insomma **si è offerta lei** di farlo
anyway   **she will do** it *in short*   **she offered** to do it **herself**

Here the interpreter explicitly helps the parties settle the disagreement. He repeatedly reassures the incoming Italian nurse that her outgoing colleague will take care of the tasks left to accomplish (lines 191 and 197), while at the same time showing sympathy towards the American nurse (line 196).

To sum up, while in the original the first person is used throughout, except for a few momentary shifts to the third person, in the role-play, despite the predominance of the first person, indirect speech is more extensively used. This shows a significant change of attitude towards a larger freedom in the use of the third person, which might be an effect of the thinking process prompted by the training seminars. In his comments, the interpreter explained his shift to indirect speech as a deliberate attempt to step into the interaction in order to solve the deadlock. An interesting finding was that, although in the original interaction Interpreter 1 sticks to direct speech, the nurses' responses differ: whereas the American nurse addresses the Italian colleague directly (see [1], line 456), the latter keeps addressing the interpreter (see [4], line 668). This seems to deny the argument that first-person interpreting favours a direct exchange between the primary parties (see Section 2).

Interpreter 2
Of the three interpreters, Interpreter 2 was the one who explicitly said that she acted on the spur of the moment and was made aware of her reporting modes only through transcript analysis. In the original interaction, she frequently shifts between direct and indirect speech. In the role-play, on the contrary, she adopts the indirect style throughout. As she pointed out, this was a deliberate choice, especially when the Italian nurse referred to her performing her nursing tasks. In this case, reflection brought about a newly acquired awareness and the intentional adoption of indirect speech as the preferred mode.

Interpreter 3
In the real-life context, the outgoing American nurse is about to leave Italy and the following day will be her last day at work. She is excited about it and the session ends with a lively exchange.

Although a conference interpreter himself – like Interpreter 1 – Interpreter 3 stated a clear preference for the third person in dialogue interpreting contexts. In doing so, he consciously disregards the first-person rule prescribed at ISMETT. This preference was confirmed in the analysis of the original interaction, where no instances of the direct style were found. Excerpt [6] provides one example of his use of the third person:

[6]
    T10   355–358
355   USn: [...] it'll be my last day I'm gonna bring- =
356   INT: =domani è l'ultimo giorno
            tomorrow it will be the last day

357   USn: I'll bring a bottle of wine tomorrow
358   INT: **porta** una bottiglia di vino ((laugh))
            *she will **bring** a bottle of wine*

The same behaviour is displayed in the role-play, with the exception of three cases, all to be found in neighbouring turns. The following sequence shows one such case:

[7]

```
        ST10 157–161
157     USn: […] it'll be my last day=
158     INT: =comunque sarà::: ⌐>il suo ultimo giorno<⌐
                anyway it will be    her last day
159     USn:                   ⌊ I'm gonna            ⌋ bring a BI::G bottle of wi::ne↑
160           ⌐ and we'll have a big party here ⌐
161     INT: ⌊ quindi porto una bottiglia       ⌋ di VI:::NO↑ ((all laugh)) e festeggiamo
                so I will bring a bottle             of wine              and we'll celebrate
```

When motivating the shift from third person (line 158) to first person (line 161), the interpreter said that in informal exchanges, especially as hilarity sets in, he becomes so engrossed in the conversation that he possibly identifies with primary speakers at an unconscious level.

5. Conclusions: From "undefining" to "redefining"?

The analysis of direct vs. indirect speech occurrences, conducted through recourse to the twin sources identified by Toury (2004) of textual products (in our case, the recorded interactions and their transcripts) and extra-textual pronouncements (i.e. the interpreters' comments on their own performances) produced a number of findings. It is worth reiterating that these findings cannot sustain any general-izations, given that they are based on the performances of just three interpreters in a very specific dialogue interpreting context.

Although the use of the first person is a prescribed rule at ISMETT, the choice of direct vs. indirect speech was found to vary from interpreter to interpreter, and in response to different interactional requirements. Firstly, two of the three in-terpreters, both with a higher-education qualification in conference interpreting, initially expressed compliance with divergent reporting modes. While in the case of Interpreter 1, the conference interpreting first-person rule was transferred to dialogue interpreting, in the case of Interpreter 3, the distinction between the two settings was deliberately marked by the use of different modes, with the indirect one being preferred for dialogue interpreting. Secondly, as a result of reflection on this aspect, all three interpreters modified, to varying degrees, their behaviour. The trend was towards a less inhibited use of the third person, whilst no shift from an indirect to a predominantly direct style was observed. Thirdly, shifts from first to third person were seen to be triggered by extended one-language turns between the interpreter and one of the primary parties (incidentally, this is in line with the findings of Dubslaff and Martinsen, 2005). Indirect speech was also the preferred mode in a situation of conflict, when the need to mediate and rebuild rapport arose. Fourthly, in a relaxed and cheerful scenario, where the bond between interlocutors was not in danger, the first person came naturally out of the identification with either primary speaker. The last two findings seem to confirm our initial assumption that rapport-building may be achieved through the use of either direct or indirect speech, depending on the specific interactional context. Finally, though brevity was identified as one of the reasons for using the first person, its consistent use by the interpreter in one of the sessions did not lead both primary speakers to communicate directly; in other words, it did not manage, in that instance at least, to "create the illusion of a direct exchange".

To sum up, the rule of the first person was not uniformly followed, not only by the three interpreters but also by their colleagues, as emerged in group discussions. Reasons were twofold: on the one hand, we noticed a lack of awareness – shared by most trainees – in using one form instead of the other, until transcripts were analysed; on the other hand, the rule was, in a few cases, outright, yet uncritically, rejected as unsuitable for face-to-face interpreting. By substituting the concept of rule with that of norm, emphasis was placed on internally generated as against externally imposed behavioural patterns. A thinking process was thus set in motion, which did not result in the consolidation of any one rule, yet raised the trainees' awareness as to the reasons for and consequences of their own reporting modes.

More generally, the concept of norm has indeed proved an invaluable didactic tool, in that it allowed trainees to "challenge the core of our received wisdom" (Marzocchi, 2005, p. 102) by leading them into the vital process of negotiation and dissent, which is where norms are to be more easily found (Pym, 1999, p. 111). However, in view of a progressive enhancement of interpreting practice, the question remains of what to prescribe and in what terms when quality is the stake. Undeniably, the inclusion of the first-person rule in healthcare interpreting codes of conduct, for example, was aimed at the much-needed professionalisation of the sector. Our view, however, is that a less simplistic solution should be found to ensure quality. Training programmes based on a theoretically-informed analysis of recorded and transcribed interpreting performances and on multi-stakeholder discussions might go some way towards making quality in interpreting a truly shared responsibility, while rendering rigid and undifferentiated prescriptions superfluous.

Owing to the universally recognised status of the medical profession, Danou (2007, p. 56) has no qualms in invoking the "art of improvisation" as "a mark of professional excellence". This "opposition to the linearity of habit" (2007, p. 50), which is presented by the author as the outcome of a long and arduous process of reflection on one's art, its principles and rules, may be too daring a proposition in our field, where non-professional practice is still all too frequent. Our hope, however, is that one day the professionalisation of dialogue interpreting will have reached so advanced a stage for this proposition no longer to sound inconceivable. In this future scenario, interpreters will perhaps be (deemed) able to "redefine" norms of behaviour as they see fit in the specific interactional context.

References

Bancroft, M. (2005). *The Interpreter's World Tour – An Environmental Scan of Standards of Practice for Interpreters*. Woodland Hills, CA: The California Endowment.

Danou, G. (2007). *Langue, Récit, Littérature dans l'Éducation Médicale*. Limoges: Lambert-Lucas.

Dubslaff, F. and Martinsen, B. (2005). Exploring untrained interpreters' use of direct versus indirect speech. *Interpreting, 7*(2), 211–236.

Garzone, G. (2002). Quality and norms in interpretation. In G. Garzone and M. Viezzi (Eds.) *Interpreting in the 21st Century* (pp. 107–119). Amsterdam/Philadelphia: John Benjamins.

Gentile, A., Ozolins, U. and Vasilakakos, M. (1996). *Liaison Interpreting: A Handbook*. Melbourne: Melbourne University Press.

Gile, D. (1999). Norms in research on conference interpreting: A response to Theo Hermans and Gideon Toury. In C. Schäffner (Ed.) *Translation and Norms* (pp. 98–105). Clevedon/ Philadelphia: Multilingual Matters.

Hale, S. (2004). *The Discourse of Court Interpreting: Discourse Practices of the Law, the Witness and the Interpreter*. Amsterdam/Philadelphia: John Benjamins.

Harris, B. (1990). Norms in interpretation. *Target, 2*(1), 115–119.

Hermans, T. (1996). Norms and the determination of translation: A theoretical framework. In R. Álvarez and M. Carmen-África Vidal (Eds.) *Translation, Power, Subversion* (pp. 25–51). Clevedon/ Philadelphia: Multilingual Matters.

Knapp, K. and Knapp-Potthoff, A. (1985). Sprachmittlertätigkeit in interkultureller Kommunikation. In J. Rehbein (Ed.) *Interkulturelle Kommunikation* (pp. 450–463). Tübingen: Narr.

Marzocchi, C. (2005). On norms and ethics in the discourse in interpreting. *The Interpreters' Newsletter, 13*, 87–107.

Merlini, R. and Favaron, R. (2003). Community interpreting: Re-conciliation through power management. *The Interpreters' Newsletter, 8*, 205–229.

Merlini, R. and Favaron, R. (2005). Examining the 'voice of interpreting' in speech pathology. *Interpreting, 7*(2), 263–301.

Meyer, B. (2002). Untersuchung zu den Aufgaben des interkulturellen Mittelns. In J. Best and S. Kalina (Eds.) *Übersetzen und Dolmetschen: Eine Orientierungshilfe* (pp. 51–59). Tübingen/Basel: Francke.

Michaux, H. (1981). *Poteaux d'Angle*. Paris: Gallimard.

Pöchhacker, F. (2004). *Introducing Interpreting Studies*. London/New York: Routledge.

Pym, A. (1999). Okay, so how are translation norms negotiated? A question for Gideon Toury and Theo Hermans. In C. Schäffner (Ed.) *Translation and Norms* (pp. 106–112). Clevedon/ Philadelphia: Multilingual Matters.

Schjoldager, A. (1995). An exploratory study of translational norms in simultaneous interpreting: Methodological reflections. *Hermes, Journal of Linguistics, 14*, 65–87.

Shackman, J. (1984). *The Right to Be Understood.* Cambridge: National Extension College.

Shlesinger, M. (1989). Extending the theory of translation to interpretation: Norms as a case in point. *Target, 1*, 111–115.

Shlesinger, M. (1991). Interpreter latitude vs. due process: Simultaneous and consecutive interpretation in multilingual trials. In S. Tirkkonen-Condit (Ed.) *Empirical Research in Translation and Intercultural Studies: Selected Papers of the TRANSIF Seminar, Savonlinna 1988* (pp. 147–155). Tübingen: Narr.

Toury, G. (1980). *In Search of a Theory of Translation.* Tel Aviv: The Porter Institute for Poetics and Semiotics.

Toury, G. (2004). The nature and role of norms in translation. In L. Venuti (Ed.) *The Translation Studies Reader* (pp. 205–218). New York/ London: Routledge.

Toury, G. (1999). A handful of paragraphs on 'translation' and 'norms'. In C. Schäffner (Ed.) *Translation and Norms* (pp. 9–31). Clevedon/ Philadelphia: Multilingual Matters.

Turner, G. H. (2007). More than token gestures: Exploring the boundaries of 'community interpreting'. Paper presented at *Critical Link 5. Quality in Interpreting: A Shared Responsibility*, Parramatta, Sydney, April 11–15.

Viezzi, M. (1996). *Aspetti della Qualità in Interpretazione.* Trieste: Sert.

Wadensjö, C. (1997). Recycled information as a questioning strategy: Pitfalls in interpreter-mediated talk. In S. Carr, R. Roberts, A. Dufour and D. Steyn (Eds.) *The Critical Link: Interpreters in the Community* (pp. 35–52). Amsterdam/Philadelphia: Benjamins.

Wadensjö, C. (1998). *Interpreting as Interaction.* London/New York: Longman.

CHAPTER 13

What can interpreters learn from discourse studies?

Helen Tebble
Monash University, Melbourne, Australia

The literature on discourse studies is vast yet the field of community interpreting has been fairly slow in making good use of it. This chapter briefly outlines three approaches to discourse analysis and emphasizes the sociolinguistic importance of the speech event. Implications of some of the findings from discourse studies of medical interpreting using the social semiotic approach (systemic functional linguistics) are discussed. They are: the generic structure of the interpreted medical consultation; interpreting everything that is said including organisational discourse markers and feedback to the patient; understanding the physician's checking strategies; and the role of cohesion in the interpreted exchange. All are relevant for high quality curriculum design and teaching of community interpreting courses; and high quality professional practice.

1. Introduction

Discourse studies are the application of discourse analytical approaches and methods to texts, be they written or spoken. Spoken texts include transcriptions of dialogue interpreting events. For this paper I will briefly overview some major topics and approaches to discourse analysis, discuss just one of each, indicating their relevance to the quality of dialogue interpreting; and then highlight some findings from our discourse studies of medical interpreting that can have a bearing on the quality of the work of a medical interpreter. The theme of this volume focuses on the quality of the interpreter's work. So we are concerned with polishing the performances of competent professional interpreters and providing theoretical justification and meaningful practice for educational courses be they for pre-service or professional development.

The use of the word 'interpreter' in this chapter will refer to professional community interpreters who interpret in consultations, interviews and small group meetings for other professionals and their clients who do not speak a language that is common to them both. The professionals use the dominant or national language of the society and the clients speak in the language of their ethnic community within the larger society or nation.[1] The interpreter is highly competent in using both languages. See Hale (2007) for further discussions on community interpreting.

2.   A brief overview of discourse analysis

Discourse analysis in its numerous forms has prevailed as the dominant area of research in linguistics for about the last thirty years and it is also dominant in other disciplines of the humanities and social sciences. When linguists study discourse they not only use concepts from linguistics, they also draw upon discourse analytic concepts from other disciplines such as sociology – especially ethno-methodology – as well as aspects of philosophy, communication studies, anthropology and social psychology. In linguistics the study of discourse brings together all the levels of language from the smallest to the largest. Such a study incorporates the letters or characters (graphemes); or sounds (phonemes) from the level of phonology, that make up the morphemes, the roots and affixes of words (the level of morphology); to the structure of sentences (the level of syntax); to the meaning of words and sentences at the level of semantics; to discourse which brings all these levels of language into use for communication (see Figure 1). Every interpreted event occurs in a situational context and within a culture. To accomplish competent interpreting each level of language is brought into play in two languages from two cultures within one situational context.

Written texts by their very nature usually comprise all the levels of language listed in Figure 1, and are usually discourses which can be subject to analysis, especially by translators. With the advent of modes of transcription of spoken language, other than the International Phonetic Alphabet, introduced by ethno-methodologists (e.g. Sacks, Schegloff and Jefferson 1978), texts of spoken discourse have become accessible to scholars other than phoneticians. This means that the spoken discourse of interpreted events (dialogues and those of small groups) can be analysed, understood and used to improve the quality of interpreters' performances in both pre-service and in-service education. Skills in discourse analysis of spoken language are no longer the province just of scholars; they need to be part of the repertoire of the professional interpreter.

---

1.   Emphasis in this chapter is given to the discourse of spoken language as distinct from the discourse of signed language.

DISCOURSE
↑
SEMANTICS
↑
SYNTAX
↑
MORPHOLOGY
↑
PHONOLOGY / GRAPHOLOGY

Figure 1. Linguistic levels of language

A discourse analyst, a student of interpreting, or a professional interpreter undertaking a professional development course could analyse a transcription of a video-recorded or audio-recorded spoken discourse that constitutes an interpreted consultation for one or more topics in discourse analysis and also take different approaches to the study of such a sample of spoken discourse.

There are different views on what discourse analysis is.[2] For the purposes of this chapter I would suggest that discourse analysis includes these topics: language in communication; pragmatics including speech act theory; discourse structures – genres; textual cohesion and coherence; message design; style; narrative; and rhetoric. Some major approaches to the analysis of spoken discourse include: conversation analysis, interactional sociolinguistics; and the social semiotic approach. One topic within the broader topic of language in communication that is vital for interpreting is understanding the nature of the actual speech event in which the interpreter performs his or her work. Interpreter trainees initially tend to want to focus just on the act of switching languages and they fail to appreciate the context, content and purpose of what they are doing. This could well be the case also of *ad hoc* or untrained volunteer interpreters.

2.1   Language in communication – scenarios for the interpreted speech event

The study of language in communication shows that the text of a speech event arises out of the situation of the discourse. Hymes' (1972) "SPEAKING" model, which is an extension and elaboration of Jakobson's (1960) model of communicative

---

2. Three useful introductory textbooks on topics and approaches to the study of discourse are Paltridge (2006), Renkema (2004) and Schiffrin (1994); and Roy (2000) usefully links discourse analysis with interpreting.

functions, draws upon the ethnography of communication and gives an anthropological slant. In summary the components of Hymes' model are:

- Setting, the time and place of the speech event
- Scene, the psychological aspect
- Participants
- Purpose
- Content
- Tone or key or pitch of speaking
- Channel of communication
- Genre

This early work from the ethnography of speaking and of communication has identified the components of the speech event. It can be used to prepare role-play scenarios for community interpreting practice and examination for pre-service[3] and in-service education. Each written scenario would specify the domain of interpreting (medical, legal, welfare, etc.); the physical setting would specify the time and place of the interpreted event; the participants with roles and fictitious names would be listed; an outline of the purpose and content of the speech event would constitute most of the text; and the scene which would describe the psychological state of one or more participants would include the tone or attitude of the speaker(s). Props that extend the channel of communication beyond the spoken word in face to face communication can include telephones, photographs, maps, x-rays, forms, letters, brochures, policy documents, etc. The genre for which the scenarios are prepared is the interpreted professional consultation or interview. Small glossaries can be provided so too can other supplementary material such as attachments with content notes and websites for additional information for actors and interpreters who could role play the scenarios. The interpreter or student of interpreting would be expected to know the subject matter (content) from a specific domain for a specific speech event.

Scenarios are not play scripts which are the texts of drama, film or literary studies. Although a few interpreted speech events or part of them are routine, for example, the delivery of a police caution when the language does not vary, in general each speech event is different. The participants are likely to be different and so will be their attitudes to each other, to the subject matter and to the event. So usually things will not be said in exactly the same way in any speech event of the same type. Play scripts are highly crafted and catch the essence of an event or of a relationship. They do not reflect the way people typically use spoken language

---

3.   Both students and staff in the course for the Master of Interpreting and Translation Studies at Monash University prepare their role play scenarios using an adaptation of Hymes' model.

with hesitations, false starts, inappropriate word choice; ungrammatical and in-complete utterances; rephrasing; auditor back channel responses; conversational repairs; and overlapping talk. When these features of spoken language occur in play scripts they are intentionally included by the playwright to serve a particular effect. They are however the very features of spoken language which interpreters need to identify and know how to interpret since it is not their responsibility to "clean up" the language of the people for whom they interpret. Quality pre-ser-vice and in-service interpreter education presupposes high competence in at least two languages before enrolment so that play scripts, which can be better used for teaching language students, are not the norm for teaching and assessment in interpreter education but well-informed scenarios are. So by understanding the nature of the interpreted speech event interpreters have a framework of the social context of their work. Such understanding can potentially result in a higher qual-ity of interpreting than if one concentrates only on trying to find equivalences in the other language. The language use of the speakers arises out of the speech situ-ation; so too must the interpreter's.

2.2   Approaches to spoken discourse analysis

Three dominant theoretical approaches to the study of spoken discourse includ-ing methods of analysis are conversation analysis, interactional sociolinguistics and the social-semiotic approach. These three approaches are mentioned because of their use by linguists in the analysis of spoken discourse and are relevant to the study of the discourse of interpreting.

Conversation analysis is used by ethno-methodologists (e.g., Boden and Zimmerman, 1991) working in sociology to analyse spoken discourse. Sacks, Schegloff and Jefferson (1978) introduced a new method of transcribing speech different from phonetics and is especially useful for understanding long stretches of talk. The concepts such as turn taking; adjacency pairs and the obligatory na-ture of the listener, for example, having to answer a question; overlapping; the way speakers correct themselves and others in conversation; opening, prolonging and closing conversations; inserted sequences; and discourse markers have been bor-rowed from conversation analysis as analytical tools by linguists. As such their use in the analysis of transcribed interpreted discourse can be of insight to both the practising professional interpreter and the trainee interpreter. The application of these concepts can truly illuminate our understanding of what we take for granted as everyday talk at work (e.g., Drew and Heritage, 1992), be it in one language or in the interpreted speech event.

Interactional sociolinguistics is another approach to the analysis of spoken discourse (see Roy, 2000) and is influenced by the work in sociolinguistics of Gumperz (1982). It gives insights especially into cultural inferences that speakers make as they engage in conversation. Interactional sociolinguistics is highly relevant to understanding intercultural communication as it occurs or breaks down when a person tries to communicate without knowing the cultural assumptions entailed in the other speaker's use of language. The contextualisation cues uttered by one speaker whose dialect is different from another speaker may be ignored or misunderstood even though both speakers claim to speak the same language. When being offered assignments to interpret for speakers of different or non-standard dialects and for speakers of low varieties (for example in some diglossic situations), interpreters need to be ethical about accepting such assignments because they need to be both linguistically and culturally competent in the dialect or variety of the speaker of the community language to be able to provide quality interpreting.

The social-semiotic approach prevails in the linguistic theory of systemic functional linguistics in the work of its founders Halliday (e.g., 1976, 1985, 1994) and Hasan (e.g., 1976, 1977, 1985) and their many students and colleagues. Drawing upon early work on the analysis of functions of language they emphasise the three fundamental variables of all social contexts: the Field, Tenor and Mode.

Each discourse arises out of its social context and has its particular configuration according to these features of Field, Tenor and Mode as shown in Figure 2. They determine the genre of that discourse. Halliday and Hasan's theory of systemic functional linguistics demonstrates how these three variables of communication in context are realised through the corresponding ideational, interpersonal and textual metafunctions of language.

The ideational metafunction links the language of the field, the content or subject matter. The interpersonal metafunction reveals the language of the tenor of the participants: their roles, status, relationships, the power relations, their informal or formal social distance; their attitudes and affectual states. The textual metafunction links the mode of communication to the use of languages, showing, for example, threads of meaning in the cohesion of the languages; as well as the status of the languages and the participants' expectations of what will be done with the languages; the rhetorical style of the speakers; and the use of the various channels of communication including non-verbal communication. Some of these features overlap with the components of Hymes' model but the theory of systemic functional linguistics addresses the social semiotic, that is, the social meanings conveyed in the grammar, vocabulary and patterns of discourse of a language as it is used by speakers in a given context. Although this theory of linguistics seems daunting when first encountered because of its jargon, it has proved to be

FIELD   What is happening
         The social activity
TENOR   Participants' roles
                status
                relationships
                power relations
                social distance
                affect, attitude
MODE   Part languages play in the speech event
                What participants expect the languages to do
                Status of languages
                Rhetorical mode – exciting, discursive
                Channel – spoken, written, signed

Figure 2. Specifications for contextual configuration (after Halliday and Hasan 1985)

very relevant for undertaking useful analyses of interpreted discourse. Such an
assessment was made for example in 1994 by the panel of scholars for Linguistics,
Discourse Analysis and Interpretation at the international conference on research
in interpreting held in Turku, Finland (Taylor Torsello, 1997, pp. 167–186). Ten
years later, in answer to the question: "Which theory or approach offers a good
general framework for analysing all the different aspects of discourse?" Renkema
answers: "The best candidate seems to be the so-called socio-semiotic approach"
(Renkema, 2004, p. 46).

Depending on one's purposes any of these topics and approaches mentioned
here can be used to analyse different aspects of the way speakers use language
to communicate and so may shed light on the performance of the interpreter at
work. Our research into medical interpreting e.g., Cocker (1999), Hirsh (2001),
Tebble (1992b, 1996a, 1998a, 1998b, 1999, 2003, 2008) and Willis (2001) has been
influenced by most of these topics and approaches, but especially by systemic
functional linguistics. So apart from reading much of the fascinating literature on
discourse analysis what can interpreters learn from discourse studies? The findings from our studies of the discourse of medical interpreting have provided the
content and methodology for a 60-hour university level course on dialogue interpreting (Tebble, 1996b). It can be a challenge for those who believe all one has to
do is practise switching languages. For those who are open to what research into
the discourse of the daily performance of qualified and NAATI accredited professional interpreters shows, it offers a new paradigm for interpreter education. For
those new to discourse studies this chapter will give an overview of just a few of
these findings.

3.   Know where you are going

If you understand the genre of the speech event for which you are interpreting then you have in mind a schema, a frame or a structure for understanding where the consultation or interview is going. You will have a good idea of the order in which things will be said and as a consequence you can pace yourself in the way you expend your energy. One of the major findings from our research into interpreted medical consultations is the description of the generic structure which is shown in Figure 3. Each stage occurs at a certain place during the speech event and is distinctly identifiable even if they sometimes occur inside one another as for example, the stages of Greetings and Introductions can. Stages in brackets are optional.

The interpreted medical consultation commences with the physician and interpreter *greeting* each other and *introducing* themselves; and the interpreter introducing the patient to the physician. The physician may however introduce the patient to the interpreter. The *contract* if stated is usually declared by the interpreter to both the physician and patient, establishing the ethical constraints under which the interpreter will work, such as interpreting everything that is said and assuring all parties that full confidentiality will be maintained. The interpreter may also advise on seating and other arrangements to ensure that everyone can see each other. The purpose of the consultation is then declared in the next stage, *stating the problem*, or elicited if it is not altogether clear why the patient is consulting the physician. *Ascertaining the facts* is typically a lengthy stage of the consultation as it comprises taking the medical history and the physical examination. If the physician decides to articulate his or her *diagnosis* while obtaining the facts about the patient's health then this stage is included. It is treated as optional since it does not frequently occur. The *exposition* or *resolution*, the stage when the physician declares his/her findings and proposed course of action for the patient, is the culmination of the medical consultation. It is the *purpose* of the speech event. It is at this stage that the physician and interpreter need to be very clear for the patient to understand what the physician has found out about the patient's health and what needs to be done. The subsequent stage of *clarifying any residual matters* can be initiated by the physician asking the patient: Is there anything else you want to ask me or check with me? The patient may also want to clarify uncertainties. The *conclusion* is typically brief and draws the consultation to a close and they *farewell* each other. The model of the generic structure of the interpreted consultation allows for the stage of *clarifying residual matters* to occur during the stages of *conclusion* and *farewell*, when the patient may have a last minute question.

Greetings
Introductions
(Contract)
Stating/Eliciting the Problem
Ascertaining the Facts
(Diagnosing the Facts)
Stating the Resolution/Exposition
(Decision by Patient)
Clarifying any Residual Matters
Conclusion
Farewells

Figure 3. Generic structure of interpreted medical consultations (after Tebble 1999: 185)

These stages of the discourse of an interpreted medical consultation are not just notional stages. They were empirically established from numerous transcriptions of professionally interpreted medical consultations. Each consultation had three cameras, one for the physician, one for the interpreter and one for the patient. The transcriptions were in English and one of the following community languages in Australia: Greek, Italian, Spanish, Serbian, Cantonese, Mandarin, Khmer and Vietnamese. Adapting the method of Sacks, Schegloff and Jefferson (1978) these transcriptions were written at the level of the spoken equivalent of the clause, that is, the tone group (Halliday, 1994). The transcriptions were translated, back translated and usually grammatically glossed. They were then subjected to the analysis of spoken discourse in the manner of Hasan (1977), Sinclair and Coulthard (1975), and Tebble (e.g. 1992a). This meant analysing each transcript (typically 100 pages of text for each consultation) for all of the various discourse structures of the interpreted consultation. This involved combining two methods from within systemic functional linguistics: that of Halliday and Hasan (1985) and Hasan (1977), who took a top down approach and just identified the genre elements in a text; and the microanalytical or bottom up approach of Sinclair and Coulthard (1975), identifying the speech act in each clause or tone group, and the structural levels above them. As shown in Figure 4 each item is on a ranked scale from the smallest unit, the speech act, to the largest discourse unit, the genre itself. The speech act occurs within a conversational move of which there are typically two that occur within a conversational exchange. One or more exchanges comprise a transaction. A transaction comprises one or typically a sequence of exchanges of a particular type; and the genre element is made up of one or more transactions on one topic. Using this method of analysis the structure of each discourse can be identified and compared, revealing patterns of generic structure. Knowing the genre that one is interpreting means knowing the stages of the speech event.

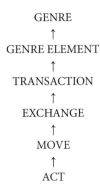

GENRE

↑

GENRE ELEMENT

↑

TRANSACTION

↑

EXCHANGE

↑

MOVE

↑

ACT

Figure 4. Hierarchy of discourse structures constituting the professional consultation or interview (Tebble, 1999, p. 184)

If you are familiar with your road map (the genre of the interpreted event) you know where you are going.

4.   Interpreting the signposts

Apart from knowing where you are going as the interpreted consultation moves through the large structural elements, the generic stages, everybody needs to know where they are at any one time. Having a schema in mind is fine for the physician and interpreter. It is like knowing the route of a journey you will take. But actually negotiating the way can require the use of signposts. The physician often uses what could be construed as signposts in the form of framing and focusing moves (Sinclair & Coulthard, 1975).

Framing moves typically comprise one or two words said with a silent beat following, for example: *OK, right, well now, good, now.* If the interpreter does not interpret these moves then the patient is at a disadvantage and the interpreter has not met the ethic of interpreting all that is said (AUSIT Code of Practice 5a i). In the following example most interpreters would interpret

D: rIght   *Framing move*
     let's get started   *Focusing move*

                                                              [E: BM, DM i]

the focusing move because it has obvious content. Both moves said by the physician are using, in Jakobson's (1960) terms, the metalingual function, or in Hymes' (1964) terms, the metalinguistic function. That is, the physician used language about language to organise, to manage the consultation; to signal that he will move to the next topic or stage. An interpreter who did not interpret what we call the physician's discourse marker "rIght" to signal the next stage of the consultation, may argue that the patient being a resident in Australia has some familiarity with English and so would recognise the word and its meaning. It is possible but not necessarily so. Or some may try to argue that there is no equivalent expression to signal that the consultation is at the next stage. The patient is disadvantaged if the framing move is not interpreted.

Framing moves do not always occur but they can be used to frame a transaction sometimes at the beginning, sometimes at the end and other times at both the start and end of a transaction. Although discourse markers (Schiffrin, 1988) can be as short as single word utterances and used with a particular rhythm and pitch they should not be underestimated by the interpreter. They can be signposts to new topics or even new stages in the consultation and make a major contribution to the coherence of the discourse. Interpreting all that is said entails interpreting not only the content but also the metalinguistic or organisational language of the consultation.

5.   Feedback

As part of the interaction between patient and physician the speakers give feedback to each other. This can occur as spoken words in a speaker's turn at talk; in auditor back channel responses (Duncan, 1974), usually para-linguistically during the other speaker's turn at talk, for example when the physician utters "*mm*" or "*mhm*" or "*yes*" during the interpreter's relaying of what the patient has just said. The interpreter who follows the ethic of interpreting all that is said does attempt to interpret the physician's feedback to the patient. The most difficult feedback to interpret would be the physician's auditor back channel feedback made while the interpreter is in the process of relaying what the patient has just said; or made by the patient while the interpreter is in the process of relaying what the physician has just said. Such interpreting can be achieved with varying degrees of success. The feedback that can and should be interpreted is that given during a turn at talk when only one person is speaking. Even if the physician's feedback is one word and appears to be routine it still needs to be interpreted. Figure 5 shows the context of a single word of feedback. The physician is using the stethoscope to listen to the patient's heart and lungs during the physical examination.

The physician's brief feedback of "good" must be interpreted. The physician's speech act expressed as "good" with low fall intonation in the follow up move is acknowledgement. The physician told the patient to take a deep breath and the patient complied. This compliance enabled the physician to obtain the information

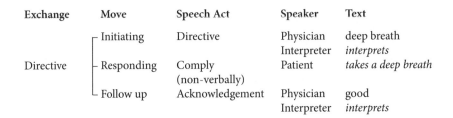

Exchange	Move	Speech Act	Speaker	Text
	Initiating	Directive	Physician	deep breath
			Interpreter	*interprets*
Directive	Responding	Comply (non-verbally)	Patient	*takes a deep breath*
	Follow up	Acknowledgement	Physician	good
			Interpreter	*interprets*

Figure 5. The place of 'good' in a directive exchange

he needed while using the stethoscope. So in the next turn at talk, the follow up move, the physician gives the patient some positive feedback in the form of the acknowledgement "good." The physician acknowledges that with the co-operation of the patient he has carried out this micro-procedure that constitutes part of the physical examination and it was successful. To paraphrase the physician: "we accomplished that brief task well." Interpreting the feedback can mean relaying expressions of rapport (Hirsh, 2001; Tebble, 1996a; and Willis, 2001). These are very important in the establishment and maintenance of trust that patients have in the physician and whether they comply with the medical advice given during the exposition stage of the consultation. Apart from interpreting positive feedback during routine use of the stethoscope, it is very important to interpret feedback during neurological examinations which may require the physician for example to conduct a set of rapid tests to check for different types of coordination, sensory and reflex responses. The patient needs as much positive feedback as possible. An example of missing out on interpreting the follow up moves containing positive feedback is illustrated in the excerpt [Gk7:16] in section 6 below. The first follow up move (Fu1 "right") containing feedback is not easy to interpret as it is uttered in the middle of the interpreter's turn at talk. However the second follow up move (Fu 2 "good") is the same as in Figure 5 and needs to be interpreted. When the physician utters this single word "good" in the follow up move it does have communicative value and needs to be interpreted.

6.   Scale of certainty

During the generic stage of ascertaining the facts, that is, when the medical history is being taken and the physical examination is being conducted, the physician elicits information and checks his or her understanding of what has been said. Two significant strategies used in professional consultations and interviews to check information are the *formulation* and the *observation*. These are concepts we have adopted from conversation analysis (Tebble, 1993). Each is the first part of the adjacency pair: formulation and decision; and observation and decision.

The formulation in English is a proposition that expresses a summary or an inference as a deduction of prior talk in the consultation. It begins with "so" and occurs in the initiating move of an exchange. The formulation is used to check understanding. It can be used with falling intonation to indicate that the speaker is pretty sure of the accuracy of what he or she is saying but not one hundred percent certain. When rising tone 2 is used with the formulation as in a question the speaker is expressing less certainty about what he or she is saying. When the physician is in even more doubt the formulation can be followed for example by a yes/no question or even a set of options with rising tone 2, hence the scale of certainty (e.g., Cocker, 1999).

In the following responding move the *decision* is used by the listener who confirms or disconfirms the content of the formulation. Sometimes the formulation is neither confirmed nor disconfirmed because it contains irrelevant and misunderstood information. In the following excerpt from a nephrology consultation with a Greek speaking patient the physician was ascertaining facts about the patient's recent treatment in hospital and was confirming by his use of the formulation that the removal of fluid from the patient's abdomen gave her some relief.

IN	Form	D:	so that's a bit better obviously since the fluid came out
		I:	τώρα αυτό είναι καλύτερα απ" τη στιγμή που έχουν
		LT:	*now this it is better from the moment that they*
		I:	αφαιρέσει το υγρό
		LT:	*have removed the water*
R	Dec	P:	ναι ναι τώρα δυο βραδυές κοιμήθηκα καλΑ
		TL:	*yes yes now two nights I slept well*
		I:	yes over the last two nights
Fu 1.	Ack	D:	right
	Dec	I:	I was able to sleep well
Fu 2.	Ack 2	D:	good ←

[Gk 7: 16]

The decision in the patient's responding move confirmed three times what the physician had deduced. It began with the emphatic repetition of the Greek word for 'yes', ναι, reinforcing the confirmation which was then justified with an elaboration: that she did get relief (was more than "a bit better") even to the extent of sleeping well for the last two nights. Prior to this procedure the patient had such discomfort that she needed sleeping tablets. All of this detailed confirmation needs to be relayed since the physician up to the point of making the formulation had only understood that the patient's condition was probably "a bit better".

The observation is one or a series of statements whose propositions are about the context of situation. It may or may not be evaluative. It is uttered with degrees of certainty to be checked by the patient. In the following excerpt the consultant physician states that she has noticed or observed in the patient's medical record what seems to be a change in the patient's medication.

IN Obs D: I see that Dr B has stopped those blood thinning tablets you were taking last year

     I: *relays in patient's language*

R Dec P: *responds in own language*

     I: no, I haven't stopped taking those tablets I've changed brands

                           [E/S: Obs.i]

In this exchange the patient's decision in the responding move disconfirms the physician's observation from the patient's record. The disconfirming decision has two negatives, "no" and "n't" and an extension (Eggins and Slade 1997:197) which contradicts the physician's observation by providing contrastive information. The patient is still taking the prescribed tablets but has switched to another brand of the same type of tablet. Being corrected during this stage of ascertaining the facts in the interpreted medical consultation is important for the physician who must obtain accurate information.

We have created a scale of certainty of expressions that physicians use to reveal their level of certainty. At one end of the scale are the formulation and observation with falling tone indicating a strong certainty which just needs a quick confirmation. At the other end of the scale is a yes/no question containing a list of items each expressed with question intonation and ending in "or" to allow for a possible additional option. For example:

D: did you apply dettol2 or a cream2 or just wash it2 or ...

                             [E: SC 20]

To understand the function of the observation, formulation and decision and how they occur in an eliciting exchange as well as where they occur can help a trainee interpreter anticipate them and rehearse them to gain a certain level of automatic recognition and ability to process them quickly when interpreting them.

7.   Cohesion in interpreted exchanges

The major categories of cohesion in English following Halliday and Hasan (1976) are: lexical, conjunction, reference, substitution and ellipsis. We have analysed the cohesion across interpreted exchanges to see how information was conveyed between physician and patient via the interpreter. Precise information can be diminished when more general words are selected. Pronouns can cause ambiguity if the nouns to which they refer are not explicit. Expressions can be substituted for others with varying degrees of accuracy and when ellipsis is used by one speaker a full reconstruction may help the meaning not to be lost.

Speaker	Move	Speech Act	Clause	Utterance
D	IN	Y/N Q	i	so is Doctor P
			ii	who first detected your BLOOD pressure
		Abort	iii	and .hhh you you had er
			iv	the problem though was the irregular heart beating +
		Y/N Q	v	is that correct[2]
I				i doctor P je ustvari pronasao da imate problem sa krvnim pritiskom a vi ste-er primetili da je da nije regularno srcani otkucaj
P	R	Ans		*Patient replies in Serbian*
I		Ans	i	yes
		Elaboration	iia, iib, iic	that's, that's how it happened
			iii	doctor P discovered that
			iv	and I realised
			v	that my er + heart beat was irregular
D	Fu	Ack		mhm

[After Cocker 1999: 58]

This excerpt from the stage *ascertaining the facts* in an interpreted medical consultation for a Serbian-speaking patient shows cohesion between the physician's initiating move and the interpreted response of the patient. The physician asks two yes/no questions. The cohesion in English takes the forms of ellipsis, lexical and reference cohesion. Lexical repetition occurs for the name of the doctor and the "irregular heart beat". Further lexical cohesion occurs with the interpreter's synonym "discovered" for the physician's use of "detected". Reference cohesion occurs with the use of the pronouns in (iia, iib, iic and iii) in the elaborated answer in the interpreted responding move. The demonstrative pronoun "that" is repeated and refers to all that the physician said in the initiating move. The use of the subject pronoun, "it" refers to the detection mentioned in clause (ii) of the physician's first yes/no question. The important cohesion is in the use of ellipsis in the answer "yes" in clause (i) of the responding move to the yes/no question, "is that correct",[2] in clause (v) of the physician's initiating move. Understanding how cohesion occurs in both languages and having different strategies for maintaining cohesive ties is vital for an interpreter who has to process so much information in both languages very quickly.

8.   Conclusion

Interpreters are people whose work is almost exclusively accomplished through talk and this means much more than just switching languages. Gone are the days when an interpreter just polished their competence in both languages, practised a few bilingual skills for memory and code switching and just role-played without any sound theoretical framework being used as feedback. A professional must be able to account for his or her work. Therefore a professional interpreter can account for his or her interpreted discourse. This means he or she will make use of discourse studies that show the intricacies of the structures that make up the texts of talk; the genres for different speech events; the complexities of turn taking; the role of metalanguage in professional communication; the necessity for cohesive interpreting; the importance of feedback; the involved checking strategies professionals use; and much more. Discourse studies are not exclusive to translation and other disciplines. They are fundamental to the knowledge and performance of the dialogue interpreter. Pre- and in-service education (rather than training) of interpreters can make excellent use of video-recordings, transcriptions and the application of relevant methods and approaches to discourse analysis to help students and practising interpreters understand how to improve and account for their interpreted discourse and so perform high quality interpreting.

Acknowledgements

1.   I acknowledge with sincere gratitude the support and encouragement for my work from Sandra Hale and members of the Critical Link 5 Organising Committee.
2.   I am forever grateful to all the interpreters, translators; and the physicians, nurses and patients from the Monash Medical Centre, Southern Health, who gave of their time as well as expertise and medical history respectively for the purposes of enabling me and my research students to study the discourse of medical interpreting. Special thanks are for Professor Barry McGrath and Sandra Nestoridis from Southern Health; and Adolfo Gentile, former Director of Language Australia's Centre for Research and Development in Interpreting

and Translating, Deakin University. The research was funded by grants from Deakin University, Language Australia, the Australian Research Council, and the Australian Commonwealth Government.

Abbreviations

AUSIT, Australian Institute of Interpreters and Translators NAATI, National Accreditation Authority for Translators and Interpreters

Ack	Acknowledgement	I	Interpreter
Ans	Answer	IN	Initiating move
Conf	Confirming move	LT	Literal Translation
D	Doctor/Physician	Obs	Observation
Dec	Decision	P	Patient
Form	Formulation	R	Responding move
Fu	Follow up move	Y/N Q	Yes/No question

Transcription conventions

Capital letters in excerpts represent stressed syllables.
+   A short untimed pause
2   Indicates rising tone as in questions.
.hhh Audible intake of breath.

References

AUSIT. (2000). AUSIT Code of Ethics. In *Ethics of Interpreting and Translation – A guide to professional conduct in Australia* compiled by NAATI, pp. 9–23. Canberra: NAATI.

Boden, D. & Zimmerman, D. H. (Eds). (1991). *Talk and Social Structure. Studies in ethno-methodology and conversation analysis.* Berkeley and Los Angeles: University of California Press.

Cocker, R. (1999). *Physicians' Checking Strategies – An analysis of the formulations and observations used by physicians in interpreted specialist medical consultations.* Unpublished BA(Hons) Thesis, Deakin University.

Drew, P. & Heritage, J. (Eds) (1992). *Talk at Work.* Cambridge: Cambridge University Press.

Duncan, S. (1974). On the structure of speaker-auditor interaction during speaking turns. *Language in Society, 2,* 161–180.

Eggins, S. & Slade, D. (1997). *Analysing Casual Conversation.* London: Cassell.

Gumperz, J. (1982). *Discourse Strategies.* Cambridge: Cambridge University Press.

Hale, S. (2007). *Community Interpreting*. Basingstoke: Palgrave Macmillan.

Halliday, M. A. K. (1985). *Spoken and Written Language*. Geelong, VIC.: Deakin University.

Halliday, M. A. K.(1994). *An Introduction to Functional Grammar*. London: Edward Arnold.

Halliday, M. A. K. & Hasan, R. (1976). *Cohesion in English*. London: Longman.

Halliday, M. A. K. and Hasan, R. (1985). *Language, Context and Text: Aspects of language in a social-semiotic perspective*. Geelong, VIC.: Deakin University.

Hasan, R. (1977). Text in the systemic functional model. In W. U. Dressler (ed.) *Current Trends in Textlinguistics* (pp. 228–246). Berlin: de Gruyter.

Hirsh, D. (2001). *Interpersonal Features of Talk in Interpreted Medical Consultations*. Unpublished MA Thesis, Deakin University.

Hymes, D. (1964). Toward ethnographies of communication: The analysis of communicative events. In P. P. Giglioli (Ed.) (1972). *Language and Social Context,* (pp. 21–44). Harmondsworth: Penguin.

Hymes, D. (1972). Models of the interaction of language and social life. In J. Gumperz & D. Hymes (Eds.) *Directions in Sociolinguistics: The ethnography of communication* (pp. 35–71). New York: Holt, Rinehart and Winston.

Jakobson, R. (1960). Closing Statement: Linguistics and Poetics. In T. A. Sebeok (Ed.) (1966). *Style in Language* (pp. 353–357). Cambridge, MA: M.I.T. Press.

Paltridge, B. (2006). *Discourse Analysis - An Introduction*. London: Continuum.

Renkema, J. (2004). *Introduction to Discourse Studies*. Amsterdam/Philadelphia: John Benjamins.

Roy, C. (2000). *Interpreting as a Discourse Process*. New York: Oxford University Press.

Sacks, H., Schegloff, E. & Jefferson, G. (1978). A simplest systematics for the organization of turn taking in conversation. In J. Schenkein (Ed.) *Studies in the Organization of Conversational Interaction,* (pp. 7–55). New York: Academic Press.

Schiffrin, D. (1988.) *Discourse Markers*. Cambridge: Cambridge University Press.

Schiffrin, D. (1994). *Approaches to Discourse*. Cambridge, MA: Blackwell.

Sinclair, J. & Coulthard, R. M. (1975). *Towards an Analysis of Discourse: The English used by teachers and pupils*. London: Oxford University Press.

Taylor Torsello, C. (1997). Linguistics, discourse and interpretation. In Y. Gambier, D. Gile, & C. Taylor (Eds.) *Conference Interpreting: Current Trends in Research. Proceedings of the International Conference on Interpreting: What do we know and how? Turku, Finland, August 25–27, 1994* (pp. 167–186). Amsterdam/Philadelphia: John Benjamins.

Tebble, H. (1992a). The genre element in the systems analyst's interview. *Australian Review of Applied Linguistics, 15*(2),120–136.

Tebble, H. (1992b). Discourse model for dialogue interpreting. In AUSIT, (1993). *Proceedings of the First Practitioners' Seminar* (pp. 1–26). Canberra: NAATI.

Tebble, H. (1993). Formulations and observations in professional interviews: Systems analysis. In A. Crochetière, J. Boulanger & C. Ouellon (Eds.), *Proceedings of the XVth International Congress of Linguists* (pp. 265–268) Vol.3. Sainte Foy, Quebec: Les Presses de l'Université Laval.

Tebble, H. (1996a). Research into tenor in medical interpreting. In *Collected Papers from "Interpreting Research"*, Editorial Committee, Japan Association for Interpretation Studies (JAIS), 2004, 37–49. Tokyo: JAIS.

Tebble, H. (1996b). A discourse based approach to community interpreter education. In AUSIT (Ed.), *New Horizons, Proceedings of the XIVth World Congress of the Fédération Internatio-*

nale des Traducteurs (FIT) (pp. 385–394) Vol.1. Melbourne: Australian Institute of Interpreters and Translators.

Tebble, H. (1998a). *Medical Interpreting – Improving communication with your patients.* Geelong, VIC.: Deakin University and Language Australia (Book).

Tebble, H. (1998b). *Medical Interpreting – Improving communication with your patients.* Geelong, VIC.: Deakin University and Language Australia (Video).

Tebble, H. (1999). The tenor of consultant physicians: Implications for medical interpreting. *The Translator, 5*(2),179–200.

Tebble, H. (2003). Training doctors to work effectively with interpreters. In L. Brunette, G. Bastin, I. Hemlin & H. Clarke (Eds.) *The Critical Link 3 – Interpreters in the Community. Selected Papers from the 3rd International Conference on Interpreting in Legal, Health and Social Service Settings, Montreal, Canada, 22–26 May 2001* (pp. 81– 95). Amsterdam/ Philadelphia: John Benjamins.

Tebble, H. (2008). Using systemic functional linguistics to understand and practise dialogue interpreting. In C. Wu, C. Matthiessen & M. Herke (Eds.) *Voices Around the World, Proceedings of the 35th International Systemic Functional Conference (ISFC). Sydney, Australia, 21–26 July 2008* (pp. 149–154). Sydney: 35th ISFC Organizing Committee.

Willis, C. L. (2001). *Linguistic Features of Rapport – An investigation into consultant physicians' linguistic use of rapport.* Unpublished BA(Hons) Thesis, Deakin University.

CHAPTER 14

Achieving quality in health care interpreting
Insights from interpreters

Ilse Blignault, Maria Stephanou[1] and Cassandra Barrett[2]
School of Public Health & Community Medicine, University of New South
Wales / NSW Transcultural Aged Care Service / NSW Transcultural Aged
Care Service

The cultural and linguistic diversity of Australian society presents an ongoing
challenge to the health care system. The 30th anniversary of the New South
Wales Health Care Interpreter Service (HCIS) provided stimulus to reflect on
the interpreter's contribution to improved health care and better health outcomes, from the viewpoint of the interpreters themselves. This paper, based on
an examination of case studies prepared by eighteen staff at one HCIS centre
in metropolitan Sydney, highlights the importance of technical skills, a professional approach and experience in achieving quality in health care interpreting.
Dealing successfully with the scope and challenges of the interpreter role, and
being a valued member of the health care team, leads to job satisfaction which
also leads to increased quality.

1.   Introduction

Australia is one of the most culturally and linguistically diverse nations in the
world. In the 2006 Census it was possible to code up to 282 countries of birth, 364
languages and 115 religious groups. New South Wales (NSW), the most popu-
lous state, is the most culturally and linguistically diverse of all Australian states
and territories. At Census 2006, 31.0% of NSW residents stated they were born
overseas, and 26.0% reported speaking a language other than English at home.
The most common languages were Arabic 2.5%, Cantonese 2.0% Mandarin 1.5%,
Italian 1.3% and Greek 1.3% (Australian Bureau of Statistics 2006).

---

1. Formerly Manager of the South East and Central Sydney Area Health Care Interpreter
Service.

2. Formerly employed at South East and Central Sydney Area Health Care Interpreter Service.

The professional practice of interpreting as it is known in Australia today developed in the wake of the Second World War. Prior to that, immigration to Australia occurred under the "White Australia Policy" with the expected result of "assimilation". The arrival of large numbers of non-English speaking refugees and migrants from post-war Europe in the late 1940s and 1950s, led to a demand for interpreters by a range of institutions and social services. Subsequent flows of newcomers from South America, Asia, the Middle East and, more recently, Africa have continued to fuel this demand.

The adoption of a national policy of "multiculturalism" in 1973 was followed by a substantial increase in government expenditure on migrant welfare and assistance (Garrett and Lin, 1990). Figure 1 provides a timeline of key events in the development of multicultural health services in Australia and NSW.

In 1977, the Health Care Interpreter Service (HCIS) of NSW was set up, initially providing a mobile workforce of twenty-seven interpreters to serve seventeen Sydney hospitals. Today, the HCIS has a workforce of over 1,000 full and part-time interpreters and contract staff and provides professional interpreting services, generally free of charge, in more than seventy languages (including Auslan or Australian Sign Language) to people using public health services across NSW. Services are available twenty-four hours a day seven days a week, depending on urgency.[3] In rural and remote regions, HCIS interpreters are able to facilitate consultations using videoconferencing. The HCIS now operates from five centres, administered by five of the Area Health Services.

At the beginning there was little clarity as to what the role of a health care interpreter should be. In 1987, the (then) NSW Health Commission issued guidelines outlining the responsibilities of health service providers when interpreters are needed, together with the role and responsibilities of interpreters. Significantly, the guidelines placed responsibility for the provision of accessible and culturally appropriate health services on the institutions themselves. The guidelines were updated and reissued in 1994 and, again, in 2006: *Standard Procedures for Working with Health Care Interpreters.*

In the Standard Procedures interpreting is defined as "the transmission of messages between two spoken languages, between a signed language and a spoken language, or between two signed languages" (NSW Department of Health 2006, p. 19). The interpreter's role is to facilitate communication between parties who do not have a language in common. This requires more than language skills; health care interpreters must also have a thorough knowledge of the culture, world view,

---

3.   Interpreting services to general practitioners and medical specialist in private practice are generally provided through the Commonwealth Government funded and operated Translating and Interpreting Service (TIS).

Policy

Service development

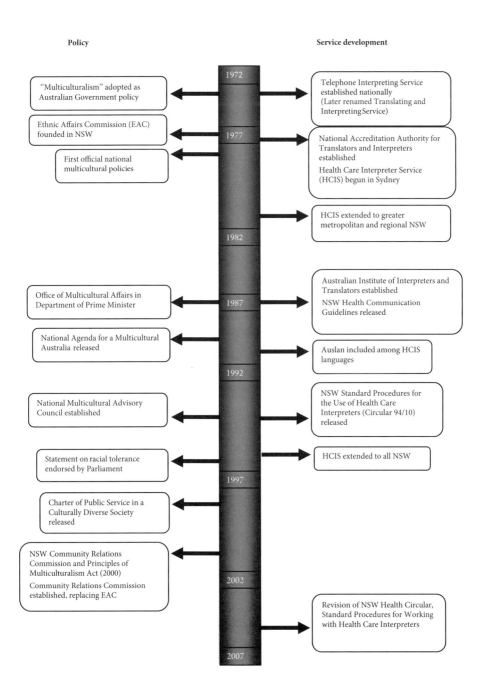

Figure 1. Timeline of key events relevant to health care interpreting in NSW

values and beliefs expressed in the linguistic structure, as well as an understanding of the conceptual frameworks within which the health professional and the patient operate. The listed benefits of using interpreters include: facilitation of accurate diagnosis and patient understanding of treatment, and health promotion and prevention programs; better management of chronic disease; improved adherence to medication; reduced hospitalisation rates; savings in unnecessary diagnostic tests and procedures and health personnel time; and prevention of misunderstandings which could result in litigation (NSW Department of Health, 2006).

The first international review of the impact of professional interpreters on the quality of health care, based on thirty-six articles published between 1975 and 2003, appeared in 2005 (Flores, 2005). This systematic review, while underscoring the need for further research, including cost-effectiveness studies, concluded that optimal patient-provider communication, patient satisfaction and outcomes, and fewest errors of clinical consequence occur when patients who are not proficient in the dominant language have access to trained medical interpreters or bilingual health providers. More recent studies support those conclusions (Brough, 2006; Fernandez et al., 2004; Mehler, Lundgren and Pines, 2004; Morales, Elliot and Weech-Maldonado, 2006; Ngo-Metzger et al., 2003; Wu et al., 2006).

Although the positive contribution of health care interpreters to the delivery of health services has been demonstrated, one issue that has not been explored is how such results are realised. What do interpreters see as the most important aspects of their work? Beyond language skills and knowledge of community norms and values and the health system, what is it that the interpreter brings to patient care? What does this mean for the patient, the provider and the interpreter himself/herself? How is quality achieved in health care interpreting? The work reported here was part of a larger qualitative study designed to explore the work of health care interpreting in a public health system from the interpreter's perspective.

2.   Method

2.1   Context

The research was led by the manager of the South East and Central Sydney Area HCIS (MS) and an academic from the University of New South Wales (IB). It followed a three-year program of research and development for all the interpreter services, funded by the Multicultural Health Policy Unit of NSW Health and the HCIS. Interpreters at the South East and Central Sydney Area HCIS were invited to contribute to a collection of case studies reflecting their experiences in the interpreter role, and drawing out the lessons for best practice.[4]

2.2   Participants

Eighteen HCIS personnel, seventeen interpreters and one administration officer, participated in the project. Some had been there at the very beginning of the HCIS, while others had joined more recently. All were employed on a full- or part-time basis with the service. Together they covered twelve language groups: Arabic, Cantonese, Croatian, Greek, Italian, Korean, Macedonian, Mandarin, Polish, Spanish, Thai and Vietnamese.

2.3   Procedure

At the first meeting, the project was explained and strategies for writing effective case studies for different purposes were presented. At subsequent meetings, the interpreters shared what they had written with others in the group and discussed the "take home message". Initially, no suggestions were made regarding content. It was left to participants to choose their own cases after discussing possibilities with a colleague. Later, the group decided it was important to reflect the breadth and diversity of interpreter experience: community health and rehabilitation as well as acute care; geriatric medicine as well as infant and child health; Auslan (the language of the deaf community in Australia) as well as ethnic community languages.

The final set of fifty narratives, including vignettes, cases and essays, covered a wide range of experiences and situations. Many were only a paragraph, while others extended over several pages. Thematic analysis (Gifford, 1998) was carried out by the two senior authors (MS and IB). All narratives were read carefully, sorted by issue and then clustered into four themes: professionalism, scope of the health care interpreter role, job satisfaction, and stress. The first three seemed particularly relevant to theme of this volume – *Quality in interpreting: A shared*

---

4. The state-wide program included workshops in quantitative and qualitative research methods, a review of published and unpublished studies and reports on health care interpreting, development of a research agenda, and a multi-site pilot study on the use of interpreters in hospital emergency departments that included interviews with health service providers and patients and their relatives, but not with interpreters. Unfortunately, attempts to obtain funding for the full study were unsuccessful.

responsibility. Narratives representative of these themes, which often overlapped, were subjected to additional scrutiny and key content and issues identified.

Several techniques were employed to increase the rigor of the research (Lincoln and Guba, 1985). Multiple data sources (authors and narratives) enabled triangulation, while project meetings provided an opportunity for "member checking" or verification with the larger group. Most of the cases required editing for presentation. This was done by CB who tried to retain the language and style of each contributor. The edited version was then returned to the author for confirmation.

3.   Results

Key findings for the three quality-related themes – professionalism, scope of the health care interpreter role and job satisfaction – are presented, in turn, below. Five cases, described in the four boxes, were selected to illustrate interpreter practice. Each case is presented in the interpreter's own words. Further information and commentary are provided in the main text.

3.1   Professionalism

Elements of professionalism were evident in almost all the cases. A fundamental underlying issue, made overt in cases that compared HCIS interpreters with family interpreters, was the requirement for formal qualification or accreditation of health care interpreters by the National Accreditation Authority for Interpreters and Translators. In-service training and continuing professional development ensure that interpreters have up-to-date knowledge of medical terminology and health system operations, thus adding to the quality of the service provided.

Resolution of complex ethical issues was a feature of several of the case studies, and the issues were readily taken up in the group discussions. Interpreters from a wide range of backgrounds join the HCIS. All bring their own personal and cultural values and, possibly, prejudices. Professional ethics are emphasised during formal training, and informally throughout their employment.

The case presented in Box 1 (*Grateful daughter*) demonstrates the value placed by a doctor, his patient and the patient's relative on a professional interpreting performance. The difference that the interpreter's assistance made to the quality of their own experience was openly conveyed to the interpreter. Firstly, the doctor recognised that a more accurate diagnosis and better understanding of the patient's condition through the interpreter leads to a more appropriate treatment plan. Secondly, the bilingual daughter of the patient acknowledged the need for more accurate and objective interpreting than she could provide, including interpreting of awkward expressions. Without the added pressure to interpret, the daughter was able to seek answers to her own questions about her mother's health. Finally, the patient, fully aware of the communication process through the interpreter, reclaimed the focus of attention in the consultation and gained insight into her daughter's concerns for her health. Increased awareness and an enhanced sense of responsibility resulted in improved patient compliance with health service provider instructions, leading to expectations of better care and outcomes.

Box 1. Grateful daughter *by Agnes Lauder*

An elderly woman had been diagnosed with stomach cancer and needed detailed investigation followed by a treatment plan. She was part of a close family and the daughter always made time to take her to these appointments, not only to assist with the transport but also to help communicate with the health professionals as her mother's English was not adequate in these circumstances. An appointment for a diagnostic scan was made and in this instance an interpreter was booked as the daughter would not be able to attend.

On arrival the interpreter was greeted by both the patient and the daughter, who at the last minute was able to be present. The daughter informed the interpreter that her services would not be needed after all. To this the interpreter replied that as the hospital made the booking she was obliged to stay until the health professional requested otherwise. In this case the professional preferred to use the interpreter.

On conclusion of the test the daughter admitted that it was easier and less stressful having the interpreter help with the instructions and procedures and that she noticed that her mother was more compliant with staff requests. She asked the interpreter if she would also be available for the oncology consultation to discuss the results. This was arranged and at the close of the interview they all voiced their satisfaction with the outcome.

The doctor commented that it was great having the interpreter as he hadn't been aware of the patient's issues and concerns and now would be able to include them in his treatment plan. The daughter remarked that for the first time her mother really listened to the doctor and was ready to comply with the treatment plan. She admitted that she would have been embarrassed to ask some of the questions and voice some of the comments her mother was making but that the interpreter communicated them with no apparent awkwardness. She was also relieved at having the opportunity to ask her own questions of the doctor, knowing that the interchange would continue to be interpreted thus keeping her mother from feeling left out and herself from struggling to keep her mother included.

The mother was happy because finally she was able to communicate those issues that were important to her and, also, learned of the real concerns her daughter was having in regards to her health.

3.2   Scope of role

Cultural competence is a complex and often ill-understood concept among health professionals (National Health and Medical Research Council, 2005). However, it is "core business" for health care interpreters who are called upon to demonstrate and, in so doing, promote cross-cultural skills and sensitivity during everyday interpreting assignments. The two examples in Box 2 exemplify the interpreter's matter-of-fact way of handling cross-cultural health encounters. The first (*Sour milk!*) highlights the problem of literal translation by individuals whose knowledge of a second language is inadequate. In Egypt and some other Mediterranean cultures, yoghurt is simply known as "sour milk" and the terms are interchangeable. Setting the social and historical context as a way of explaining or justifying a patient's answer is the essence of the second illustration (*1912: Memory test*). This particular anecdote relates to an answer given by a Greek patient during psychological testing. In the experience of many elderly Greeks, the commencement of WWI dates from the beginning of the Balkan Wars which started earlier but merged into WWI. In this case failure of the health care interpreter to intervene, outside the interpreting process, by adding an explanation would lead to a wrong assessment.

Box 2. Cultural issues in communication

Sour milk! *by Madlen Labbad*

An Egyptian mother went to an Early Childhood Centre. While talking about the food recommended for children the mother said in English, "I gave my son sour milk, he liked it very much". The nurse was alarmed. "Sour milk? No, no, sour milk is bad for your child", she said, thinking it was rotten milk. The interpreter asked the mother what it really was and reassured the nurse, "She meant yoghurt!"

1912: Memory test *by Marie Marshall*

As part of a research program for memory testing, participants were asked a number of questions over a period of a few months. On being asked "When did WWI start?" many Greek subjects answered "1912". This was marked as being wrong. In fact the Balkan Wars that merged with WWI started in 1912.

Many of the case studies described sensitive or personally difficult situations. Box 3 (*Don't tell the patient!*) deals with an end-of-life experience. A frail elderly patient learned about the terminal nature of her illness through the interpreter's sensitive approach and appreciated the fact that this enabled her to prepare spiritually for her approaching death. Giving information to a patient about a terminal diagnosis is not easy in any circumstances. In cultures where conveying such news directly to a patient is unacceptable, there is added complexity. Health care interpreters are familiar with this problem. Consequently, they are apprehensive about situations where they are likely to be pressured by relatives to withhold information regarding the true nature of their condition from the patient. The attitude and demeanour of the interpreter can make a difference for all concerned. Being empathetic does not preclude the interpreter from acting professionally and within the code of ethics.

Box 3. Don't tell the patient *by Ann Nguyen*

> Vietnamese people are generally shy and scared of many things. Many are brought up in a way which uses punishment and scare tactics as discipline. As a result we usually think that the elderly, being old and sick, would be fearful of facing their own death. Therefore, many Vietnamese families try to protect old patients with terminal illness by not telling them the diagnosis or that their time is nearly up.
>
> Many family members often approached me outside the cubicle and told me not to break the bad news to the patient. I could only say: "I have to interpret whatever the doctor says but, if you like, I can interpret for you with the doctor. You can make your request and it's up to the doctor to decide".
>
> But one day, I met an old lady in a hospital ward. Even though she did not know exactly what her illness was she could feel her health diminished day by day. She was alone on that day. She told the doctor: "If I knew that my life was near the end, I would put all my effort to pray to Buddha who would take me to Buddha Kingdom at the time of death. I would not waste my time involved in worldly matters any more." And the doctor told her the truth.

Most case studies dealt with single episodes of care. The final example (Box 4: *Long-term patient*) shows how quality in health care interpreting was achieved in the context of an extended and satisfying professional relationship with a long-term patient and his family. The interpreter, who was involved throughout the continuum of care, did not follow instructions passively but became an active member of the treating team. Apart from the expected interpreting services, she took the initiative in translating documents which proved useful for the patient's rehabilitation. She provided moral support to the family and acted as a resource person for staff, explaining how to engage appropriate language services within and outside the public health system. By demonstrating flexibility in a range of situations, she managed to overcome a number of ethical challenges, contributing to a successful outcome for all.

Box 4. Long-term patient *by Vera Crvenkovic*

A young man of eighteen was admitted to the Spinal Unit, following serious injuries that left him a complete quadriplegic. A recent refugee from war-torn former Yugoslavia, he had arrived in Australia with his widowed mother and ten-year-old sister just a few months earlier. Their English was almost non-existing. They were registered with the Service for the Treatment and Rehabilitation of Torture and Trauma Survivors (STARTTS). The Red Cross, who provide emotional support, accommodation and financial help for people in this kind of situation, had just started to work on their case. They were totally lost in this new country, having spent years of running from one part of former Yugoslavia to another and spending most of that time in refugee camps. They were haunted by horrible flashbacks and dreams, but determined to make a new start in this country. When I met them, they did not need only sound linguistic support, but lots of understanding and strong moral support as well.

To overcome obvious linguistic and cultural differences hospital staff started to book health care interpreters for all hospital procedures and consultations. During the thirteen months of his stay in the Spinal Unit I made at least three or sometimes even more visits per week. On top of my booked assignments, I made numerous regular voluntary visits, classified as "ward rounds".

The patient went through a thorough rehabilitation program and I was present for his many dental appointments, physio and occupational therapy sessions. I interpreted and initiated several sessions with the Unit's psychologist for both the mother and the patient. There were also many appointments with the Unit's social worker who was involved in the family's accommodation and financial needs, cooperating with various government and voluntary organisations.

When the time came to leave the hospital I accompanied the patient and his mother, with the social worker, to several nursing homes, this being an option for his future accommodation. I helped the consultant nurse in teaching them both how to contact the outreach nurses, get medication and to be aware of risks and dangerous signs, how to change catheters and other problems which would have to be properly addressed once they were on their own. I also translated relevant information for their post-discharge needs.

I still maintain professional contact with the patient and his family. The local Outreach Services organise extensive telephone interviews with the patient and his family members using our Service. From time to time they have follow-ups in the hospital's Spinal Unit and other recommended clinics. Although the patient's and his mother's command of English has improved, we continue to be booked to interpret for every appointment at the hospital. This case has been one of the most rewarding experiences in my twenty-eight years as a HCIS interpreter. In fact, it was an extraordinary experience for all concerned.

3.3   Job satisfaction

In all the case studies collected, including the examples given here, the effectiveness of the interpreter's intervention was a source of great job satisfaction. The ability to combine technical skills and a professional approach with the lessons of experience led to a higher quality of care for the patient than would otherwise have been possible. Discussions by study participants reinforced this theme: achieving quality enhances the interpreter's satisfaction which, in turn, increases quality in health care interpreting.

4.   Discussion

In this small study we sought to understand what it is that the interpreter brings to a health care encounter that makes a difference for those involved, and how quality is achieved from an interpreter's point of view. The project grew out of a service-wide program of research and development, as well as an interest in promoting individual and organisational learning through writing and reflection.

Generalisability is not a goal in qualitative research, thus it is not necessary to have a large and representative group of participants (Lincoln and Guba, 1985). Nevertheless, the study had a number of limitations. Only one of the five NSW HCIS centres was involved. The participants were self-selected; all were employed by the HCIS on a full- or part-time basis and all were highly experienced. All the narratives dealt with face-to-face encounters, and none with interpreting over the telephone or via videoconference. Further research is needed to explore these issues, including the experiences of sessional staff and interpreters from new and emerging language groups where expectations of quality may be different.

NSW Department of Health Guidelines stipulate that a professional health care interpreter brings more than language skills to their work; the cultural mediator aspect of their role is also important. However, for newly qualified interpreters entering the health system what this means in practice is far from clear. The first HCIS interpreters to be employed learnt about the interpreter role, and its complexity and boundaries, largely through a process of trial and error. To the degree that their approach was instinctive rather than prescribed, quality was inevitably going to be variable.

Subsequently, the HCIS developed competency standards, a feature of increasing professionalism in interpreting worldwide (Bancroft, 2005). Some NSW HCIS centres (including the one involved in this project) attempted to introduce a performance management system, but assessment of quality remained problematic. Linguistic accuracy, a key factor in quality, is almost impossible to assess unless a sufficiently qualified bilingual person can be present at the consultation, a situation which rarely occurs. In the absence of objective measures, interpreters and others rely on subjective impressions. For example, has the doctor received sufficient information to be able to make a good diagnosis? Does the patient feel comfortable in asking questions? Is everyone confident that privacy and confidentiality will be maintained?

Despite the performance management system, health care interpreters mainly self-assess their performance, even though this is unreliable. In doing so, they tend to employ technical criteria; for instance, whether they knew and were able to convey all the medical terms used by the doctor, or whether they understood the dialect spoken by the client. Additionally, they rely on informal feedback received from health care providers and patients. A call from either party to book the same interpreter for a follow-up appointment is taken as confirmation of satisfaction with their performance. This may be true, but occasionally a patient may show preference for an interpreter who treats them kindly while waiting, displays the culturally expected level of respect, or is prepared to carry out small favours such as calling a taxi after the consultation. Such behaviours are not part of the formal role of a health care interpreter, and can be the source of collegial conflict. Some interpreters refuse to become involved beyond their strict interpreting assignment, as they feel this diminishes their professional status.

Stepping outside the (occasionally conflicting) boundaries of the role defined by professional associations and employer organisations can, indeed, do more harm than good. An inexperienced interpreter may fall into the trap of encouraging dependency on behalf of the patient or assuming other roles such as counselling or advocating. However, the boundaries are not always "black and white". In such cases, high quality is achieved by operating effectively within the "grey areas" as illustrated in the final case presented, even though this can be contentious. Some may question whether it is the interpreter's role to offer moral support, although this may simply be a matter of "being there". Others may challenge an individual for offering her/his services voluntarily in an industrial environment where the profession is viewed as undervalued and, certainly, under-remunerated.

The links between job satisfaction and quality of care (and staff retention) are well established in the health sector (e.g. Bartram, Joiner and Stanton, 2004; DeVoe et al., 2002; Harris et al., 2007). The scope and challenges of the health care interpreter role, although sometimes anxiety-provoking or personally distressing, are a major source of work satisfaction. The importance of organisational and collegial support in such cases should not be under-estimated. In assignments dealing with refugees who have experienced torture and trauma, for instance, formal debriefing can help prevent vicarious traumatisation (Valero-Garces, 2005). Participation in case conferences and professional development activities with other health professionals provides opportunities to share insights about improving the quality of health care overall. A culture that supports reflection and exchange of lessons learned, as demonstrated in this project, produces benefit across the health service.

Quality and safety have become "buzz words" within the health sector, and risk management has become a more prominent feature of health administration. Concern to reduce rates of adverse events has focused attention on the interpreter's role in reducing communication errors between service providers and patients who do not speak the same language (Divi et al., 2007). Language services in health must be adequately resourced. Establishing common benchmarks for health care interpreter services and individual interpreter performance, though difficult, should be high on the agenda of all stakeholders.

In an increasingly mobile and diverse world multicultural policies are more necessary than ever (United Nations Development Programme, 2004). Inclusive programs and services build a stronger and more stable society. Throughout the health system, health care interpreters play a vital role in meeting the needs of people from diverse linguistic and cultural backgrounds. Enhancing the quality of health care interpreting will enhance the quality of health care provided, contributing to better health outcomes for all.

Acknowledgements

We are grateful to all the staff at South East and Central Sydney Area HCIS who contributed to this project, in particular to Vera Crvenkovic, Madlen Labbad, Agnes Lauder, Marie Marshall and Ann Nguyen whose work is reproduced here. Thanks are due to the two anonymous reviewers who provided comments on an earlier version of this paper.

References

Australian Bureau of Statistics. *2006 Census QuickStats: New South Wales*. Canberra: ABS. Retrieved 5 April 2009, from http://www.censusdata.abs.gov.au

Bancroft, B. (2005). *The interpreter's world tour: An environmental scan of standards of practice for interpreters*. Woodland Hills, CA: The California Endowment. Retrieved 5 April 2009, from http://www.hablamosjuntos.org/resources/pdf/The_Interpreter's_World_Tour.pdf

Batram, T., Joiner T. A., and Stanton P. (2004). Factors affecting job stress and job satisfaction of Australian nurses: Implications for recruitment and retention. *Contemporary Nurse, 17*(3), 293–304.

Brough, C. (2006). *Language services in Victoria's health system: Perspectives of culturally and linguistically diverse consumers*. Melbourne: Centre for Culture Ethnicity & Health. Retrieved 5 April 2009, from http://www.ceh.org.au/downloads/final_report.pdf

DeVoe, J., Fryer, G. E., Lee-Hargraves, J., Phillips, R. L. and Green, L. A. (2002). Does career dissatisfaction affect the ability of family physicians to deliver high-quality patient care? *Journal of Family Practice, 51*, 223–228.

Divi, C., Koss, R. G., Schmaltz, S. P. and Loeb, J. M. (2007). Language proficiency and adverse events in US hospitals: A pilot study. *International Journal for Quality in Health Care*, *19*(2), 60–67.

Fernandez, A. et al. (2004). Physician language ability and cultural competence: An exploratory study of communication with Spanish speaking patients. *Journal of General Internal Medicine*, *19*(20), 167–174.

Flores, G. (2005). The impact of medical interpreter service on the quality of health care: A systematic review. *Medical Care Research and Review*, *62*(3), 255–299.

Garrett, P. and Lin, V. (1990). Ethnic health policy and service development. In J. Reid and P. Trompf (Eds.) *The health of immigrant Australia: A social perspective* (pp. 339–380). Sydney: Harcourt Brace Jovanovich.

Gifford, S. (1998). Analysis of non-numerical research. In C. Kerr, R. Taylor and G. Heard (Eds.) *Handbook of Public Health Research Methods* (pp. 543–553). Sydney: McGraw Hill.

Harris, M. F. et al. (2007). Job satisfaction of staff and the team environment in Australian general practice. *Medical Journal of Australia*, *186*(11), 570–573.

Lincoln, Y. S. and Guba, E. G. (1985). *Naturalistic Inquiry*. Beverly Hills, CA: SAGE.

Morales, L. S., Elliot, M. and Weech-Maldonado, R. (2006). The impact of interpreters on parents' experiences with ambulatory care for their children. *Medical Care Research and Review*, *63*(1), 110–128.

Mehler, P. S., Lundgren, R. A. and Pines, I. (2004). A community study of language concordance in Russian patients with diabetes. *Ethnicity & Disease*, *14*(4), 584–588.

National Health and Medical Research Council. (2005). *Cultural Competency in Health: A guide for policy, partnerships and participation*. Canberra: NHMRC.

Ngo-Metzger, Q., Massagli, M. P., Clarridge, B. R., Manocchia, M. and Davis, R. B. (2003). Linguistic and cultural barriers to care. *Journal of General Internal Medicine*, *18*(1), 44–52.

NSW Department of Health. (2006). *Standard Procedures for Working with Health Care Interpreters*, Doc No. PD2006_053. Sydney: NSW Health. Retrieved 5 April 2009, from http://www.health.nsw.gov.au/policies/pd/2006/PD2006_053.html

Wu A. C., Leventhal, J. M., Ortiz, J., Gonzalez, E. E. and Forsyth, B. (2006). The interpreter as cultural educator of residents: Improving communication for Latino patients. *Archives of Paediatrics & Adolescent Medicine*, *160*(11), 1145–1150.

United Nations Development Programme. (2004). *Human Development Report 2004: Cultural liberty in today's diverse world*. New York: UNDP.

Valero-Garces, C. (2005). Emotional and psychological effects on interpreters in public services: A critical factor to bear in mind. *Translation Journal*, *9*(3). Retrieved 5 April 2009, from http://accurapid.com/journal/33ips.htm

CHAPTER 15

Research ethics, interpreters and biomedical research

Patricia Kaufert, Joseph M. Kaufert and Lisa LaBine
Department of Community Health Sciences, University of Manitoba

This paper is based on a project with the title Centering the Human Subject in Health Research: The Meaning and Experience of Research Participation. This paper looks at research interpreters and research workers who are influenced by both professional and ethical codes and broader research policies which govern the ethical conduct of clinical and community-based research. It is based on a review of the research ethics literature and a series of semi-structured in-depth interviews with fourteen key informants including researchers, interpreters and members of Research Ethics Boards (REBs). These interviews were completed with individuals with direct experience working across language barriers, sometimes as interpreters and sometimes as researchers; it is these interviews that provide the framework for this paper. It asks two main questions: (1) What are the differences and similarities between interpreters working in research and medical interpreters; and (2) How do the codes and policies governing research ethics compare with the professional codes of ethical conduct applied to interpreters.

To answer the first question we revisit the three models of the medical interpreter: the interpreter as conduit, the interpreter as cultural broker, and the community embedded interpreter (Avery, 2001). We provide a brief description of each model and discuss the roles of interpreters, focusing on language and relationships. We also examine the implications of language barriers for research ethics, focusing on informed consent and the technical and ethical challenges of translating consent forms from one language to another. We then compare the professional codes of ethical conduct developed for medical interpreters by their own profession with the rules and regulations issued by government policy and research funding agencies and implemented by Research Ethics Boards. Lastly, we look at the question of community consent and at the roles played by some interpreters in speaking "for" a researcher and a research project.

1.   Introduction

This paper takes the theme of the Critical Link 5 Congress and explores how it applies in the context of an interpreter working on a health research project. Research is increasingly governed by codes and bodies of law which lay down the rules and regulations governing the interaction between human subjects and researchers. Many of these rules apply to communication and negotiation of informed consent. The implementation of these rules is the responsibility of the researcher and other members of a research team, including interpreters. However, the literature on interpretation and the development of professional codes of conduct for interpreters assumes a clinical setting in which the role of the interpreter is to facilitate communication between health professionals and patients. We use this paper to discuss the commonalities between these professional codes and research ethics codes, but we also focus on the differences that arise because the bodies responsible for research ethics do not understand the complexities of language and interpretation. We also recognize that the body of research and practice ethics within the professional interpreter community may not yet have fully engaged the impact of the diversity of roles and diverse methodologies that language interpreters working in the field of health research engage.

This paper utilizes data collected through a joint initiative between researchers at the University of British Columbia and the University of Manitoba.[1] The title of the project is *Centering the Human Subject: Understanding the Meaning and Experience of Research Participation*, and the primary focus of the project is on research as seen from the standpoint of human subjects. Their experiences cannot be understood, however, without examining their relationships with researchers and frontline research workers, or without studying the impact on the conduct of research of Research Ethics Boards in Canada, or Institutional Review Boards (IRBs) in the United States.

This paper looks at interpreters as a subgroup within the research worker category. Our interest in interpreters grew partly out of previous research on medical interpreters (JK) and partly out of the recent emphasis in research ethics on improving communication with research participants. However, very little attention within the research ethics literature was being paid to the impact of language barriers on communication in research.

The material for this paper is taken from an extensive review of the research ethics literature and from a series of semi-structured interviews with researchers, research workers and members of REBs. Several of these interviews were completed with individuals with direct experience of working across language barriers, sometimes as interpreters and sometimes as researchers; it is these interviews that provide the framework for this paper. We asked two questions; first, what are the differences and similarities between interpreters working in research and medical interpreters? The second is how do the codes and policies governing research ethics compare with the professional codes of ethical conduct applied to interpreters?

To answer the first question we revisited three models of the medical interpreter: the interpreter as conduit, the interpreter as cultural broker, and the community embedded interpreter (Avery, 2001). Part One provides a brief description of each model and a summary of the differences between these models and the roles of research interpreters. Part Two of the paper explores some of the implications of language and language barriers for research. Part Three uses the informed consent process as a practical example of the potential for conflict between the professional codes of ethical conduct developed for medical interpreters by their own profession and the rules and regulations that govern the administration of informed consent. Part Four explores the role that interpreters have played in facilitating research projects and negotiating community consent as the basis for developing a new and expanded model of the interpreter in research.

2.   Methods

The interviews with Chairs and members of REBs, ethicists and policy makers were shared between the two sites of the project, but the interviews with human subjects were largely done by colleagues at the University of British Columbia. We took responsibility for interviewing the majority of researchers and research workers.

Using a purposive sampling approach, we first constructed a matrix based on different types of research methods (quantitative, qualitative and participatory action) and disciplines (clinical, epidemiological, the social sciences). This matrix served as a general guide to recruitment. We have completed (or have planned) thirty-two interviews, fourteen of which are used in this paper. These fourteen included ten researchers, six social scientists and five health professionals. (Some individuals had more than one identity, which explains why some individuals were counted more than once.) At least eight spoke one or more languages other than English, with a roughly even split between indigenous and other languages. Seven of these eight had acted as interpreters at some time in their careers, and five of these seven were still professionally involved with interpreting. One researcher learned enough of the language spoken at his research site to do his own translation and transcriptions.

The first interviews followed a very open format as people talked about their careers and their relationships with research subjects, researchers, research workers, REBs and the communities in which they had done their research. We added more structured questions over the course of interviewing; however, each interview also included some questions to the background and expertise of that particular individual.

3.   Three models of interpreting

Avery (2001) sees model building and role definition as closely linked with the process of professionalisation within medical interpreting, including the establishment of standards of competence, the development of codes of ethical practice, training and credentialing initiatives. The models discussed by Avery include:

– The "conduit" model based on the assumption of a neutral interpreter;
– The active interpreter working as a cultural mediator or broker, who manages cross-cultural/cross-language communication;
– The interpreter embedded in their own cultural-linguistic community (Avery, 2001, p. 10)

4.   The interpreter as conduit

The concept of the "neutral" interpreter reflects the assumption that the sole function of the interpreter is to serve as an instrument, or "conduit", for transmitting messages (Putsch, 1985). This model emphasizes the importance of exact translation of everything that is said by the physician or by the patient. Dysart-Gayle writes: "The ideal of accurate, faithful and thorough interpretation is expressed in the use of the metaphor of the interpreter as a conduit transmitting information without distortion between provider and patient" (Dysart-Gayle, 2005, p. 92).

Widely criticized for not making any allowance for differences in education, social class, power imbalances or disparate belief systems (Kaufert and Putsch, 1997), the conduit model has also been accused of substituting a "misleading neutral literalism for essential 'nuanced interpretation'" (Solomon, 1997, p. 92).

The model has been modified and now allows interpreters to take on slightly more active roles; for example, an interpreter can check whether a patient truly understands the implications of giving or withholding consent (Roat, 1995; Putsch, 2005). Despite such revisions, there is still a considerable difference between the degree of flexibility allowed to interpreters in this model relative to the second model, the interpreter as cultural broker.

5.   The interpreter as cultural broker

The cultural broker model goes beyond bilingual competence and accurate message transmission and leaves the interpreter free to take on other roles (Verrept and Louck, 1995; Kaufert and Koolage, 1984). For example, this model recognizes that interpreters often possess both cultural and community knowledge as well as knowledge of health care institutions and medical culture. They are, therefore, well equipped to take on the roles of mediator, or even advocate, between their own culture and biomedical culture.

Cultural mediation is not without risk and its critics have questioned the implications of this model for ethical practice and the maintenance of standards of professional competence. Dysart-Gayle states:

> Those who resist the expansion of interpreter roles argue that while the code of ethics provides fairly clear definitions of the expanded roles, there is no discussion about how and when an interpreter is to move away from the default mode of information transmission and assume the tasks of the expanded roles, nor does it provide interpreters with parameters for assessing the effectiveness of their performance of these roles.   (Dysart-Gayle, 2005, p. 92)

Various attempts have been made at revising this model; for example, the International Medical Interpreters Association (originally the Massachusetts Medical Interpreter Association (MMIA)) introduced the concept of the "interpreter as manager of the cross-cultural/cross-language mediated clinical encounter" (MMIA, 1997). The MMIA included recommendations for interpreters on such topics as not being drawn into alliance with either participant, or on the importance of maintaining communication flow and pace. They also proposed standards of practice based on client well being, the development of shared meanings, and overcoming communication barriers.

This model gives the interpreter responsibility in such areas as identifying cultural barriers and the resolution of cultural differences. However, there is no acknowledgment of the significance of the relationships between interpreters and their own community (Avery, 2001).

6.   The embedded interpreter

The "embedded interpreter" model draws on the experience of interpreters recruited from small, tightly integrated cultural communities and who continue to maintain their ties with their own community. In Avery's view, it is the closeness of the relationship between the interpreter and the community which is pivotal:

"The interpreter has to have credibility as a member of the community in order to have credibility as an interpreter" (Avery, 2001, p. 11).

Avery (2001) associates this model with community interpreters from non-Western cultures and with interpreters from First Nations and Indigenous communities. In her view, this model of the interpreter takes a "qualitative leap that uniquely differentiates it" from two previous models. She writes: "While it recognizes that the core function of the interpreter is the transmission of messages from one language to another, it assumes that the person performing the function is there as a whole person embedded in the social fabric of her community" (Avery, 2001, p. 10).

Critics object that this model includes functions well outside the professional and ethical definitions of practice for health interpreters. Dysart-Gayle writes:

> More concretely they point out that interacting with or on behalf of patients outside the context of the clinical interview compromises confidentiality and invariably leads to patient requests for advice, recommendations, clarifications, and other actions that will put the interpreter in the position of what informants frequently referred to as practicing medicine without a license.
>
> (Dysart-Gayle, 2007, p. 240)

It is easier to compare medical with research interpreters by looking at what each of these models have in common rather than at their differences. Expanding the role definitions from conduit to embedded does not fully engage the diverse role and alternative sources governing ethical practice among interpreters working in research.

7. The research interpreter

We have used the term "Research Interpreter" as shorthand for a professional interpreter hired to work on a research project, sometimes for a single interview, or as a permanent member of a research team whose project is targeting a population with limited language access.

Avery (2001) describes medical interpreting as occurring in a health care setting and sees all attempts at defining the medical interpreter as "centred on the limits of what interpreters could do as part of their role and the nature of the relationship of the interpreter with both the patient and the provider" (Avery, 2001, p. 4). She also describes the relationship between patient, provider and interpreter as based on a common goal, the health of the patient.

The assumption that interpreters work almost exclusively in hospitals is not applicable to research interpreters. Some do, but clinical research in North

America has a long history of excluding non-English speaking subjects from their research and has had, until recently, relatively little need for interpreters (a small group of experienced nurse researchers interviewed for this project could not recall having ever worked with an interpreter on a clinical research project). Only three of the fourteen individuals, whose interviews formed the basis for this paper, were attached to large teaching hospital and these respondents were administrators of medical interpreter programs. Two of the researchers we interviewed had used interpreters when working on international projects on population health, health promotion and traditional healing; however, the majority of interpreters and researchers spoke of their experiences working in communities in Northern Canada in which Indigenous languages were spoken, particularly by the elders.

It is not only the settings that are different. There are fundamental differences in the relationships inherent in research relative to those formed through the delivery of medical care. For example, the common goal in research is the production of knowledge, not health. There are multiple codes for medical interpreters, some produced by their professional organization and some developed by the organization in which they are hired. They are part of the process of professionalisation, although some argue that they are designed to "integrate interpreters into the clinical culture, coordinating their work with other practices within the clinic. Most obviously, the code outlines an interpreter's obligation to conform to standards of hospital practice" (Dysart-Gayle, 2005, p. 93).

The complex system of ethical regulation and REB/IRB oversight was set up to protect the human subject. They are backed by real sanctions, the most powerful being the refusal of research funding agencies to release funds unless the project has gone through the process of ethical approval. The Principal Investigators are responsible for seeing these codes are followed, but they apply to everyone working on a project, including interpreters.

However, REBs do not define the interpreter's role, nor specify their qualifications. Dysart-Gayle was writing about trained and certified medical interpreters, but probably no more than two of the fourteen interviews we are using for this paper were with individuals with this level of qualification. The interpreters in Aboriginal languages had some training but also years of experience. The three researchers with experience in interpreting were bilingual. We included them in this analysis because their descriptions of their experiences offered some valuable insights into the process of working across language barriers.

Finally, although the three models differ greatly in their approach to contact between interpreters and patients, they are all focused on the centrality of the encounter between physician, patient and interpreter. This triadic structure is replicated in research whenever the research design calls for the researcher, the research subject and the interviewer to meet together, but there are other models.

For example, some survey designs train the interpreter in the use of a questionnaire, but then the interpreter works alone to conduct the interview. As we will discuss later in the section on community consent, the interpreter may speak not to a single subject, but to a focus group, or to a Chief and Council, or at a public meeting. In addition to issues of ambiguity in role definition and ethical regulation, research interpreters also engage language barriers in research communication.

8.   The implications of language and language barriers for research

An administrator of a multi-language interpreter program was very concerned about the importance of language barriers for research: "I think that one of the biggest challenges in research is having the researchers understand the complexity of what they are hoping to carry out" (413). Later in the interview, she said: "Researchers do not always understand the complexity of trying to translate or interpret what is said. They kind of underestimate that and don't always build it into their budgets" (413).

These comments stemmed from her work experience, but also from a deep commitment to language. She was very critical of those who had no understanding of the differences between languages and who saw the translation from one language to another as a simple technical exercise. She talked about why translating a research instrument from English to French was sometimes easier than doing the same translation from English into Spanish, and why it was much more difficult if the language was Punjabi or Arabic. Drawing on her experiences when asked to translate a research instrument, she said: "Unfortunately the instruments they give you to translate or to interpret are already poorly constructed. The questions are ambiguous and it comes to the fore when you try to translate these things and you think what does this really mean" (413).

The problem is partly a matter of vocabulary, but more importantly it concerns conceptual differences between languages.

The assumption underlying that two people speaking the same language should roughly agree on translation is relatively fundamental to interpreting and also the assumption underlying the use of back-translation. However, the people we interviewed who were working with Aboriginal languages had a different perspective and talked about language as a constantly changing entity as new words come in, such as the translation of HIV/AIDS into Cree, and old words were lost. The Director of an Aboriginal Interpreter Program also described changes from one generation to the next.

> Many of the old people learned the written language as used in the Bible but current uses of syllabics has changed a lot….[and] is done by people who don't know the old usages and the elders can't understand the current documents. … So the requirement that a written translation is in syllabics may mean you only reach one generation (412).

The teaching of languages in schools hastened the process of standardization, but differences in dialect were still common among the more isolated communities and particularly among elders. One interpreter talked about the need for patience in finding the "right" word in the sense of being the word that was understood.

They also wanted to talk about the social, political and ethical dimensions of how language was used. A researcher/interpreter talked about holding a meeting in a community that had maintained its Cree language. She said, "All ages speak Cree and it is more ethical to speak in the Cree language with a group like that, although they understand English" (411). In this context, she was using "ethical" as coterminous with "respectful". Another interpreter told a story when she was much younger and faced with translating for a male cancer patient: "I could not directly translate the word penis in Cree because it would be disrespectful to the elder. I had to refer to the place where the urine comes from. You don't name the body parts out of respect for the elder and they understand" (412).

One informant with experience as both a researcher and interpreter described the importance of going through the long process of greetings at the beginning of a meeting. Not to have done so would display a lack of respect. An anthropologist described how the young men taking part in his study preferred to tell their stories in English rather than Afrikaans, although this was the language in which they had been educated. They claimed that English was "the language of liberation" enabling them "to speak beyond their borders" (414).

A physician/researcher described his observation of the extended time period that an interpreter spent in discussion with elders. The interpreter consulted the elders about a question of researchers understanding of cultural context in references to the spiritual dimension of palliative care and dying.

> It was more making sure I understood the whole concept of spiritual beings and the history of naming and cultural contexts of when does death actually occur and the struggles to try to make sure I really understood what they were trying to say, especially the elders who were trying to define death or when you define death (311).

These are very different examples, but they do illustrate the point made by the administrator quoted at the beginning of this section that "one of the biggest challenges in research is having the researcher understand the complexity of what they are doing" (413).

9.   Interpreters, informed consent and research

This section focuses on the challenge of enabling Research Ethics Boards REB/ IRB to understand the complexity of research interpreters' roles in the context of their relationships with individuals and communities. The central theme was on the problems of translation and interaction with individuals in negotiation and negotiation of informed consent.

Every informant referred to issues of interpretation of informed consent and nearly all complained; sometimes about the length, sometimes about the language, and sometimes about the REB committee that had asked for changes in the consent form. To understand why informed consent has become such an issue in the relationship between researchers and REBs requires a brief review of the research ethics literature. The preoccupation with informed consent traces back to the Belmont report and its definition of autonomy as "respect for persons". "Respect" included treating potential research participants as autonomous agents "capable of deliberation", who should be able to "enter into research voluntarily and with adequate information". A more recent definition of autonomy describes it as "giving prospective participants the facts they need to make an informed choice about study enrolment" (Dresser, 2001). The key components are:

–   provision of full information about risks and benefits of the research process;
–   capacity of the participant to understand information presented;
–   the accessibility of the information presented (including both language level and appropriate linguistic format);
–   insuring participants are in a situation where real voluntary choice can be exercised (Meissel, Roth and Litz, 1977)

The realization that consent forms were often signed with little understanding of their content has been relatively recent and has stimulated a new interest in language and communication in the research ethics literature. However, very little of this concern has extended to language barriers or interpreters. When "interpreters" and "language barriers" were entered as key words into a literature search, there were very few "hits" and many of the papers we found were by social scientists writing on ethics and research in developing countries. A study commissioned by the US National Bioethics Advisory Committee focused on the experience of researchers working in developing countries, who had submitted their projects to American based IRBs (Dawson and Kass, 2005). There were some very interesting comments on language and the importance of getting at the underlying concepts rather than insisting on a direct translation unlikely to be understood. However, while a few of the researchers participating in this study said that they had learned the language of their research subjects, the majority had not and would have used interpreters. Yet there is no mention of interpreters in the paper or their contributions as language mediators.

A search of recent reports, guidelines and regulations – the grey literature of research ethics – was more successful, but all the references were confined to sections on informed consent and dealt with the practical, as distinct from the philosophical, aspects of language barriers. For example, the Canadian Tri-Council Policy Statement recommends the involvement in the consent process of an "intermediary not involved in the research study, who is competent in the language used by researchers as well as that chosen by the research subject" (Article 2.1). In the United States, Federal regulations stipulate that consent "shall be in a language understandable to the subject or the representative". The Office of Human Subject Research (OHSR) recommends having an interpreter present during the consent process; however, interpreter is defined simply as "someone who is independent of the subject (i.e., not a family member)" (Office of the Interpreter General, 2000). There is no suggestion that researchers should hire or consult with trained and certified interpreters.

The administrator contended that: "Some of the consent forms that are imposed by the ethics review committee are not understandable in English, French or any other language" (413).

A clinician/researcher complained that the increasing technicality and complexity of the language used in informed consent forms was making them inaccessible to anyone with limited language proficiency (305).

Another researcher clinician with years of experience was equally disturbed by the increasing length of these forms and reflected on their evolution over the course of his career:

"Well, over fifteen years of submitting to the REB, I can identify the order of magnitude of changes in terms of the length of the consents. The first consents that I put together back in 1990/1991 were one-pagers and they were typically approved at the first meeting" (403).

Continuing his comments on the shorter consent form, he said: "I think one of the concerns that I had with some of the templates is that it's sort of a procrustean approach to informing individuals, and sometimes the important aspects get lost in all the detail" (403).

Along with his complaints, he also gave us an insight into how he worked with his interpreter.

> [The consent forms] are all written in English and Inuktitut. So what I do is I go over the English language version with the interpreter who goes over the Inuit Consent form with the participant and most in my recollection ask for the Inuktitut translation regardless of their age and their conversational capacity in English (311).

The complaints about the length and complexity of informed consent forms was not restricted to these fourteen interviews; they occurred also in the interviews we did with researchers, research workers and even members of REB committees. Some suggested that REBs had become fixated on the consent form itself without paying enough attention to "the accessibility of the information presented" (Meissel, Roth and Litz, 1977). Others blamed researchers who wanted their ethical approval letter and were unwilling to negotiate the content of the consent form with the REB. This conclusion is based partly on our experience talking with researchers and partly on a study done in the United States. A survey of thirty IRB websites belonging to top-ranked medical schools and hospitals in the United States illustrates the consequences of focusing on informed consent to the exclusion of other language issues. The websites were searched for information provided to researchers by the IRB on factors to consider when their proposed study involved "human subjects with Limited English Proficiency [LEB]" (Resnik and Jones, 2006). Almost all sites (97%) carried information on translating consent forms, but only 20% discussed the legal and ethical problems with enrolling human subjects when there is a language barrier between the researchers and the researched, and only 7% provided guidance on translating research tools. Resnik and Jones (2006) see these figures as evidence that IRBs have not addressed "several important questions relating to language barriers in research", but focus only on those requirements which are mandatory.

In the final section of this paper, we look at community consent as used in First Nations communities as a potential model for a different approach to the use of interpreters in research.

10.   Community consent

Canadian REBs require evidence that a First Nation community has been consulted and has agreed to a research project before the REB will give it ethical approval. This usually means that the researcher must formally present the proposed project to the community at a public meeting, as well as at a formal meeting with the Chief and Band council, and have a letter from the Council approving the project. Having some one who is a trusted and respected member of the community speak at these meetings in support of the project is a major advantage. This role is often taken by the interpreter.

The following quotation describes the importance of these meetings:

> For our work with First Nations communities I've always been present at the
> first meeting where the research coordinator [Interpreter] is introduced and we

discuss what the expectations are from participants, and what we need from the community and at the same time try to indicate how we're going to work with the community to bring information back and what the benefits are to the community. We've been pretty good at that (403).

The interpreter who undertakes this role is often chosen by the community health committee, who select the interpreter they think, is best for the job (311). Another researcher described the importance of selecting an interpreter who had experience, prestige and community trust:

> I think so because on occasion their status or stature is called upon when there are really significant issues. I can remember one very recently where there were issues of the whole community being consulted regarding end of life decision making and organ donation. The individual that I regarded as being at the top of the hierarchy of interpretation was in fact the one that was called in despite the fact that there were other individuals in the health centre who were also trained interpreters but perhaps not of the same stature (403).

There is a tradition of interpreters playing pivotal leadership roles in small remote Northern communities. In terms of research, some have played formal roles in facilitating agreements on the ethical and resource-related terms of research; they have also played less formal roles in terms of the advice they have given researchers on language, but also on the social and cultural aspects of communication. They have often been essential in recruiting research subjects and as a general liaison between the community and the researcher.

11.   Conclusion

The idea of the interpreter being chosen based on a community assessment of their experience, language proficiency, status and trustworthiness is very close to the earlier description of the embedded community interpreter: "The interpreter has to have credibility as a member of the community in order to have credibility as an interpreter" (Avery, 2001, p. 11).

In writing this paper, we have tried to stress the importance of the social aspects of language and language barriers. We also came to recognize how little attention has been paid to language interpretation and the role of interpreters in maintaining ethical relationships with human subjects, researchers and ethical review bodies. The codes of ethical practice for medical interpreters stress the absolute value of accurate and precise translation. However, the message from our interviews with researchers and interpreters is that there must be accuracy in communicating more complex conceptual meanings of the message. These meanings must be expressed in terms that are comprehensible at the level of the individual for whom the message is intended. In the case of an elder, this may mean using "dialect" rather than the newly standardized Cree term for diabetes, or taking time to understand the elder's concept of death when doing research on palliative care.

In their turn, some Research Ethics Boards have been so concerned with ensuring that every possible risk is included in the consent form, they lose sight of the original purpose of informed consent in the protection of the human subject. As is now realized, this purpose is not achieved by using a consent form which a third of the study population cannot understand.

The paper by Dawson and Kass (2005) recommends the use of advisory committees made up of researchers and members of the community in which the research is set. Their role would presumably include the review of informed consent forms as well as all the research instruments. This idea comes out of the experience of researchers working in developing countries but could be extended to other settings.

Based on some of the principles and the experience of community consent, we would advocate the inclusion of interpreters, playing their role as cultural brokers but mediating the gap between the researcher and the research subject/research community. This would entail a broader concept of the role of the interpreter, but it would also have to include the education of REBs and researchers in the importance of language in research.

Acknowledgements

The research described in this paper was supported by a Canadian Institutes for Health Research Grant (2005–2010): "Centering the Human Subject in Health Research: Understanding the Meaning and Experience of Research Participation." The project is directed by Dr. Susan Cox (P.I.) and Dr. Michael McDonald (Co-P.I.) from the Maurice Young Centre for Applied Ethics, University of British Columbia. Co-Investigators Dr. Patricia Kaufert and Dr. Joseph Kaufert are based in the Department of Community Health Sciences at The University of Manitoba. Research team members from UBC and UMan include Ms. Lisa LaBine (U Man), Dr. Monica Morris Oswald (U Man) Dr. Cathy Schuppli (UBC), Ms. Christina Preto (UBC), Ms. Kim Taylor (UBC), Dr. Darquise Lafreniere (UBC), Dr. Anne Townsend (UBC) and Ms. Natasha Damiano-Paterson (UBC).

References

Avery, M. (2001). The role of the health care interpreter. Retrieved April 2001 from *National Council on Interpretation in Health Care*: http://www.ncihc.org, 1–15.

Bell, J., Whiton, J. & Connelly, I. S. (1998). *Final Report: Evaluation of NIH implementation of Section 491 of the Public Health Service Act, mandating a program of protections for research subjects*. Contract NO1–00-2-2109: Arlington, VA: James Bell Associates.

Dawson, L. & Kass, N. E. (2005). Views of US researchers about informed consent in international collaborative research. *Social Science and Medicine, 61*, 1211–1222.

Desser, R. (2001). Beyond disability: Bioethics and patient advocacy. *The American Journal of Bioethics, 1*(3), 50–51.

Dysart-Gale, D. (2005). Communication models, professionalisation, and the work of medical interpreters. *Health Communication, 17*(1), 91–103.

Dysart-Gale, D. (2007). Clinicians and medical interpreters negotiating culturally appropriate care for patients with limited English ability. *Family Community Health, 30*(3), 237–246.

Kass, N., Dawson, L. & Loyd-Berrios, N. (2003). Ethical oversight of research in developing countries. *IRB: Ethics & Human Research, 25*(2), 1–10.

Kaufert, J. & Koolage, W. (1984). Role conflict among culture brokers: The experience of Native Canadian medical interpreters. *Social Sciences and Medicine, 18*(3), 283–286.

Kaufert, J. & O'Neil, J. (1990). Biomedical rituals and informed consent: Native Canadians and the negotiation of clinical trust. In G. Weisz, (Ed.), *Social Science Perspective on Medical Ethics* (pp. 41–64). Philadelphia: University of Pennsylvania Press.

Kaufert, J. & Putsch, R. (1997). Communication through interpreters in healthcare: ethical dilemmas arising from differences in class, culture, language and power. *Journal of Clinical Ethics, 8*(1), 71–87.

Kaufert, J. & O'Neil, J. (1998). Culture, power and informed consent: The impact of Aboriginal health interpreters on decision-making. In D. Coburn, C. D'Arcy & G. Torrance (Eds.), *Health and Canadian Society* (pp. 131–146). Toronto: University of Toronto Press.

Marshall, P. A. (2003). Human subjects protections, Institutional Review Boards, and cultural anthropological research. *Research Anthropology Quarterly, 76*(2, Spring), 269–285.

Marshall, P. A., et al. (2006). Voluntary participation and informed consent to International genetic research. *American Journal of Public Health, 96*(11, November), 1981–1999.

Massachusetts Medical Interpreters Association and Education Development Centre (1997). *Medical interpreter's standards of practice.* (pp. 1–23). Andover, Massachusetts.

McGee, G. & Johnson, S. (July 2007). Has the spread of HPV vaccine marketing conveyed immunity to common sense? *The American Journal of Bioethics, 7*(7), 1–2.

Medical Research Council of Canada, the Natural Sciences and Engineering Research Council of Canada & the Social Sciences and Humanities Research Council of Canada (1998). *Tri-Council Policy Statement: Code of Ethical Conduct for Research Involving Humans.* Prepared by the Tri-Council Working Group. Ottawa: Government of Canada.

Meisel, A., Roth, L. & Lidz, C. (1977). Toward a model of legal doctrine of informed consent. *American Journal of Psychiatry, 34*(1), 3–45.

National Council on Interpreting in Health Care (2004). *A National code of ethics for interpreters in health care.* Working Paper. Retrieved July 2004 from: http://www.ncihc.org

Office of the Inspector General: Department of Health and Human Services (2000). *Protecting human research subjects: Status recommendations.* Boston Regional Office OE-01-97-00197. Retrieved April 2001 from: http://www.dhhs.gov/progorg/oei

Putsch, R. W. (1985). Cross-cultural communication: The special case of interpreters in health care. *Journal of the American Medical Association, 254*(23), 3344–3348.

Putsch, R. W. (2005). *Language access in health care: Domains, strategies and implementations for medical education.* Concept Paper. Seattle, Washington: Cross-Cultural Health Care Program.

Putsch, R. W. & Joyce, M. (1990). Dealing with patients from other cultures. In H. K. Walker & J. Hurst (Eds.), *Clinical Methods* (pp. 1050–1055). Boston: Butterworths.

Resnik, D. B. & Jones, C. W. (2006). Research subjects with limited English proficiency. *Accountability in Research, 13*, 157–177.

Roat, C. E. (1995). *Bridging the Gap: A Basic Training for Medical Interpreters, 40 Hours for Multilingual Groups.* Seattle, Washington: Cross Cultural Health Care Program.

Solomon, M. (1997). From what's neutral to what's meaningful: Reflections on a study of medical interpreters. *Journal of Clinical Ethics, 8*(1), 88–93.

Verrept, H. & Louck, F. (1995). *Health advocates in Belgian health care.* Brussels: Unpublished report.

Contributors

A/Prof Sandra Hale
Leader, Interpreting & Translation
Research Group
University of Western Sydney, Australia
s.hale.@uws.edu.au

A/Prof Ludmila Stern
Deputy Head, School of Languages and
Linguistics, Coordinator of MA in
Interpreting and Translation Studies
(MAITS)
University of New South Wales, Australia
l.stern@unsw.edu.au

Dr Uldis Ozolins
Lecturer in Translating & Interpreting
Royal Melbourne Institute of Technology
University Melbourne
Australia
uldis.ozolins@rmit.edu.au

Stephanie Jo Kent
American Sign Language/English Interpreter
Ph.D. Candidate in Communication
University of Massachusetts Amherst, USA
stephaniejo.kent@gmail.com

Eva N. S. Ng
School of Chinese
The University of Hong Kong
Hong Kong
nsng@hku.hk

Isabel Abril Martí
Facultad de Traducción e Interpretación
Universidad de Granada, Spain
miabril@ugr.es

Jieun Lee
Lecturer
Department of Linguistics
Macquarie University, Australia
jieun.lee@ling.mq.edu.au

Waltraud Kolb
Centre for Translation Studies
University of Vienna, Australia
waltraud.kolb@univie.ac.at

Dr Jemina Napier
Senior Lecturer, Coordinator Translation
& Intepreting Programs
Department of Linguistics
Macquarie University, Australia
Jemina.Napier@mq.edu.au

Prof David Spencer
Associate Dean (Academic)
Faculty of Law & Management
La Trobe University, Australia
David.Spencer@latrobe.edu.au

Dr Helen Tebble
Adjunct Senior Research Fellow
Interpreting and Translation Studies
School of Languages, Cultures and
Linguistics
Faculty of Arts
Monash University, Australia
Helen.Tebble@arts.monash.edu.au

Dr Michael S. Cooke
Principal of Intercultural Communications
Australia
intercult@netspeed.com.au

Dr Ilse Blignault
Senior Research Fellow at the School
of Public Health and Community Medicine
University of New South Wales, Australia
i.blignault@unsw.edu.au

Maria Stephanou
Manager, NSW Transcultural Aged
Care Service
Australia
maria.stephanou@hotmail.com

Cassandra Barrett
Communications Officer
NSW Transcultural Aged Care Service
Australia
Casandra.barrett@email.cs.nsw.gov.au

Juan Miguel Ortega Herráez
Department of Translation and
Interpreting Studies
University of Alicante, Spain
Greti Research Group
University of Granada, Spain
juanmiguel.ortega@ua.es

Dr Patricia Kaufert
Professor, Department of Community
Health Sciences
Faculty of Medicine
University of Manitoba, Canada
email-kaufert@cc,umanitoba.ca

Lisa LaBine, MSc
Department of Community Health Sciences
at the University of Manitoba, Canada
labine_lisa@hotmail.com

Roberta Favaron
PhD student
Centre for Translation Studies
University of Vienna, Austria
r.favaron@gmail.com

Index

Benjamins Translation Library

A complete list of titles in this series can be found on *www.benjamins.com*